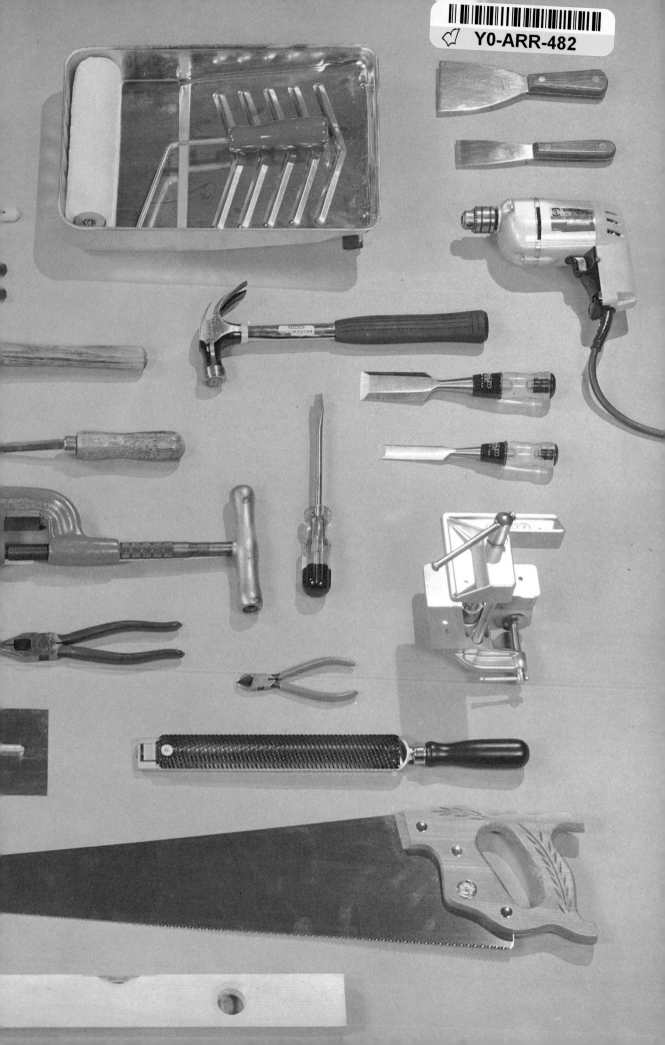

THE
PRACTICAL
HANDYMAN'S
ENCYCLOPEDIA

THE PRACTICAL HANDYMAN'S ENCYCLOPEDIA

THE COMPLETE

ILLUSTRATED

DO IT YOURSELF

LIBRARY FOR HOME & OUTDOORS

VOLUME ONE

GREYSTONE PRESS/NEW YORK

YOUR PRACTICAL HANDYMAN'S ENCYCLOPEDIA

OVER 100 expert authors, artists, designers, and photographers and 12 years of painstaking labor were necessary to produce these 3,456 pages of the most massive and comprehensive do-it-yourself encyclopedia ever created for the home handyman.

• All major building projects—including entire homes, cabins, boats, furniture—were actually constructed from the ground up, photographed in step-by-step detail, drawn to exacting dimensions, thoroughly tested by actual use, and proven to save your building dollars before they were accepted for this work.

• Every home repair—including automobile, television, appliance, electrical, heating and plumbing repairs—was performed with tools, parts and materials available to every home craftsman and requiring no special skills or training.

• Each home modernization project—including room and garage additions, new kitchens and bathrooms, attic and basement finishing —was carefully designed to add beauty, practicality and solid financial value to your home.

• Every home maintenance job—including painting, plastering, furniture refinishing,

lawn care, masonry work—was expertly planned to save you substantial time and labor yet produce professional results.

• All hobbies and family fun ideas—including photography, gardening, hi-fi, patios and play areas, barbecues, water sports—were created to allow you luxury pleasures at minimum cost.

• In short, in this encyclopedia you will find hundreds of fine projects to bring more fun into your life, to provide more of the good things to make your entire family happy, and to keep you profitably busy for a joyous lifetime!

• The authorities selected to write this encyclopedia have not only acknowledged professional stature in their respective fields, but are best-selling authors whose clear and concise explanations of technical subjects have won them a vast approving audience of Americans who have benefited from their expert advice to enjoy finer homes and a more abundant life. A board of editors with decades of practical experience in do-it-yourself techniques was appointed to organize and edit this practical work—the most useful library of practical how-to-do-it information ever assembled.

THE PUBLISHERS

CONTRIBUTING AUTHORS

FRED RUSSELL
Dean of automotive writers. Nationally syndicated columnist. Famous AAA Motor Club writer. Best-selling author.

T. H. EVERETT
Horticulturist, New York Botanical Garden. World famous lecturer and writer on gardening and landscaping.

HANK WIEAND BOWMAN
Author of "Encyclopedia of Outboard Motorboating," dozens of books. Famous boating expert, newspaper columnist.

ROBERT HERTZBERG
Former Editor-In-Chief, Mechanix Illustrated. Electronics authority. Well-known TV and radio author.

PETER GOWLAND
Renowned Hollywood glamour photographer. Author of dozens of best-selling books on all phases of photography.

WALTER IAN FISCHMAN
How-To Columnist, New York Daily News. Articles in Popular Science, Mechanix Illustrated. Author of how-to books.

BILL BAKER
Author of do-it-yourself furniture books. Articles appear in Popular Science, True, Mechanix Illustrated.

SIMON NATHAN
Contributor to U.S. Camera, Popular Photography, Good Photography. Author of best-selling photography books.

ROBERT BRIGHTMAN
Crafts and Hobbies Editor, Mechanix Illustrated. Feature writer on home improvement and how-to subjects.

DAVID X. MANNERS
Building Editor, House Beautiful magazine. Author of hundreds of articles on do-it-yourself subjects.

ART MARGOLIS
Writer on TV Repairs, Popular Science magazine. Author of television books.

JACKSON HAND
Author of outdoor furniture books. Formerly with Better Homes & Gardens.

LOUIS HOCHMAN
Author of books on refinishing furniture. Contributor to Mechanix Illustrated.

TOM RILEY
Feature writer for Field & Stream, Better Homes & Gardens. Author of top-selling how-to-do-it books.

BILL MOORE
Shopwork Instructor, New York City schools. Furniture building expert.

R. J. DeCHRISTOFORO
Leading author of books on power tools, building, home how-to subjects.

BERNARD GLADSTONE
Home Improvement Editor, New York Times. Well-known how-to-do-it expert.

HAL KELLY
Designer of championship racing boats, family runabouts, cruisers, etc. Writer for major boating magazines.

HI SIBLEY
Long renowned furniture and home repair expert. Writer for Popular Mechanics, Mechanix Illustrated, Popular Science.

HENRY CLARK
How-to artist and designer. Pioneer expert in do-it-yourself diagrams.

RUDOLPH MATERN
Famed architect. His hundreds of home designs are nationally known.

GLEN L. WITT
Naval Architect. Expert designer of all types of family boats.

GRIFF BORGESON
Author and expert on hot rod and automotive subjects.

ARTHUR M. WATKINS
Writer, authority on home heating.

JOSEPH MARSHALL
Author of numerous books, hundreds of articles on stereo and hi-fi subjects.

GROFF CONKLIN
Author of home air conditioning books.

ALFRED MORGAN
Well-known electrical repairs authority.

JOHN L. LACEY
Craftsman and wood carving expert.

We have listed here only a few of the famous authors who have contributed to your Practical Handyman's Encyclopedia.

CONTENTS OF THIS ENCYCLOPEDIA

The following contents lists only major subjects. For a complete,
cross-referenced index of the entire encyclopedia, see last volume.

BEDROOM ADDITION

By Harold Kelly

Thoughtful planning and low-cost but good-quality materials helped make this a successful project.

WITH TWO growing boys in the family, we found that we had to add a room to our old house. The structural problems won't be discussed here, except to say that they existed. Every old house and differing local zoning laws present individual problems. As for the finishing, we wanted good-looking and inexpensive materials that could be handled by the average home handy man.

Most of the structural and exterior

Most of framing and exterior work was done by carpenters. Center photo, simple sliding aluminum windows are installed. Right, pump jack proved great time-saver.

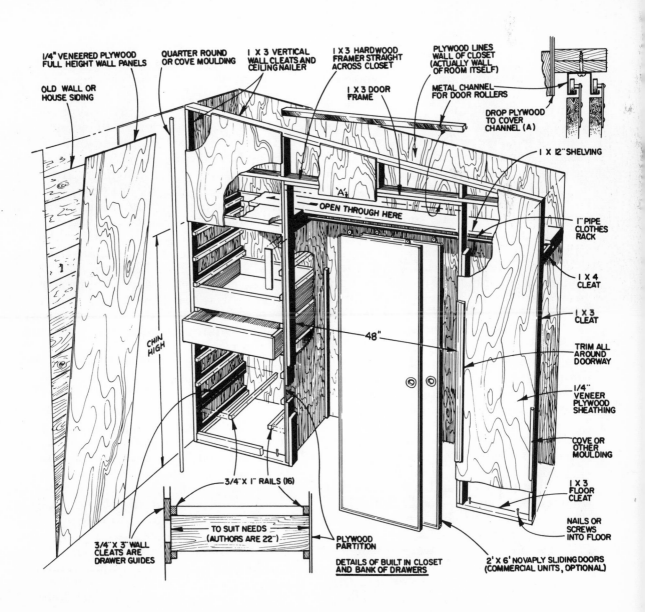

1/4" VENEERED PLYWOOD FULL HEIGHT WALL PANELS

OLD WALL OR HOUSE SIDING

QUARTER ROUND OR COVE MOULDING

1 X 3 VERTICAL WALL CLEATS AND CEILING NAILER

1 X 3 HARDWOOD FRAMER STRAIGHT ACROSS CLOSET

1 X 3 DOOR FRAME

PLYWOOD LINES WALL OF CLOSET (ACTUALLY WALL OF ROOM ITSELF)

METAL CHANNEL FOR DOOR ROLLERS

DROP PLYWOOD TO COVER CHANNEL (A)

1 X 12" SHELVING

A

OPEN THROUGH HERE

1" PIPE CLOTHES RACK

1 X 4 CLEAT

1 X 3 CLEAT

CHIN HIGH

48"

TRIM ALL AROUND DOORWAY

1/4" VENEER PLYWOOD SHEATHING

COVE OR OTHER MOULDING

1 X 3 FLOOR CLEAT

NAILS OR SCREWS INTO FLOOR

3/4" X 1" RAILS (16)

TO SUIT NEEDS (AUTHORS ARE 22")

3/4" X 3" WALL CLEATS ARE DRAWER GUIDES

PLYWOOD PARTITION

DETAILS OF BUILT IN CLOSET AND BANK OF DRAWERS

2' X 6' NOVAPLY SLIDING DOORS (COMMERCIAL UNITS, OPTIONAL)

Far window is to become medicine chest in bathroom which can be seen through nearer window; this one will be door into hall.

With all electrical work in, insulation comes next. Be sure to insulate around all windows; they must be well caulked outside.

work was done by professional carpenters who were familiar with the zoning law requirements, and who could get the room under wraps before the rainy season began.

The room addition measured approximately 8x22 feet. Two large aluminum sliding windows were installed, as was a closet at each end of the room. We handled all the electrical work, putting in three wall plugs and two ceiling lights, each on its own switch. Cost of all electrical materials, including the flush lights, was only $35.

All insulating material was put up in about two evenings. For the ceiling we used insulation faced with aluminum on one side, and a low-cost rock lath was nailed to the ceiling beams. All walls were covered with plywood. For this we chose a light-colored wood called Japanese Ash, put out by U. S. Plywood Corporation; it is tough-wearing and low-cost, and is excellent for almost any type of room.

For wood trim, light-colored Korina was used. This also is made by U. S. Plywood. Here's a good tip: Before installing plywood and trim, give them about three coats of a good quality, hard-wearing, clear finish such as Satinlac, Fabulon, or brushing lacquer.

Plywood and trim were finished off in the author's shop, brought up to the room, and, there, cut to size and fitted on the spot. The plywood was nailed to

the wall studs with 1-in. brads, after the stud locations were carefully marked off.

Next came the floor covering. Linoleum was used.

For the ceiling, acoustical-type square panels were employed to silence the noise that children invariably make. Brand used was Armstrong Cushion-tone, which is attractive, inexpensive, and simple to attach. We chose the type that is fastened to the ceiling with an adhesive paste. The ceiling was marked off to locate the panel positions, and the panels requiring it were easily trimmed to size with a matte knife.

The only trick to applying the acoustical panels is to get the paste in four even pats per square. The panels stick easily to the ceiling, and the holding quality of the cement paste is amazing. After the ceiling is in place, you can walk around and push up the squares a bit to make sure you get it nice and even.

Between the windows we attached one sheet of pegboard, painted off-white to match the ceiling. Pegboard is perfect material for a child's room, and my sons use it to display their prize toys, etc. Be sure to space the pegboard at least ½ in. away from the wall so that hangers can be hooked in place.

Where there once was an old bathroom window we installed a large, deep medicine cabinet. Translucent Alsynite was used for sliding doors. A fluorescent bulb inside acts as a night light—a

Ceiling light is in place; notice simple framing for holding light box. Each end of room has a light with its own switch.

Either hand or hammer type of staple gun can be used. However, if you miss with a hammer type, you tear up the insulation.

Low-cost rock lath is nailed into place with large-headed nails after the insulation has been installed. Note how lath is staggered. This material can be cut easily with a matte knife, making the cut on each side and right through the paper backing. After cuts are made it is simple to snap off the excess.

Plywood wall panels are nailed in place with 1-in. brads. Measure off location of wall studs before attaching the plywood.

Brads are then countersunk with nail set and holes are carefully filled, using a natural colored wood dough to match wood.

To cut out holes for the switch boxes, a Porter Cable "Homemaster" was used; it does job well and in a matter of seconds.

After the plywood was in place, switch covers were put on quickly before kids could have a chance to start exploring.

All plywood panels were coated with Satinlac before they were installed; now a touch-up where wood dough covers nails.

Here in author's shop all wood is given three coats of Satinlac before being cut to size; it's quicker and easier this way.

Be sure to use aluminum reflecting material behind radiator; this will reflect the heat out, increase radiator's efficiency.

The trick in putting up Armstrong Cushiontone is to apply the adhesive paste in four neat piles on back of each square.

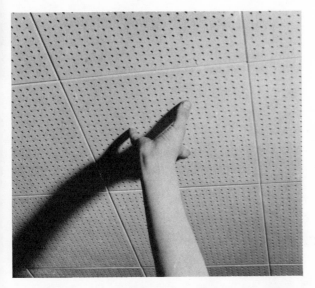

Panels are pushed into place and hold to rock lath quite firmly; when all are in place you should check them for evenness.

Now that ceiling is installed, flush light box is adjusted to fit snugly to ceiling. More photos appear on following pages.

small item, but an important one for any bathroom, we felt. Shelves are glass, and old, heavy plate glass was ideal for these. For complete details on the medicine chest, see the accompanying drawings. Incidentally, an adequate-sized medicine cabinet is a surprisingly expensive item if you go to buy it. It's one item that it definitely pays to make.

At each end of the room, we built a 2-foot deep closet. Both closets are similar in construction, but a row of drawers was built into one of them to hold shirts, other clothing, and for general small item storage.

The sliding closet doors can be purchased in several sizes. Made of Novaply (a water-resistant, laminated wood product for interior furniture and panel use), the doors remain flat and warp-free through years of use. The doors can easily be cut down in height, and we did so in order to keep them in scale with the rest of the room.

Refer to the drawings and photographs on the next six pages.

The boys have been living in their new room for almost a year now, and the room is standing up very well indeed under the wear and tear they put it to. Everything points to this having been a completely successful project, one well worth the expense and elbow-grease.

Adding room to your house and finishing it properly is like putting money in the bank. You get the principal (and perhaps even more) back if you sell the house, and the interest is in the years of pleasant use you've had from the room. •

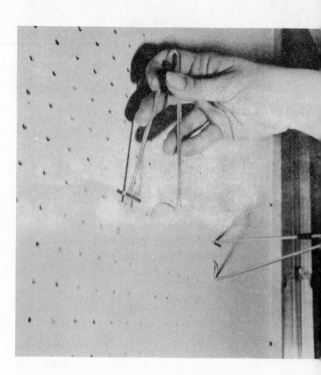

Pegboard is screwed to the wall with roundhead screws. These look unobtrusive and neat, so there's no need to conceal them.

Pegboard hangers come in many styles, shapes, are just slipped in place. Use ½-in. spacer strips in-between board and the wall.

Left, closet at this end of the room is for older boy. Combination dresser, desk and bookcase holds all his other belongings.

For uniform heat, use same type of heater as in rest of house. This hot-water radiator has air bleeder.

Here's the pegboard in use, with a sampling of some of things the kids will display on it over the years.

See additional photos on following page

Small fluorescent light in the medicine chest is used for a night light. It's a valuable item; get it in your hardware store.

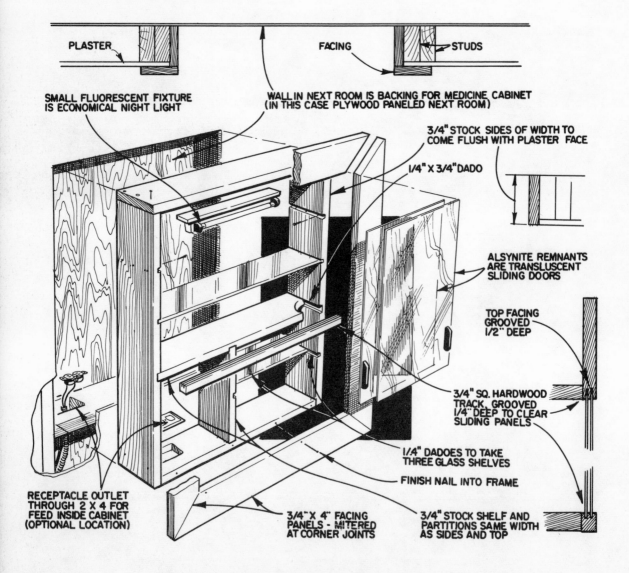

PLASTER

FACING — STUDS

SMALL FLUORESCENT FIXTURE IS ECONOMICAL NIGHT LIGHT

WALL IN NEXT ROOM IS BACKING FOR MEDICINE CABINET (IN THIS CASE PLYWOOD PANELED NEXT ROOM)

3/4" STOCK SIDES OF WIDTH TO COME FLUSH WITH PLASTER FACE

1/4" X 3/4" DADO

ALSYNITE REMNANTS ARE TRANSLUSCENT SLIDING DOORS

TOP FACING GROOVED 1/2" DEEP

3/4" SQ. HARDWOOD TRACK, GROOVED 1/4" DEEP TO CLEAR SLIDING PANELS

1/4" DADOES TO TAKE THREE GLASS SHELVES

FINISH NAIL INTO FRAME

RECEPTACLE OUTLET THROUGH 2 X 4 FOR FEED INSIDE CABINET (OPTIONAL LOCATION)

3/4" X 4" FACING PANELS - MITERED AT CORNER JOINTS

3/4" STOCK SHELF AND PARTITIONS SAME WIDTH AS SIDES AND TOP

Sliding doors in medicine cabinet slip right into grooves. Top grooves are deeper than at the bottom for easier installation.

Finished cabinet has modern and attractive appearance in bathroom. Screws on inside of sliding doors hold handle in place. Glass shelves allow the light to illuminate the whole cabinet, and door is translucent to give soft room light throughout night.

Shelves for closet are put in place before the outside trim is nailed on. See drawing on page 15 for closet construction details.

Take your time and be careful when you're nailing the closet sections near ceiling; it's easy to hit and mar ceiling panels.

Note that section used for drawers goes only to eye-level height; space above it is used for the storage of blankets, etc.

After closet walls are in position, trim is nailed on. Trim comes with door unit. Storage space has already been put to use.

Trim is put on with 1-in. brads which are covered with natural wood dough and later touched up with same finish as walls.

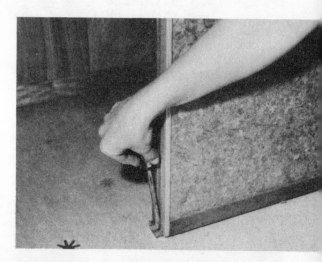

Door guides are fastened down after doors are hung. Note that linoleum floor covering is put down before building closets.

Above, two of the storage drawers are in place. Check photo and drawing below for full construction details of the drawers.

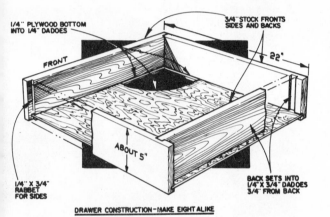

1/4" PLYWOOD BOTTOM INTO 1/4" DADOES

3/4" STOCK FRONTS SIDES AND BACKS

FRONT

22"

ABOUT 5"

1/4" X 3/4" RABBET FOR SIDES

BACK SETS INTO 1/4" X 3/4" DADOES 3/4" FROM BACK

DRAWER CONSTRUCTION—MAKE EIGHT ALIKE

Right, most of drawers are accessible to youngster. We hope he'll learn to use them.

Below, drapery rod supports are screwed to window frames—no window shades!

Right, draw drapes cover the window, are of same color as wall, don't "break up" room.

Aerial or Tuner Problem

by Art Margolis

An infallible test for determining which is causing your trouble

SOME discussion of the raster man-ufacturing plant will be of value to us here. The horizontal, high voltage and vertical sections of the TV provide the light source on the phosphor screen just as the lamp in a movie projector provides light on the movie screen.

While the raster is necessary, it is boring to sit and stare at it, unless there is a picture. The picture information in a movie projector comes from the film obstructing the light and producing light spots and dark spots on the screen.

The picture information inserted into the raster comes through the air from the TV studio in the form of electromagnetic pulsing waves. These invisible forces are intercepted by your TV antenna, funneled down your antenna wire and fed into the antenna terminals of your TV set. The TV processes these tiny bits of electronic information and injects it into the electron ray in the picture tube. The ray then produces light spots and dark spots on the TV screen.

Let's examine how a scene at the TV studio can get out into the air.

A TV camera takes a moving picture of the programming at the studio. The photo sensitive plate inside the camera's picture

The first step in isolating confusing front end trouble is to attach a pair of rabbit ears, as shown here.

All of the passengers, picture (P), sync (V, H) and sound (S) are loaded into the carrier wave, as shown.

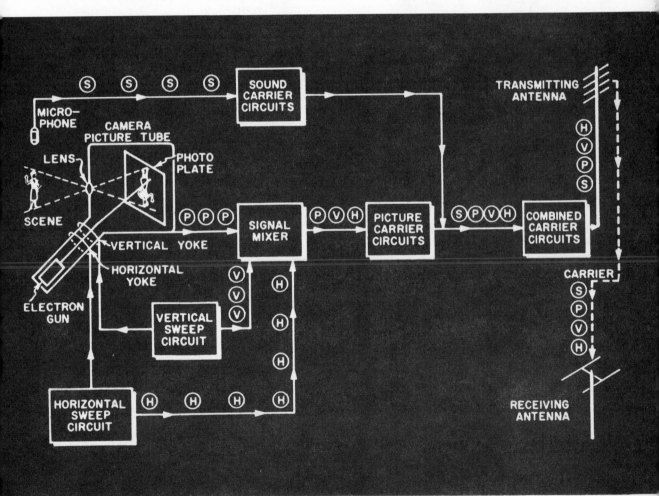

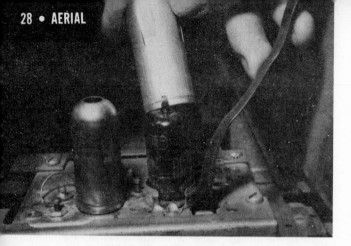

The first circuitry to receive the signal is the tuner. Note the aerial wire going into the tuner unit.

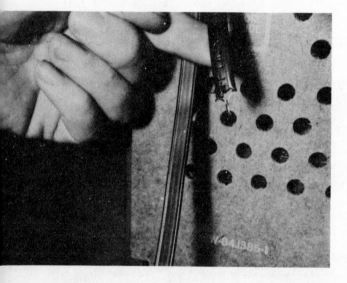

Disconnect your outdoor antenna wire and short leads. Then attach pair of rabbit ears for test.

tube is electrically altered by the light that is focused on it. An electron gun similar to the one in your picture tube, fires a ray through a yoke, scanning the photographic plate with a 15,750 CPS horizontal rate and a 60 cycle vertical rate.

The ray hits either dark spots or light spots according to the scene that is coming through the lens. A wire leads out from the plate. If the ray hits a light spot a small voltage is developed and a small voltage emerges from the wire. If the ray hits a dark spot a heavier voltage is developed.

The signal voltage represents each picture frame in terms of millions of tiny spots ranging from light to dark. The signal voltage at this point is ready to be processed for beaming out on the air waves.

This is where the carrier wave comes in. Each TV station is known by its frequency. Each TV station has a different frequency. As you flip your channel selector you are tuning in a different station each time. The station's designated frequency or carrier is developed by an oscillator set to run at that frequency in the transmitter. It is called the carrier wave because the picture signal is impressed on it for transmission to your set.

The carrier wave is invisible. It exists at the same time as we do but in different dimension. While we have length, breadth and height, a carrier wave has amplitude and frequency, both electromagnetic characteristics. If we graph it, it looks like "A".

In addition to the video we also must have audio. Thus there is a microphone near the camera. It picks up the sound of the scene. The sound is also impressed on the carrier wave, but in slightly different fashion so the sound and picture voltages won't mix. While the picture signal affects

Unmodulated carrier wave is developed at transmitter and runs at assigned frequency, as shown.

The picture signal is impressed on the carrier and modulates the hills and valleys called amplitude.

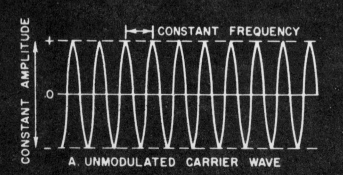

A. UNMODULATED CARRIER WAVE

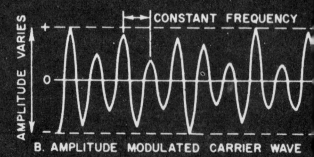

B. AMPLITUDE MODULATED CARRIER WAVE

the height or amplitude of the carrier the sound affects the frequency. The frequency as we mentioned before is one of the carriers' dimensions and is represented by the distance between the hills and valleys shown on the drawing. Since the audio is varying the frequency, it is said to be frequency modulated (FM).

The video signal, on the other hand, is amplitude modulated (AM) because it affects the other carrier dimensions' amplitude. The fact that the picture and sound are respectively AM and FM helps keep them from interfering with each other.

In addition to transmitting sound and picture, another passenger must be loaded aboard the carrier wave: sync.

In your TV the vertical oscillator runs free and automatically. That's not good enough. For unless your vertical oscillator draws the beam down at precisely the exact time as the camera is doing so at the TV station, your TV picture will roll. So, at the end of every second picture, the studio inserts a vertical locking or sync pulse into the video voltage. This transmitted vertical pulse, upon arrival at your TV is separated from the composite TV signal and sent to the vertical oscillator. At precisely the end of the picture information it is applied, and locks the vertical sweep into step, preventing flopover.

The horizontal sync works in a similar fashion. In order for you to see a picture and not a screenful of horizontal lines, the 525 lines must be drawn and whipped back precisely in time with the picture being scanned at the studio. So, at the end of every line of video information a horizontal sync pulse is placed into the video voltage. This pulse gets into your TV, is separated from the video and is presented to the hori-

zontal oscillator at precisely the end of each line of video. The pulse makes the oscillator fire precisely when it should and the yoke whips the electron beam back for the next line to begin.

This is the way all the passengers, picture, sync and sound, are loaded into the carrier and radiated from the transmitting antenna. Your TV antenna absorbs some of the radiation and funnels it down to your set.

The Infallible "Aerial or Tuner?" Test: The first circuitry the loaded carrier runs into as it leaves your antenna system is the front end or tuner of your TV. Subsequently, antenna troubles and tuner troubles cause similar symptoms of trouble. This can cause you to troubleshoot the antenna system when actually you have tuner trouble or vice versa.

If you have any of the prescribed symptoms there is a test you can perform to steer you correctly.

Disconnect the antenna wire from the antenna terminals and short the leads protruding from the antenna wire together. Sometimes aerial trouble will radiate into the TV even if the aerial is not connected to the TV. With the wires shorted this possibility is reduced.

Attach a substitute indoor antenna onto the TV terminals. Examine the picture you receive with the substitute antenna.

If your trouble ceases at this point and you receive the normal reception you usually get with this substitute antenna, chances are the trouble is in your original, now disconnected, antenna.

However, should the trouble remain even with the substitute aerial, chances are good you have tuner trouble rather than antenna problems. •

The audio signal in contrast, modulates frequency of the carrier, that is, the distance between the hills.

The total transmitted modulated carrier contains AM picture information and FM sound, as shown.

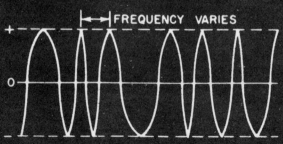

C. FREQUENCY MODULATED CARRIER

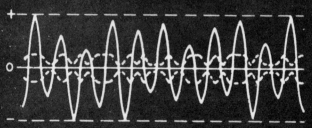

D. MODULATED TV CARRIER WAVE

- - - - - - SOUND—CONSTANT AMPLITUDE, FREQUENCY CHANGES

———————— PICTURE—CONSTANT FREQUENCY, AMPLITUDE CHANGES

How to Air Condition An Existing House

by Arthur M. Watkins

Salvage as much as possible from your present heating system, check insulation, shade, wiring—then find the most suitable cooling unit.

WHEN a large five-year-old St. Louis house was air-conditioned last year the owners learned how to reduce the cost by 15% and thereby saved $325. They started out with an air-conditioning bid for $2,350. Then they called in an engineer to look over the small print in the contract. But he also gave the house a once-over and even hoisted himself into the attic to look around.

Although the house was insulated the engineer advised the owners to double the attic insulation and also add outside shading devices over two large window areas. This would cost $285, he estimated. But then a smaller air-conditioning system

could be used and it was later bought for only $1,740, all told. The owners thus made a net saving of $325. Since the smaller cooling system consumes less electricity to keep the house at 75° during summer, operating costs are also lower and extra savings mount up every year.

This St. Louis story shows that it really pays to insulate thoroughly and shade an existing house. In addition, engineers, who have accumulated a wealth of information on existing houses, suggest the following check list before air conditioning:

►*How well is your attic insulated?* Biggest cooling problem is almost always from

the huge heat load on the roof that builds up furnace-like temperatures in an attic. Engineers find most attics "inadequately insulated." So your first step should be a thorough attic investigation. As much as six inches of bulk insulation laid over the ceiling or the equivalent in aluminum foil insulation will usually pay for itself. Most houses today have less than three inches of insulation, if any at all. The gable ends of the attic should also be opened up with large ventilating louvers.

►*Are large windows shaded from direct sun rays?* If not, they should be protected by outside shading devices. Remember that ten times as much sun heat invades a house through glass as through an equal area of insulated wall.

►*Are the walls insulated?* Although it may be more costly to insulate the finished walls of an existing house, it will still pay when measured against cooling savings. Walls should get three inches of insulation and this can usually be blown in.

►*Can existing heating ducts be salvaged for cooling?* Because cooling generally calls for bigger ducts than those needed just for heating, have a trained dealer measure your existing ducts to see if they are big enough. "Heating ducts almost always work out," says one top engineer, "but some modifications may be needed." You

A two-story home in Fort Wayne, Indiana, was fitted with new, year-round equipment as shown in the photograph at right.

Photos courtesy of General Electric

Neat ductwork for new, cooler-heater hugs basement ceiling. After installation, winter heating oil costs actually dropped 25%.

Add-on cooling unit is used with existing forced-air heating system. Cooling-coil section is atop furnace. Carrier Corp.

Steady supply of refrigerant for add-on cooling unit is pumped from the air-cooled compressor outside.

may need a bigger trunk line in the basement or an extra duct run to a big room facing south. ("The easiest room to heat in winter is often the hardest to cool in summer.") Ductwork is the most expensive part of the installation so it rates thorough advance planning.

►*Can you keep the existing warm air outlets?* Proper air diffusion is far more important for cooling than heating. Air conditioning usually calls for a double-deflection type of air outlet—one with both vertical and horizontal louvers that can be opened, closed or slanted so the right amount of air is diffused in the right direction for each room. If your warm air outlets are plain metal grilles with fixed louvers they probably should be replaced.

►*Is the furnace blower big enough for cooling, too?* In about half of the cases, yes. If so, you can save by buying a stripped-down summer cooler that hooks up the furnace fan.

►*What can you do if your house has hot-water heat or no central heat?* You can put in a chilled-water system, console units or window units. In many houses, however, engineers say that a ductwork system is still your best bet, furring down the ducts in a central hall, for instance, with short ducts branching out to the rooms around. The hot water boiler remains for heating.

►*Is the present wiring adequate?* Most air-conditioning systems need at least a separate 220-volt, 30-ampere circuit wired straight from the main electric board. The board itself should normally have a capacity of at least 60 amperes for the whole house, preferably 100 amperes. The size of the board is usually marked on the cover. Another solution is a gas-operated air conditioner which only needs a relatively small amount of electricity to run its blower.

►*Which is the best cooling system for a particular house?* — There are six principal types, all but one being the same as used in new houses. Here are the advantages and disadvantages of each:

The Add-On Unit

This was designed especially for adding cooling to an existing forced-air heating system. As shown on page 39, a cooling-coil section is put above the heater and pipe-connected to the cooling compressor, which is usually located outside. Refrigerant is pumped to and from the cooling coil section is put above the heater and blower works the year round. In summer, the house air is pulled through the furnace (which is then inoperative), blown through the add-on cooler for air conditioning and distributed through the existing ducts.

The add-on unit is the most inexpensive if you start with a good forced-air heating system. For one thing, you usually save the cost of a cooling fan by using the furnace fan. For another, you use the ductwork already installed. And the remote compressor section can be bought with an air-cooled condenser so no water is needed. Total installation costs start at about $1,200 for a 2-ton size, the more complex the installation the higher the cost.

The Attic Cooler

The horizontal attic cooler is good for existing houses where space is at a premium. Actually the unit not only can go in the attic but can also be suspended from a closet or basement ceiling. If a house has heating ducts the unit can be tied into them for distributing cool air. If a house has hot water heat, the unit can be centered in the house and only short supply ducts need be installed to get air to all rooms. Cooling is then independent of the heating.

The Small Duct System

This system gives the advantage in many old houses of using small 3½-inch or four-inch round ducts that can be easily inserted within existing partitions. This eliminates much of the cutting and patching in houses where conventional ductwork would normally mean expensive alterations. Thus the small duct system can be a natural in a house without any heating ducts to start.

The basic cooling equipment used is similar in size and cost to conventional equipment except that the air blower may be somewhat larger to deliver air at higher than normal velocities. This is because the smaller ducts require faster air speeds to handle the same overall cooling load handled by bigger ducts with relatively low air velocities. But the slightly increased fan horsepower used makes very little difference on overall operating costs.

Frigidaire
A combination heater-cooler takes less space than furnace and provides complete air conditioning.

Horizontal unit is designed for addition to existing warm-air ductwork in attic, closet, basement.
Lennox Furnace Co

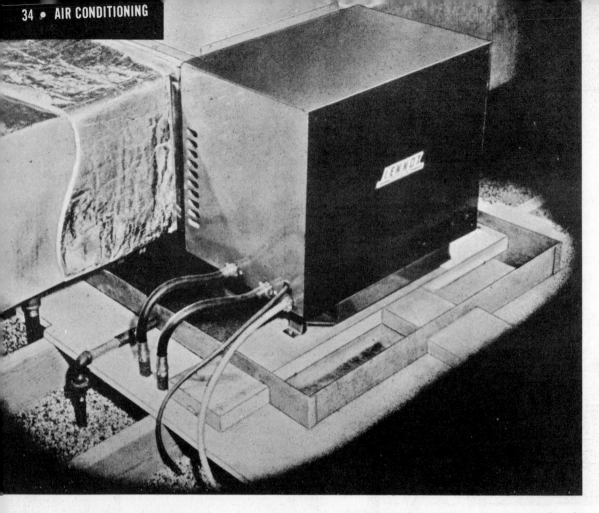

Installation of horizontal unit is shown above. It contains refrigerating apparatus and a fan as well.

A second type of horizontal unit is designed for houses without warm air ducts (the ducts are added).

Carrier Corp.

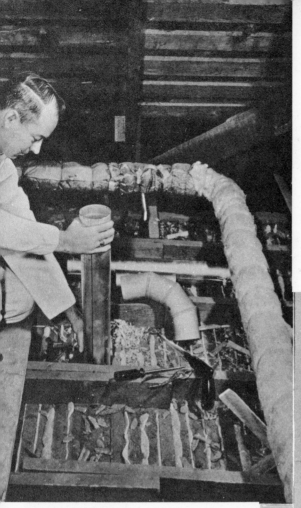

Prefabricated 3½-in. round ducts facilitate duct installation in existing houses. They are inserted within partitions. The Coleman Co.

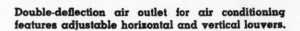

Double-deflection air outlet for air conditioning features adjustable horizontal and vertical louvers.

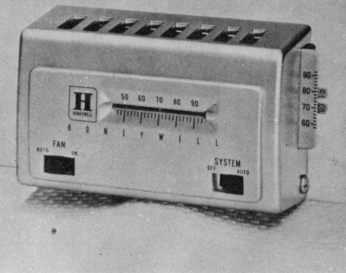

New year-round thermostat should replace old one. This one switches system from heating to cooling. Minneapolis Honeywell Regulator Co.

Chilled-Water Air Conditioning

This system is combined with an existing hot water heating system and no ducts are needed. But in an existing house it is essential that all the pipes be insulated before chilled water is pumped through. Otherwise condensation will drip from the pipes and cause havoc to paint and plaster. Because it is a tough job to reach all the hidden pipes in an old house and then insulate them, the chilled-water system may be an expensive proposition. On the other hand, ductwork may be out of the question in some old houses and chilled water can then be a blessing.

Room Air Conditioners

Room coolers are the easiest way to add air conditioning, especially in doing it piecemeal. But when a whole house is to be air conditioned the total cost can be much higher than the cost of installing a complete central system at one crack. Furthermore, the operating costs of a battery of room coolers will be higher than for a central system because a number of little compressors all running at one time are less efficient than one large compressor. And an odd array of room coolers sticking out of windows will add little to the appearance of any house.

On the plus side, room coolers can save you money if you only want to air condition part of a house and not all the rooms. Some of the new models can be recessed into a wall like a TV set or built into shelves to lick the problem of unsightliness. Most engineers, however, still recommend a central system to air condition the whole house. •

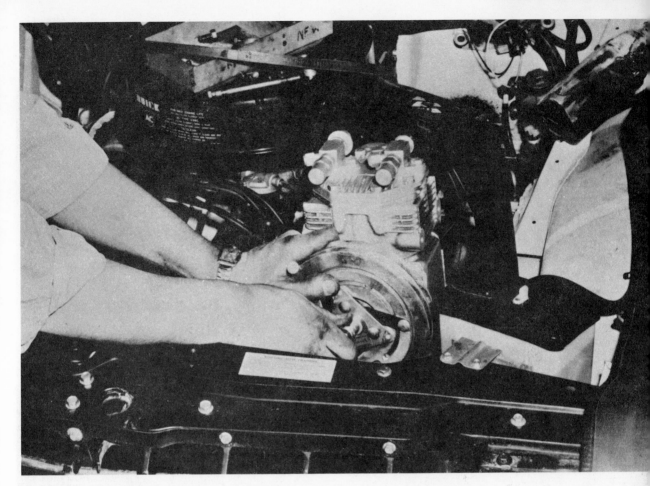

Compressor and adapter kit for Vornado's air conditioner is easily located at the side of the engine.

Car Air Conditioning

What to know about car air conditioning

WITH MORE than a half million air conditioners being installed on cars annually it's a foregone conclusion that there will need to be a lot more attention paid to the cooling system and engine efficiency. And unless there is a better understanding of how air conditioners work a lot of motorists are going to be mighty hot and bothered over their summer cooling.

Fortunately the breakthrough is conveniently afforded by a tour of inspection of the kitchen's electrical refrigerator. Here we find the same basic plan as in the car air conditioner except for the pump or compressor which is driven by the engine of the car instead of by an electric motor. Here, briefly, are the essential steps in car cooling:

The compressor picks up the heated re-frigerant vapor from the system and discharges it into a condenser which is located just ahead of the engine's radiator. Immediately, the vapor goes into liquid form, throwing off heat into the passing air currents. From here the liquid refrigerant goes to the receiver, and then through an expansion valve into the evaporator where it boils and goes back into vapor. The process of turning the liquid into a gas cools the evaporator and the air surrounding it. Finally, the vapor is drawn back into the inlet of the compressor to start the cycle all over again.

Ice cools by absorbing heat as it melts. A refrigerant cools by absorbing heat during its process of changing from liquid form to vapor. Keep in mind also that transfer of temperature always is from a warm object to one that is cooler.

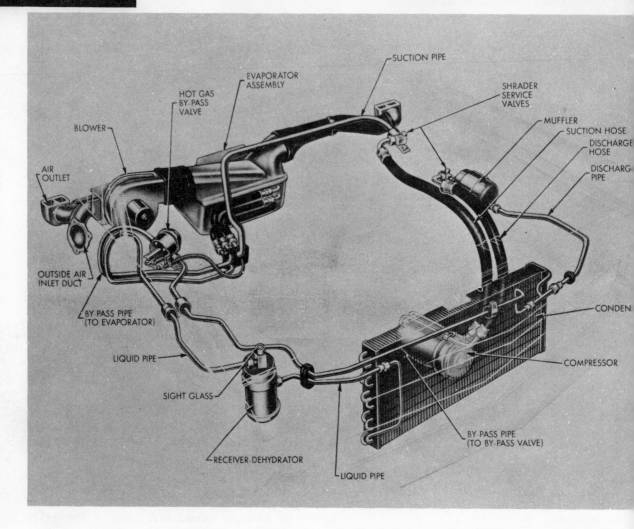

AIR OUTLET

BLOWER

HOT GAS BY-PASS VALVE

EVAPORATOR ASSEMBLY

SUCTION PIPE

SHRADER SERVICE VALVES

MUFFLER
SUCTION HOSE
DISCHARGE HOSE
DISCHARGE PIPE

OUTSIDE AIR INLET DUCT

BY-PASS PIPE (TO EVAPORATOR)

LIQUID PIPE

SIGHT GLASS

RECEIVER-DEHYDRATOR

LIQUID PIPE

BY-PASS PIPE (TO BY-PASS VALVE)

CONDEN

COMPRESSOR

Details of this factory-installed air conditioner, from Buick Motor Division, include a receiver dehydrator, a small muffler, hot gas by-pass valve, blower, compressor, service valves and sight glass.

All this seems simple enough, but the problem is the fact that in an automobile we have to saddle all this load on top of the car's cooling system at the very time when things are already at the sizzling point. Putting it frankly, the air conditioner is no better than the efficiency of the car's cooling system. Let the car develop trouble and the chances are that there will at least be a temporary halt in cooling comfort.

The air conditioner usually is independent of the car's ventilating and heating system. There's always a blower wheel or a fan designed to move air across the evaporator coils and into the car's body. Ducts are provided for even distribution of cooled air when the system is factory installed; and if it is one added to the car there would be louvers to provide for variations in aiming of cold air flow. Systems vary somewhat in their details. You may, for instance, find a small muffler between the compressor and the condenser.

Compressors may be of the rotary or the reciprocating type. There may be a fusible plug at the bottom of the receiver which will allow refrigerant to escape before its temperature exceeds 231 degrees Fahrenheit.

After leaving the condenser, the liquid refrigerant is forced into the receiver (a reservoir) so that there is always a sufficient supply to be fed to, and then through, the evaporator. This receiver is also a dehydrator for removing all traces of moisture.

Obviously the compressor must be equipped with a means of disengagement when no cooling is needed, or if cooling becomes excessive while the system is in operation. A magnetic clutch with thermostatic switch control is the popular way of handling this. The compressor also has a reservoir for its own lubrication, and there is the matter of its drive belt which usually should be adjusted for ½-inch deflection midway between the compressor and the

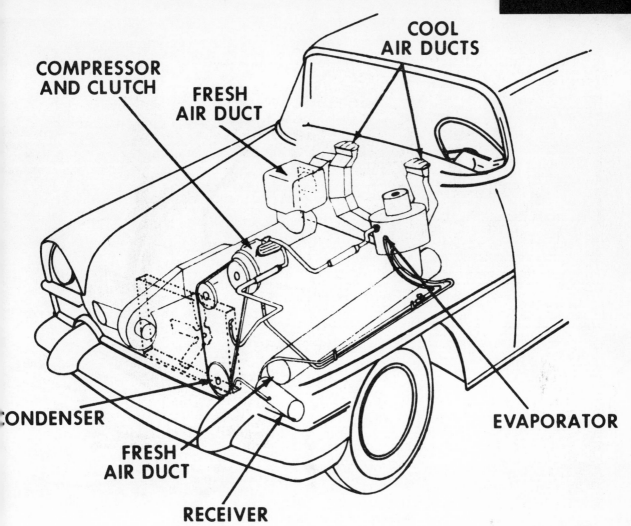

COMPRESSOR AND CLUTCH

FRESH AIR DUCT

COOL AIR DUCTS

CONDENSER

FRESH AIR DUCT

RECEIVER

EVAPORATOR

This sketch of a typical air conditioner simplifies its many components and shows their relationship.

pulley from which the drive is received.

Not only does the compressor rob the engine of some of its power, but heat given off by the condenser passes through the engine's radiator core at the very time the latter needs cooler air. Many cars with automatic transmissions also have an oil cooler at the bottom of the engine radiator so that the transmission's efficiency may be impaired by operation of the air conditioner. That everything works out as well as it does is a tribute to the skill of the car makers and the air conditioner manufacturers. But no system will operate satisfactorily unless certain rules are followed.

If you keep the conditioner on Manual for continuous operation on a very humid day the evaporator will ice up, and that will cut off air flow through this vital unit of the system. Under such conditions it is better to set the conditioner for Automatic operation.

On some cars the heater core is close to the evaporator and the temperature of the

cold air entering the driving compartment is adjusted by the amount of coolant passing through the core of the heater. Here it is possible to freeze the heater's coolant unless ethylene glycol antifreeze is used in summer. In other words, antifreeze should be used in such cases, not to raise the boiling point of the engine's coolant, but to protect the heater core against freezing!

Owners of cars with air-cooled engines can buy compact air conditioners. These can be installed without altering the engine's cover or making body modifications.

Much needs to be cleared up regarding use of long-lasting antifreeze in cooling systems of water-cooled cars with air conditioning. Consider the case of John H. With a 60 per cent solution of ethylene glycol in the system the boiling point was raised to 231 degrees. He rightly figured that the engine would run hotter with the conditioner operating, and he knew this antifreeze would thus help prevent coolant

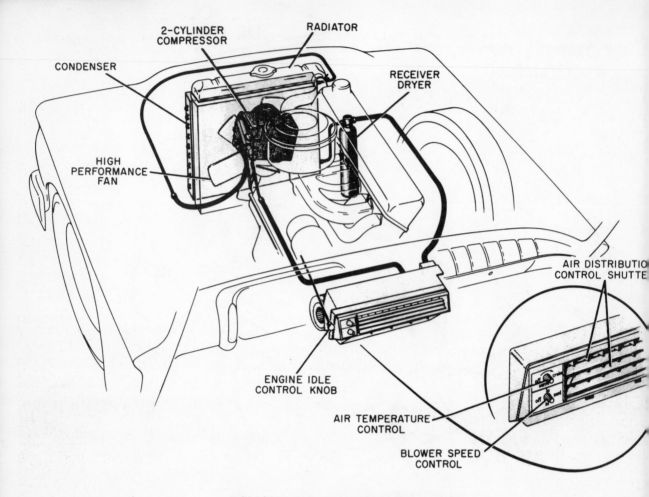

2-CYLINDER
COMPRESSOR

RADIATOR

CONDENSER

RECEIVER
DRYER

HIGH
PERFORMANCE
FAN

AIR DISTRIBUTIO
CONTROL SHUTTE

ENGINE IDLE
CONTROL KNOB

AIR TEMPERATURE
CONTROL

BLOWER SPEED
CONTROL

VALIANT AIR CONDITIONING UNIT

loss out the overflow, but he failed to figure that this was covering up urgent need for service. The engine did not immediately lose coolant, but it ran much too hot. This thinned down the oil, brought on clicking of the hydraulic valve lifters, and pinging. Then, on a long hill, things began to happen. Suddenly the engine's temperature hit the danger point, the automatic transmission began slipping and the radiator pressure cap's valve opened up. A real mess.

Use of long-lasting antifreeze is important to air conditioning success, but be sure the cooling system is in top form. Make certain that ignition timing is on the nose, that there is no slippage in the automatic transmission and that the engine operates on high enough octane gas.

Few motorists realize that the effectiveness of any cooling system depends upon the number and size of the passengers carried. Body heat is extra work for the heat transfer system. Often it is on a hot day when you feel like loading the car

with friends and relatives for a trip, and that's when insufficient cooling is likely to be the result, especially since the engine also is working harder. If the car has been standing in the sun, you should always drive a mile or two with the windows open to get the inside temperature down to normal before switching on the air conditioner.

During traffic stops it is better not to use the conditioner. Prolonged idling at temperatures above 90 degrees will cause excessively high compressor pressure. Switch off the system when climbing long grades. It is a good idea to test the system's efficiency with the aid of a thermometer held at an air outlet, with the conditioner switched on and the engine running around 1500 rpm. Without the thermometer test we often are mistaken as to just how effective the conditioner is.

In winter always operate the system twice a month so as to keep oil around the seal in the compressor. Unless this is done there will be leakage of refrigerant from

Below is the dash panel of the 1961 Valiant showing the air conditioning outlet. On the opposite page is the outlet in relation to working parts, with a detailed drawing of air shutters and control knobs.

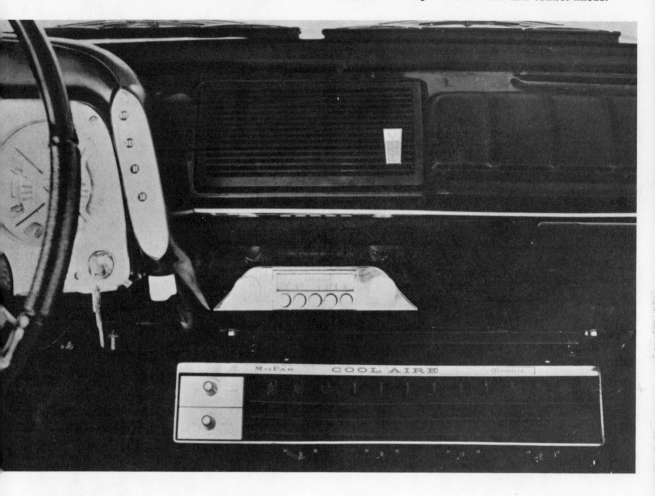

the system and insufficient cooling, later. Incidentally, when the system does not seem to be doing a good job, check the ducts of the car's heater and defroster. Air may be entering here.

A blown fuse for the blower will, of course, make the system ineffective. Failure will also result if the clutch doesn't get into the act when the conditioner is turned on, or doesn't cut in when the automatic control calls for more compressor action after a rest period. The magnetic clutch draws only 1.8 amperes, but the blower on High draws as much as 7.5 amperes.

You can observe the refrigerant flowing into the system by looking at the sight glass atop the receiver while the cooling control is set at maximum and the engine is running at 1500 rpm. If foam appears, the refrigerant supply is low. Add more refrigerant until bubbles disappear. Depending on the system's capacity, a little more refrigerant should then be added for good measure. Because refrigerant must be handled carefully (it is highly dangerous if it gets into the eyes), owners are urged to leave the actual job of adding refrigerant to a mechanic who specializes in this work. Safety goggles should be worn when working on any part of the system. Keep this in mind if you are doing motor work and might accidentally open up one of the air conditioner lines. Have your goggles nearby.

It will help the system do a better job on a summer day if you remember to keep the engine's radiator and the evaporator free of accumulations of leaves and dead insects. Make sure, too, that the fan belt is tight enough and that the engine has sufficient oil of the type it requires. Just because you can get more breeze with a convertible going at top speed is no reason to overlook the fact that you'll get more efficient artificial cooling in a closed car if you don't push its engine too hard. To keep cool, take it easy. •

Infrared Burglar Alarm

Any break in the invisible beam between these low-cost kit units sounds a continuous alarm.

By R. J. Capotosto

SETTING up a foolproof electronic burglar alarm is easy with two inexpensive Knight-Kits made by Allied Radio Corp., 100 N. Western Ave., Chicago, 80, Ill. The heart of the system is an ultra-sensitive photoelectronic relay which costs only $12.95 in kit form. This "eye" is positioned to intercept an imperceptible beam of light which crosses the only path a burglar might take and it triggers the alarm the instant he breaks the beam. Stepping out of the beam avails him nothing—the alarm continues to sound.

Two kits-one for the relay and one for the light source-comprise a complete system.

Mounting ot parts precedes wiring. The relay terminal is shown being mounted in position.

A variable resistance type photocell reacts to changes in the intensity of the light beam.

The subchassis is completely wired. It should be checked before mounting in main chassis.

There are springs on mounting screws of the sealed-beam light source for adjustment.

A red filter reduces the visibility of the light beam. It is slipped under retaining ring.

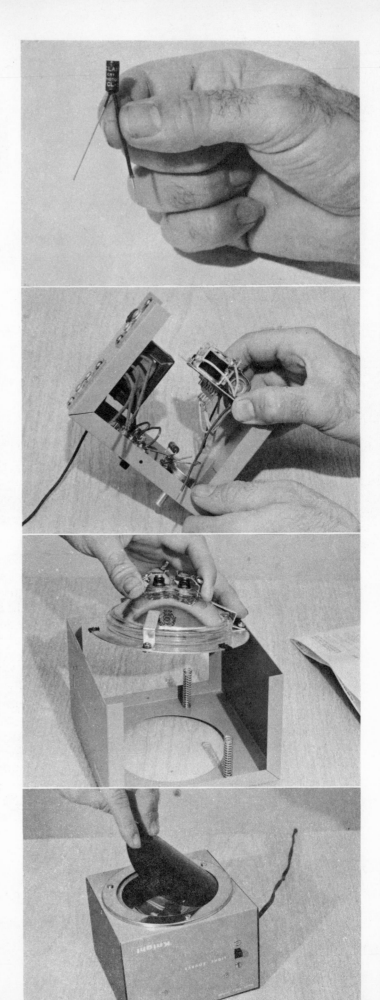

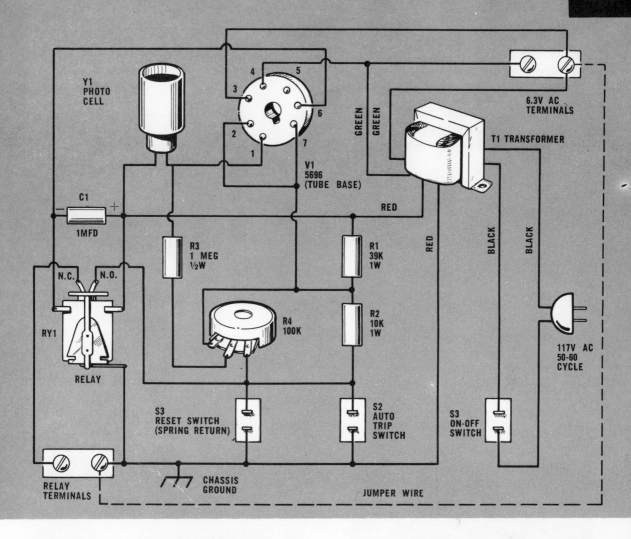

Actually, any light beam may be used with the photocell but the Knight-Kit sealed beam light source is handy and inexpensive at just $7.75. The inclusion of a transformer also allows the lamp to operate at five volts, which extends its useful life. To cut down the light so that it is almost invisible at close range,. a red filter is supplied. Yet the photocell

The completed units, including a small chime alarm in the middle, are ready to be installed.

will still operate at distances up to 150 feet away. For completely invisible light, a Wratten No. 70 filter which is sold at most photo supply houses may be employed. This will still allow operation up to 50 feet distant. An interesting application is to use mirrors to bend the light beam around corners. In this way, a door and one or more windows can be protected by a single installation. The setup, of course, may also be used to open garage doors, turn on lights or to announce visitors. It may even be employed to count assembly-line production in a factory.

Complete instructions for assembly of the photoelectronic relay and the light source are supplied with the kits and you should be able to complete the job in an evening or two. For an alarm you can hook up a loud bell or a chime which is also available for $4.70. Then sleep in peace. •

Tub Enclosure

ATTRACTIVE, smart and honestly functional, this bathtub enclosure will give your bathroom that up-to-date look. The basic materials used are aluminum angle and storm sash (or "Y" rails as they are called here). The two sliding door panels are of translucent plastic sheeting. The doors move at the touch of a finger and let in lots of light. It's easy to step in and out of the tub, too, because of the generous width of the doors.

You'll find the unit easy to make if you use the materials and follow the procedure suggested here. The length of your aluminum pieces will of course depend upon the size of your own bathroom and upon your own wishes. Plastic panels such as Reso-lite which can be worked with woodworking tools are available under several trade names. These panels come in many colors and will transmit up to 90% of the visible light. They can be purchased in either corrugated form or in flat sheets. The flat sheet of course is the proper one for this particular tub enclosure design.

TOP AND BOTTOM TRACKS

Start with your top and bottom tracks. After looking at the detail drawings shown here, cut these aluminum angles (⅛ x ¾ x ¾ inches) to the proper size on your table saw. Rivet the two angles together solidly.

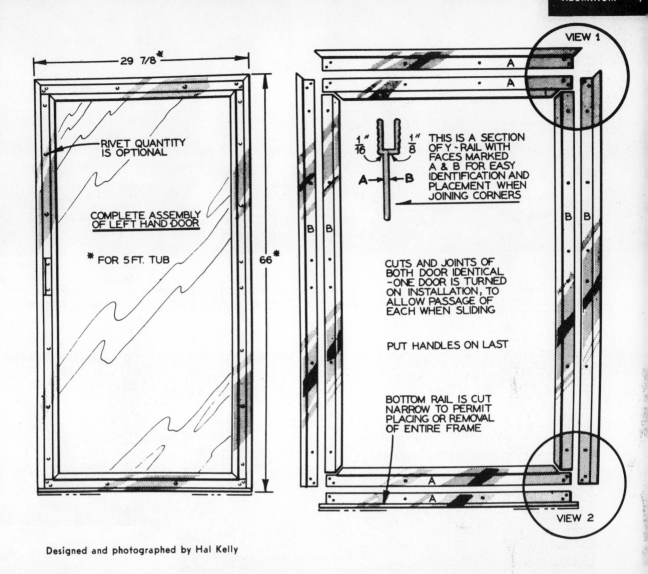

29 7/8*

RIVET QUANTITY IS OPTIONAL

COMPLETE ASSEMBLY OF LEFT HAND DOOR

* FOR 5 FT. TUB

66*

1/16"   1/8"

THIS IS A SECTION OF Y-RAIL WITH FACES MARKED A & B FOR EASY IDENTIFICATION AND PLACEMENT WHEN JOINING CORNERS

A ► ◄ B

VIEW 1

CUTS AND JOINTS OF BOTH DOOR IDENTICAL —ONE DOOR IS TURNED ON INSTALLATION, TO ALLOW PASSAGE OF EACH WHEN SLIDING

PUT HANDLES ON LAST

BOTTOM RAIL IS CUT NARROW TO PERMIT PLACING OR REMOVAL OF ENTIRE FRAME

VIEW 2

Designed and photographed by Hal Kelly

For water-tight bathing comfort, build yourself this bathtub enclosure. It's attractive, smart, and honestly functional.

Remember that the end of the rivet is peened into a countersunk hole so that the rivet is flush with the surface of the aluminum angle. This will enable you to cement the track to the tub edge. Drill your weep holes in the bottom track next. Then use your file, sandpaper, and steel wool on all rough or sharp edges.

Cementing the bottom track to the tub is a simple job. Just use two lines of masking, Scotch, or some similar tape spaced ¾ inch apart along the edge of the tub. Cover the area between tapes with tile cement. Place the bottom rail in position with a little pressure so that the cement is pushed into the pores of both surfaces. Do not

To make bottom tracks, fit two lengths of angle together as shown in drawings; join by riveting.

Drill holes for riveting; centerpunch, then add rivets as you go to keep tracks properly aligned.

Top and tub side of tracks can be trimmed to the desired width on table saw after being riveted.

Saw your storm sash members or "Y" rails to correct over-all length with handsaw or table saw.

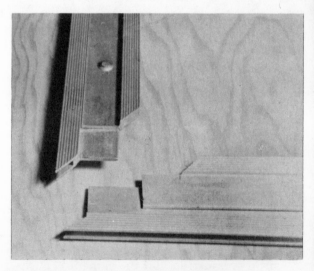

If you have a planer-jointer, run your tracks and "Y" rails through it to secure a true edge.

Cut miters as shown in detail drawing and join storm sash members to form sliding door frame.

Cut translucent plastic panel to required size; form frame around it and rivet corners to secure.

Upset rivets on inside of door frame, leaving clean, rounded rivet heads on outside of frame.

install the top rail until the doors are finished.

THE SLIDING DOOR

At this point a careful study of the detail drawings of the door corners will save you time, energy, and even money. Saw your storm sash or "Y" rails to the correct over-all length first. Note that the chan-

nel section of the "Y" rail which slides over the bottom track has been reduced to ¼ inch and that there is a $\frac{3}{16}$-inch space left between the top of the upper "Y" channel and the upper track. This will enable you to remove and install the doors whenever you wish by simply lifting the doors up and pulling them out at the bottom.

This bottom "Y" rail can be sawed to

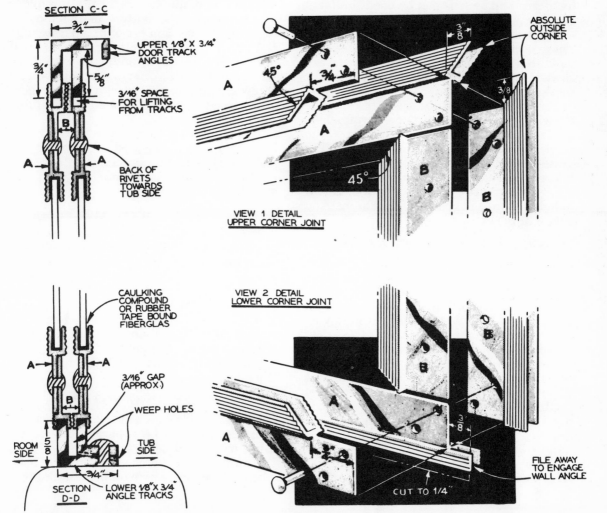

SECTION C-C

¾"

¾"

5/8"

UPPER 1/8" X 3/4" DOOR TRACK ANGLES

3/16" SPACE FOR LIFTING FROM TRACKS

B

A   A

BACK OF RIVETS TOWARDS TUB SIDE

VIEW 1 DETAIL
UPPER CORNER JOINT

45°

3/4"

A

A

B

45°

B

3/8"

3/8"

ABSOLUTE OUTSIDE CORNER

CAULKING COMPOUND OR RUBBER TAPE BOUND FIBERGLAS

A   A

B

3/16" GAP (APPROX.)

WEEP HOLES

ROOM SIDE

5/8

TUB SIDE

¾"

SECTION D-D

LOWER 1/8" X 3/4" ANGLE TRACKS

VIEW 2 DETAIL
LOWER CORNER JOINT

B

B

A

A

3/8"

CUT TO 1/4"

FILE AWAY TO ENGAGE WALL ANGLE

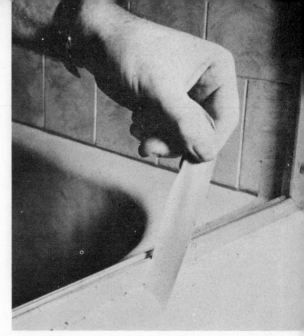

To cement bottom tracks to tub edge, first apply tile cement between two strips of masking tape.

Place bottom tracks in position, seating firmly; let dry, then strip off tape with excess cement.

the correct width on a table saw and then sanded. It can also be run through a planer-jointer a few times (if such a machine is available to you) to secure a true or straight edge. If necessary, of course, a hand saw and a plane can be used similarly for this purpose.

Mark and saw your corner miters next. These corners can be sawed on a table saw or with a hacksaw. Once the corners are sawed and fitted together they can be marked for drilling.

The pair of rails lettered "A" in the drawing can be marked, centerpunched, drilled, and riveted together before the corner joints are drilled and riveted. The same procedure can be followed with the pair of rails marked "B" in the detail drawing. You can use a C-clamp or wood screw to hold the rails in position for drilling. Any vise will do the job, too.

RIVETING THE DOOR FRAMES

It's a good idea to buy rivets which are the correct length. Add to the thickness of the materials to be riveted together a distance equal to about two times the thickness of the rivet. This will give you, under any circumstances, the over-all length of the rivet to be used. If your aluminum rivets are too long you can easily cut them down with a pair of pliers or saw them shorter in a vise. A quick method of getting the right size rivet hole is to check the shank of your twist drill against the body of your rivet. They should be the same size.

Place your rivet in the hole with the rivet head on a solid steel surface. This can be the head of a hammer held in a vise, or a steel stake as shown here.

INSTALLING SIDE ANGLES

Measure these for length carefully. Remember that the top angle track must be $\frac{3}{16}$ inch above the bottom of the top "Y" channel (see section c-c of detail drawing). If your walls are of plastic tile just drill pilot holes through both the aluminum angle and the tile. Then insert self-tapping screws. You can secure a tighter bond with some tile cement applied to the aluminum angle also.

The aluminum corner braces ($\frac{1}{16}$ x $\frac{3}{8}$ x 2 inches) can be riveted or screwed into place with self-tapping screws; the protruding ends can be nipped off, filed, and sanded.

THE TOP TRACK

The top track is installed last. Mark and cut it carefully. Then mark the location of holes for the corner braces and fasten them into place.

DOOR HANDLES

Since the position of the door handles is important, mark their location with the doors in place. Then remove the doors, mark and drill, and rivet the handles to the doors.

FINISHING NOTES

Use a file first on any edges which are rough or need to be rounded. Follow the filing with sandpaper and fine steel wool. Light rubbing with fine steel wool will leave a bright, uniform finish on the aluminum. •

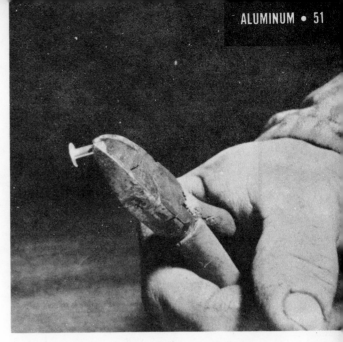

Use head of a nail punch to get at rivets when securing angle inserts in corners of door frame.

If the aluminum rivets you have are too long, you can easily cut them down with a pair of pliers.

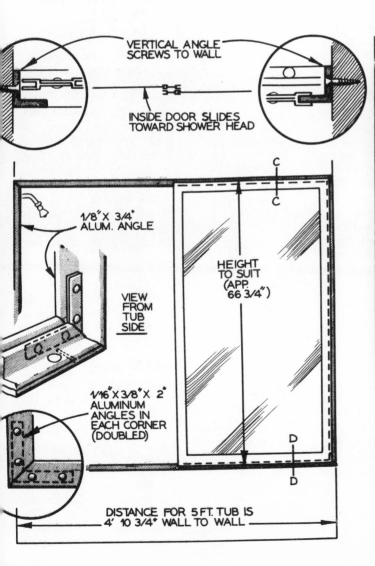

VERTICAL ANGLE SCREWS TO WALL

INSIDE DOOR SLIDES TOWARD SHOWER HEAD

1/8″ X 3/4″ ALUM. ANGLE

VIEW FROM TUB SIDE

HEIGHT TO SUIT (APP. 66 3/4″)

C C

1/16″ X 3/8″ X 2″ ALUMINUM ANGLES IN EACH CORNER (DOUBLED)

D D

DISTANCE FOR 5 FT. TUB IS 4′ 10 3/4″ WALL TO WALL

Mark the positions of the door handles with the doors in place, then remove doors and attach handles by riveting.

Fireplace Set

Colorful, lightweight, and quite easy to make, you'll find these fireplace tools make themselves at home on any hearth.

Only Do-It-Yourself Aluminum plus a whitewash brush, a ball of dyed jute cord, and miscellaneous screws are needed to build this modern fireplace set.

COLORFUL, lightweight and easy to make, you'll find these fire-place tools make themselves at home on any hearth. Only Do-It-Yourself Aluminum plus a whitewash brush, a ball of dyed jute cord, and miscellaneous screws are needed to build this modern set.

To get started, cut the handles to length, 22 inches for the poker, 21 inches for the shovel, and 18 inches for the broom. Before bending the shovel and broom handles apart, fasten them together with No. 8 x ¾-inch sheet metal screws. Wedge the two rods apart, and bend to fit the shovel's scoop and the brush. Rough out the flat parts at the ends with a hacksaw or coping saw; then file to fit snugly along the sides of both brush and shovel's scoop.

You'll want to shape and form both pieces of the poker and hook rods before joining them. Taper ends of both pieces on a jointer, jig, or band saw, or by hand with a hacksaw; rasp and file smooth. Bend the

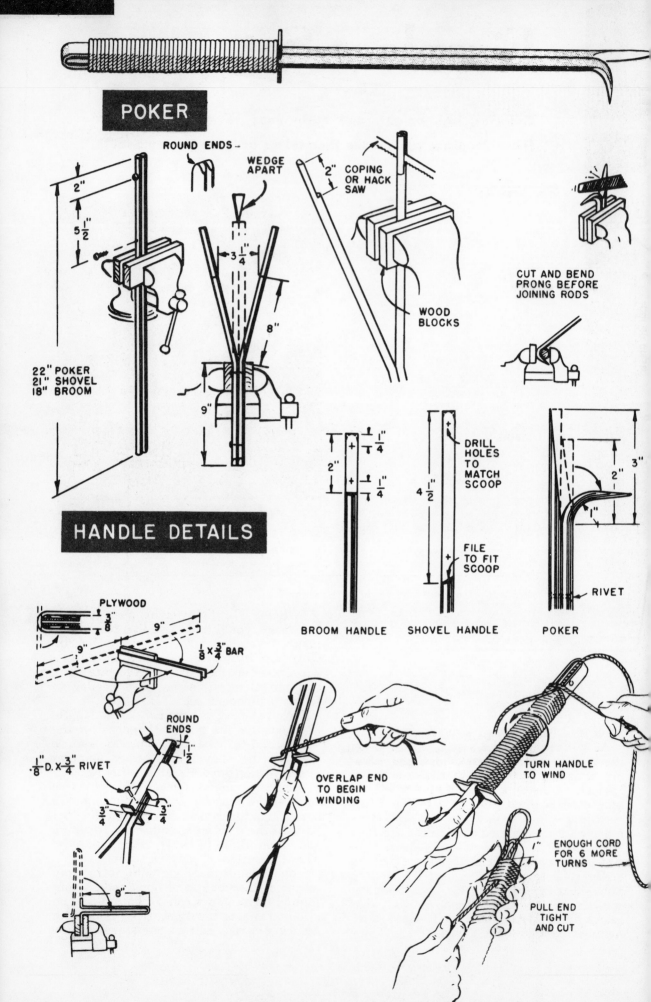

POKER

ROUND ENDS

WEDGE APART

COPING OR HACK SAW

2"

2"

5 1/2"

3 1/4"

8"

9"

WOOD BLOCKS

CUT AND BEND PRONG BEFORE JOINING RODS

22" POKER
21" SHOVEL
18" BROOM

HANDLE DETAILS

DRILL HOLES TO MATCH SCOOP

FILE TO FIT SCOOP

RIVET

2"

3"

2"

1/4"

1/4"

4 1/2"

BROOM HANDLE   SHOVEL HANDLE   POKER

PLYWOOD
3/8"

9"

9"

1/8 x 3/4" BAR

ROUND ENDS
1 1/2"

1/8" D. x 3/4" RIVET

3/4"   3/4"

8"

OVERLAP END TO BEGIN WINDING

TURN HANDLE TO WIND

ENOUGH CORD FOR 6 MORE TURNS

1"

PULL END TIGHT AND CUT

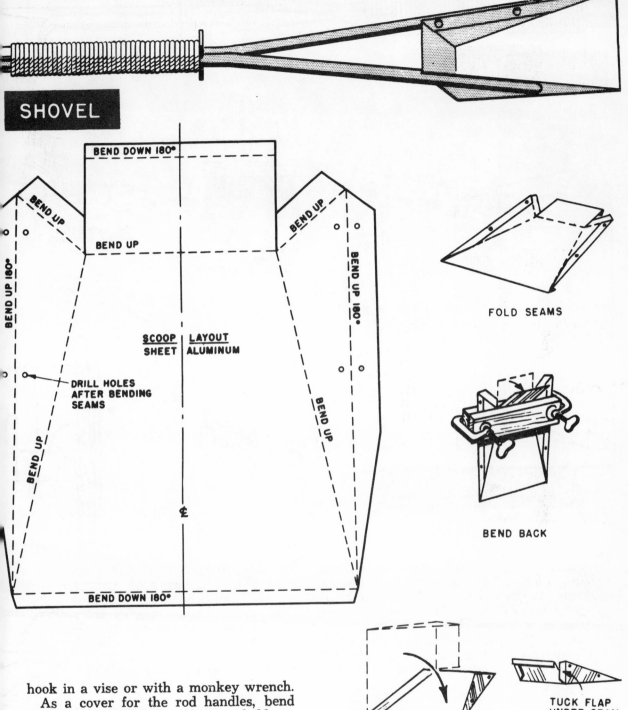

SHOVEL

BEND DOWN 180°

BEND UP

BEND UP

BEND UP 180°

BEND UP 180°

SCOOP LAYOUT
SHEET ALUMINUM

DRILL HOLES
AFTER BENDING
SEAMS

BEND UP

BEND UP

₵

BEND DOWN 180°

FOLD SEAMS

BEND BACK

hook in a vise or with a monkey wrench.

As a cover for the rod handles, bend the ⅛ x ¾-inch bar over the rounded handle ends and fasten it to the rods with ⅛-inch diameter x ¾-inch rivets. Wrapping cord of dyed jute, or venetian blind cord in a color to match your room's decorative scheme, is used to wind the handles.

To make the shovel scoop, make a full-size pattern and trace it onto a plain sheet of Do-It-Yourself Aluminum. The aluminum sheet can be easily cut with ordinary scissors or tin snips. Bend up the edge seams first between hardwood blocks, then hammer flat on a bench with a mallet (ex-

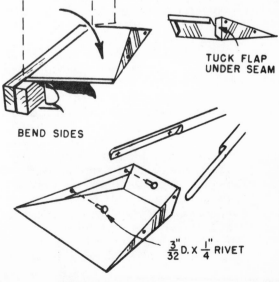

TUCK FLAP
UNDER SEAM

BEND SIDES

$\frac{3}{32}$" D. X $\frac{1}{4}$" RIVET

SCREW TO HANDLE

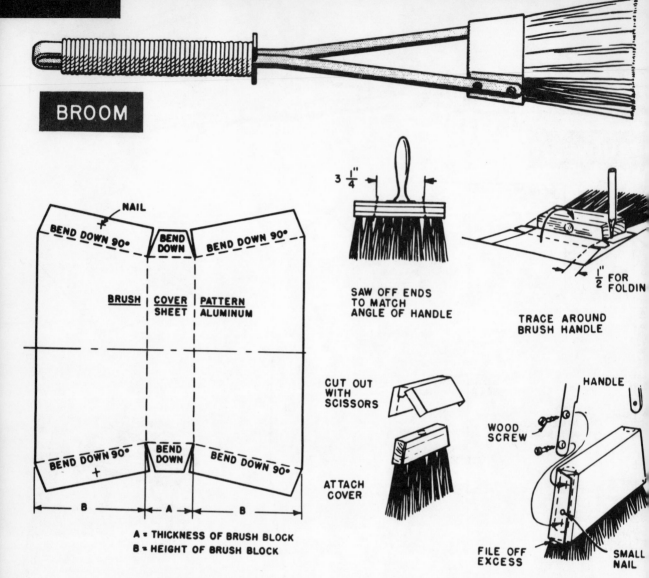

BROOM

NAIL

BEND DOWN 90° **BEND DOWN** **BEND DOWN 90°**

BRUSH **COVER SHEET** **PATTERN ALUMINUM**

BEND DOWN 90° **BEND DOWN** **BEND DOWN 90°**

B — A — B

A = THICKNESS OF BRUSH BLOCK
B = HEIGHT OF BRUSH BLOCK

$3\frac{1}{4}''$

SAW OFF ENDS
TO MATCH
ANGLE OF HANDLE

$\frac{1}{2}''$ FOR FOLDING

TRACE AROUND
BRUSH HANDLE

CUT OUT
WITH
SCISSORS

ATTACH
COVER

HANDLE

WOOD
SCREW

FILE OFF
EXCESS

SMALL
NAIL

cept along top of back). Bend up back and sides, tucking flaps under back edge seam. Fasten the back flaps with 3/32-inch diameter x ⅛-inch aluminum rivets (cut down from ¼-inch length). Attach the scoop to the handles with two 3/32-inch diameter x ¼-inch rivets along each side. Countersink holes in rod on outside and file flush after driving head.

Lay out the hood for the brush by rolling it on the aluminum sheet, marking the sides and allowing at .least ½ inch along each end. See half-size pattern for reference. Screw the ends of the handle through the overlapped ends and into the wood with No. 6 x ¾-inch flathead screws, countersunk flush in the handle rods.

The frame is bent from one rod, with a lap-joint at the bottom. File out the lap joint after cutting off the short ends left over and fasten with two ⅛-inch diameter x 7/16-inch rivets (cut down from ¾-inch length). Countersink holes and file both sides smooth after driving head. If you

shouldn't happen to have a 6-inch piece of 1/16 x 1 x 1-inch angle for the notched support bar, bend up an angle from a doubled sheet of aluminum. Rivet the lips on the underside of the support bar with 3/32-inch diameter x ¼-inch rivets. •

MATERIALS LIST

No. Reqd.	Size	Use
2	3/8" dia. x 22" rod	poker
2	3/8" dia. x 21" rod	shovel
2	3/8" dia. x 18" rod	brush
1	3/8" dia. x 72" rod	stand
1	1/16 x 1 x 1" angle x 6" long	support bar
3	1/8 x 3/4 x 18" bar	handles
1	.020 x 8 x 8" sheet	shovel scoop
1	.020 x 5-1/2 x 3-1/4" sheet	brush cover
6	No. 8 x 3/4" sheet metal screws	
8	1/8" dia. x 3/4" aluminum rivets	
4	No. 6 x 3/4" flathead wood screws	
10	3/32" dia. x 1/4" aluminum rivets	
1	whitewash brush	
1	200" ball of 3/32" dyed jute cord	

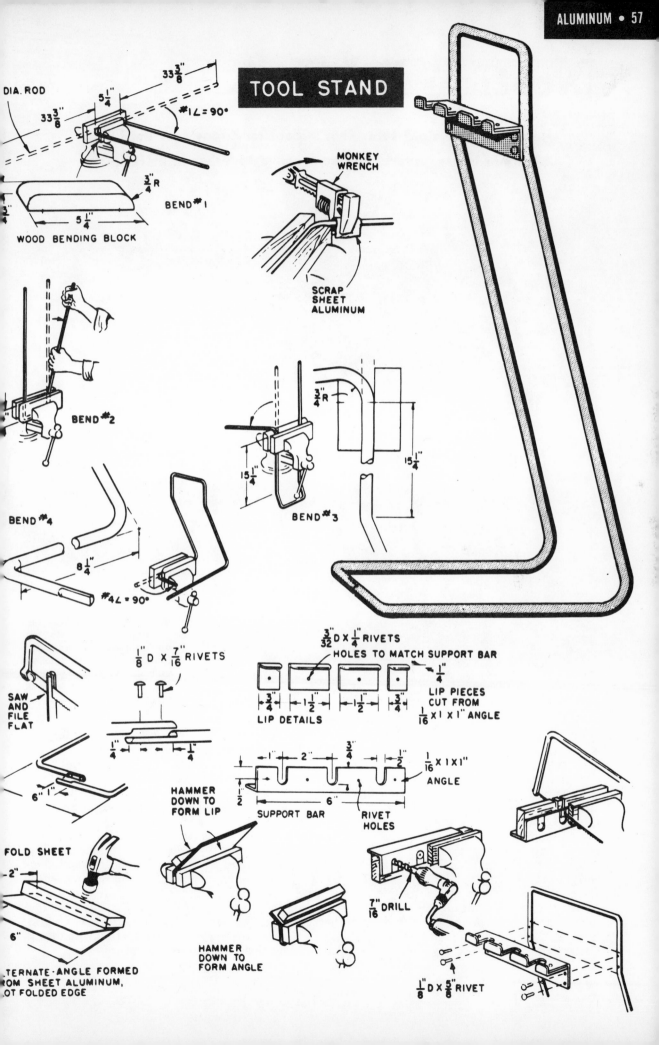

TOOL STAND

DIA. ROD

$33\frac{3}{8}$"

$33\frac{3}{8}$"

$5\frac{1}{4}$"

#1∠ = 90°

$\frac{3}{4}$"R

BEND #1

WOOD BENDING BLOCK

$5\frac{1}{4}$"

MONKEY WRENCH

SCRAP SHEET ALUMINUM

BEND #2

$\frac{3}{4}$"R

$15\frac{1}{4}$"

$15\frac{1}{4}$"

BEND #3

BEND #4

$8\frac{1}{4}$"

#4∠ = 90°

SAW AND FILE FLAT

$\frac{1}{8}$" D X $\frac{7}{16}$" RIVETS

$\frac{1}{4}$" $\frac{1}{4}$"

$6\frac{1}{4}$"

HAMMER DOWN TO FORM LIP

$\frac{3}{32}$" D X $\frac{1}{4}$" RIVETS

HOLES TO MATCH SUPPORT BAR

$\frac{1}{4}$"

$\frac{3}{4}$" $1\frac{1}{2}$" $1\frac{1}{2}$" $\frac{3}{4}$"

LIP DETAILS

LIP PIECES CUT FROM $\frac{1}{16}$" X 1 X 1" ANGLE

1"   2" $\frac{3}{4}$" $\frac{1}{2}$"

$\frac{1}{2}$"

6"

SUPPORT BAR

$\frac{1}{16}$" X 1 X 1" ANGLE

RIVET HOLES

FOLD SHEET

2"

6"

ALTERNATE ANGLE FORMED FROM SHEET ALUMINUM, NOT FOLDED EDGE

HAMMER DOWN TO FORM ANGLE

$\frac{7}{16}$" DRILL

$\frac{1}{8}$" D X $\frac{5}{8}$" RIVET

Nesting Table

Here's a lightweight table that's ideal for today's casual living. When not in use, several can be stacked together in little space.

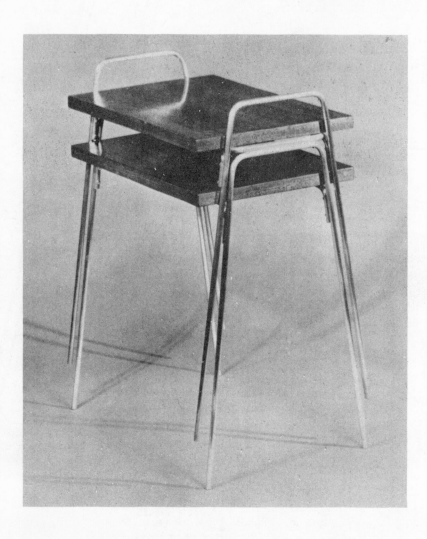

Braces, secured to the underside of the table top and extending between the table legs, keep stacked tables from scratching the top of table just below.

LIGHTWEIGHT tables are handy for glasses and a magazine alongside a favorite chair. They fit in with today's casual living for serving television snacks. When not in use, they nest together in little space. The brace, Part A, keeps stacked tables from scratching the top of table below. And they're easy to make from Do-It-Yourself Aluminum.

You'll need a pair of each of the three rods, Parts A, B, and C. Cut one pair of Parts B and C from one 6-foot length of ⅜-inch diameter aluminum rod. Form both braces, Parts A and B, with their ends bent at right angles around a form block. Center the rod for the leg, Part C, on the

form block and clamp in vise. Bend legs so bottom ends are 12 inches apart.

Begin the assembly by filing flat sections on the inside of the side braces, Part B. File away about ⅛ inch, leaving ¼ inch thickness. C-clamp the side brace to the inside of the leg, Part C, and drill ⅛-inch diameter holes through both for rivets. Countersink the hole on the outside of the legs, so end of rivets can be formed into the opening. Insert ⅛-inch diameter x ¾-inch aluminum rivets from the inside of the side braces. Form the head on the outside of the leg, forcing the metal into the countersink. File off the remaining rivet head flush with the bar.

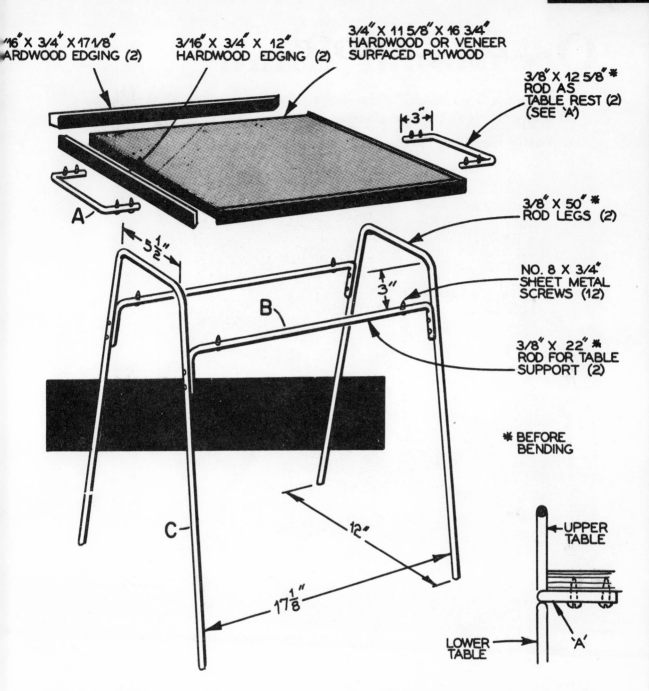

16" X 3/4" X 17 1/8"
HARDWOOD EDGING (2)

3/16" X 3/4" X 12"
HARDWOOD EDGING (2)

3/4" X 11 5/8" X 16 3/4"
HARDWOOD OR VENEER
SURFACED PLYWOOD

3/8" X 12 5/8" *
ROD AS
TABLE REST (2)
(SEE 'A')

3"

A'

3/8" X 50" *
ROD LEGS (2)

5 1/2"

3"

NO. 8 X 3/4"
SHEET METAL
SCREWS (12)

B

3/8" X 22" *
ROD FOR TABLE
SUPPORT (2)

C

12"

17 1/8"

* BEFORE
BENDING

UPPER
TABLE

LOWER
TABLE

'A'

The wood table top is next. You can make this out of solid hardwood, but a ¾-inch hardwood veneer plywood is less costly and will be less likely to warp. To hide the plywood's end grain, fit $\frac{3}{16}$ x ¾-inch edging strips of matching wood around the edges, mitering them at corners. Apply glue to the strips and to the edge of the plywood. Hold the edging strips in place with ¾-inch brads until the glue sets.

Sand the table top carefully. Either set the brads around the edges or pull them out. Seal the wood with shellac or lacquer for a clear finish and sand with 6/0 garnet paper. For an open grain wood, like oak or mahogany, apply coat of filler, let dry and sand smooth. Fill the brad holes around the edge with matching stick shellec. Finish with two coats of pale or "rubbed effect" varnish.

Assemble the top by drilling $\frac{5}{32}$-inch diameter holes up through side brace, Part B, for screws into top. Pilot drill $\frac{3}{32}$-inch diameter holes into underside of top for screws. Fasten top to side braces with No. 8 x ¾-inch aluminum sheet metal screws. Insert end brace, Part A, through legs under top. Outside of end brace should be flush with outer plane of legs. Screw end brace, Part A, to the underside of the table top the same way that you did the side braces. •

Occasional Chair

This smart, sleek-looking aluminum frame chair is upholstered with a plastic material, making it suitable for use both indoors and out.

Designed by John W. Davies

THIS chair is an appropriate project for the beginner as well as for the advanced craftsman. The simplicity of the design and the ease with which it may be constructed recommend it especially to the neophyte aluminum worker. These same features, of course, guarantee that you'll have a smart, sleek-looking chair. Plastic upholstery makes it suitable for use outdoors as well as indoors.

ARMS AND LEGS

So that both sets of arms and legs will be formed alike, begin by making a full-size layout of one set on wrapping paper. Then, when forming the arms and legs,

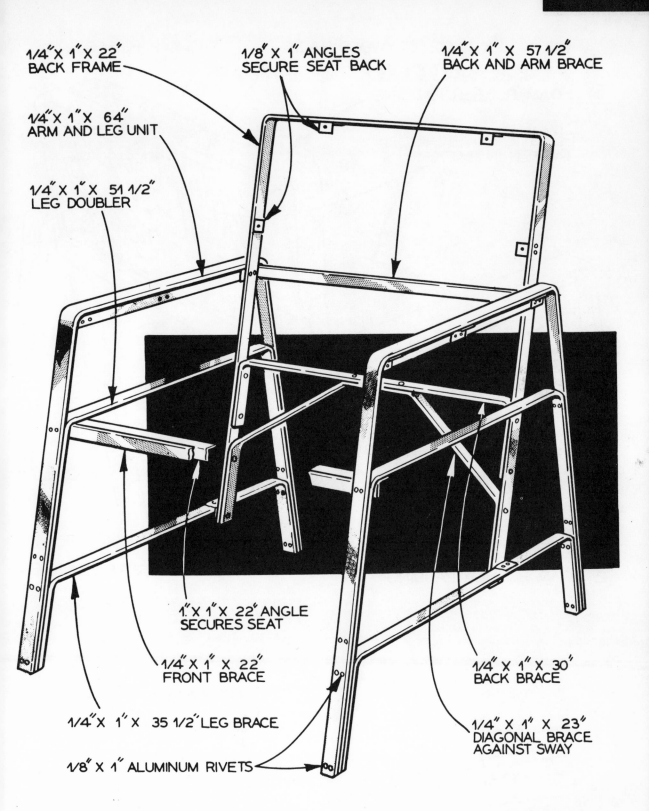

1/4" X 1" X 22"
BACK FRAME

1/8" X 1" ANGLES
SECURE SEAT BACK

1/4" X 1" X 57 1/2"
BACK AND ARM BRACE

1/4" X 1" X 64"
ARM AND LEG UNIT

1/4" X 1" X 51 1/2"
LEG DOUBLER

1" X 1" X 22" ANGLE
SECURES SEAT

1/4" X 1" X 22"
FRONT BRACE

1/4" X 1" X 30"
BACK BRACE

1/4" X 1" X 35 1/2" LEG BRACE

1/4" X 1" X 23"
DIAGONAL BRACE
AGAINST SWAY

1/8" X 1" ALUMINUM RIVETS

check them against the drawing. Do not trim these pieces to *exact* length until both sides have been formed. This will help you to get both sides equal.

Form all your bar stock around a piece of 1-inch steel pipe. You can use a short length of water or gas pipe for this purpose. Clamp the pipe in a vise. Bend the bar slowly, checking with your drawing until desired bend is achieved. If possible, keep the bar on a horizontal surface while bending so that the bar will not twist.

Now proceed to locate your rivet holes. Mark them accurately and centerpunch each one before drilling. You can put the bars in a vise to drill the rivet holes. Notice

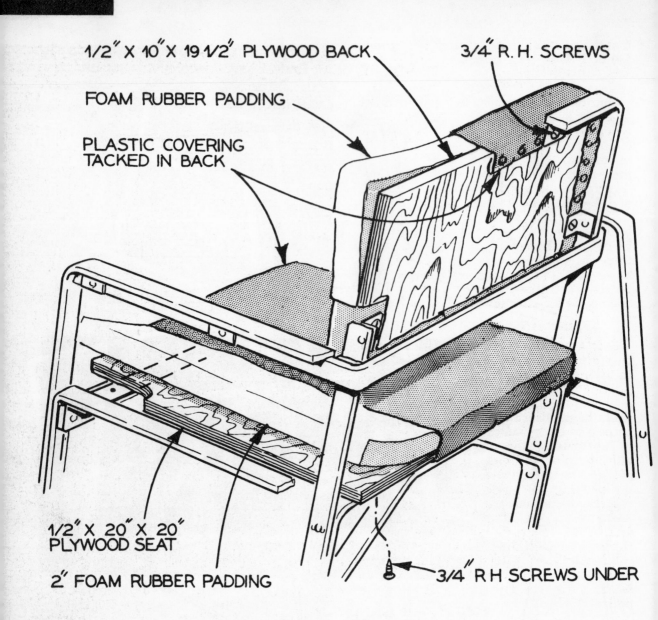

1/2" X 10" X 19 1/2" PLYWOOD BACK

3/4" R. H. SCREWS

FOAM RUBBER PADDING

PLASTIC COVERING
TACKED IN BACK

1/2" X 20" X 20"
PLYWOOD SEAT

2" FOAM RUBBER PADDING

3/4" R H SCREWS UNDER

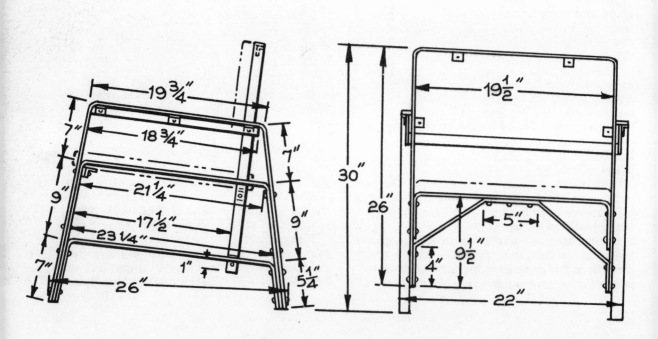

19 3/4"

7"

18 3/4"

7"

21 1/4"

9"

17 1/2"

9"

23 1/4"

7"

1"

26"

5 1/4"

30"

19 1/2"

26"

5"

4"

9 1/2"

22"

that the rivets are used in pairs, two at each joint. File smooth to finish.

CHAIR BACK

You can saw the back frame and brace to exact length after forming. Form the two pieces carefully. Now cut a number of aluminum angle braces from ⅛ x 1 x 1-inch stock. File edges smooth, then rivet the angles to the chair back as indicated. (Angle braces are also used under arms and to attach seat back to leg braces.)

The diagonal brace which gives the back of the chair additional rigidity can be cut and formed at this time. Rivet all three back pieces together. Remember, however, that aluminum angle braces must be riveted to the lower ends of the main back piece for attachment to the leg braces.

FRONT AND BACK BRACES

Saw these three pieces to exact length only after they have been given a trial fit in their positions on the chair.

After these braces have been formed and sawed to fit, lay out your rivet holes and drill them, inserting fillets between arm brace and back frame.

The ends of the back-and-arm brace must be filed to fit the bend in the arm stock. Mark this curve with a sharp tool before filing.

Mark, centerpunch, and drill all holes for rivets which are to hold the arms to the arm brace. Note that the rivet holes in the top surface of the chair arms have been countersunk so that the rivets can be peened into them. This will enable you to file and sand the top surface of the arms perfectly smooth.

PLYWOOD BACK AND SEAT

These two pieces of plywood are ½ inch thick and must be upholstered before being fastened to the chair. Cut foam rubber to the shape of the plywood and cement it to the wood with rubber cement.

The upholstery material can be whatever you wish to use. However, a plastic covering will prove useful both indoors and out. Tack the covering to the plywood with short upholstery tacks or carpet tacks.

Both seat and back can be anchored to the frame of the chair with either ¾-inch wood screws or self-tapping screws.

RIVETING NOTE

If the rivets you have on hand are too long, just cut them down with a pair of cutting pliers. If your rivets are too short, you can substitute aluminum machine screws; both ends of these screws can be peened over and sanded smooth. •

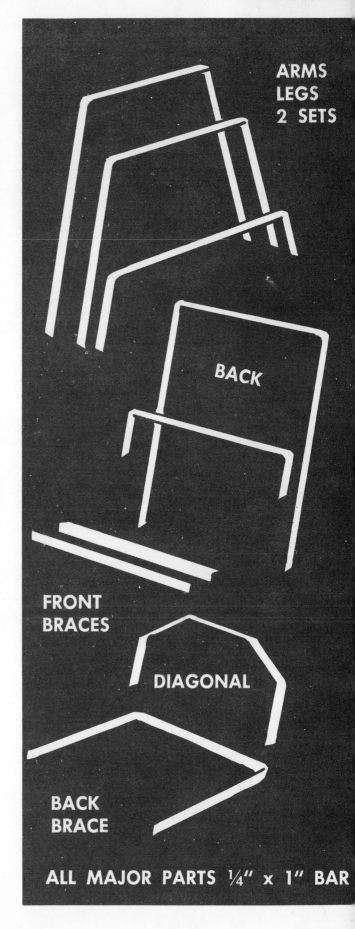

ARMS
LEGS
2 SETS

BACK

FRONT
BRACES

DIAGONAL

BACK
BRACE

ALL MAJOR PARTS ¼" x 1" BAR

File Desk

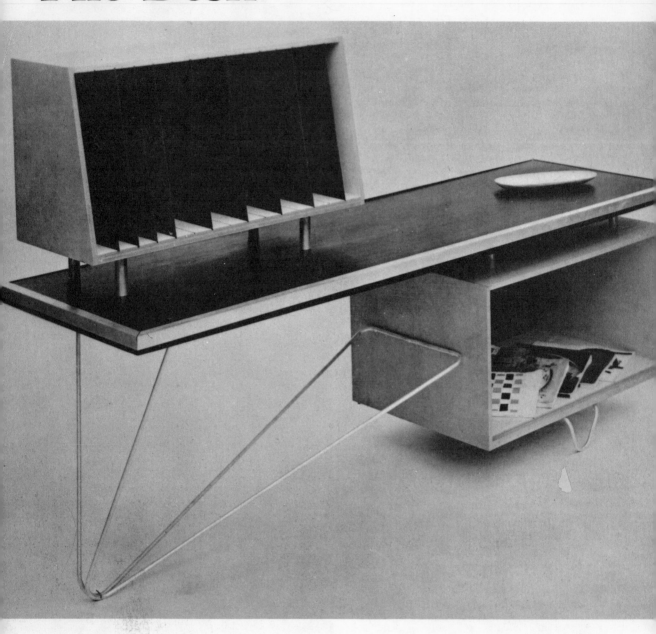

THE design of this desk skillfully utilizes large rectangular shapes together with triangular and smaller cylindrical ones. The light, gleaming aluminum also offers a sharp contrast to the dark wood of the desk top and the masonite separators in the upper, file box.

A feature worth noting is that the wood parts can be quite inexpensive. The two box-like structures are made of plywood. The top of the desk can be made of a solid hardwood, or of cheaper wood covered with veneer. Formica or linoleum of a modern design could also be used. The plans call for aluminum tubing (with dowel inserts) to be used to separate the desk top from the two box-like structures. Instead of tubing, however, solid rods or bars might be artfully shaped and used.

DESK TOP

As the desk top is just two feet wide, you can easily make it with three boards (¾ x 8 x 72 inches) doweled and glued together. Reinforce the top with a frame, or blocking as it is called here, made from ¾ x 4-inch stock. Glue and screw this frame to the underside of the desk top. After planing the edges and squaring the top, chamfer the top edges to permit the angled surfaces of the aluminum edging to sit flush against the wood.

Admittedly more decorative than functional, this striking desk of ultra-modern design will add beauty and excitement to any setting.

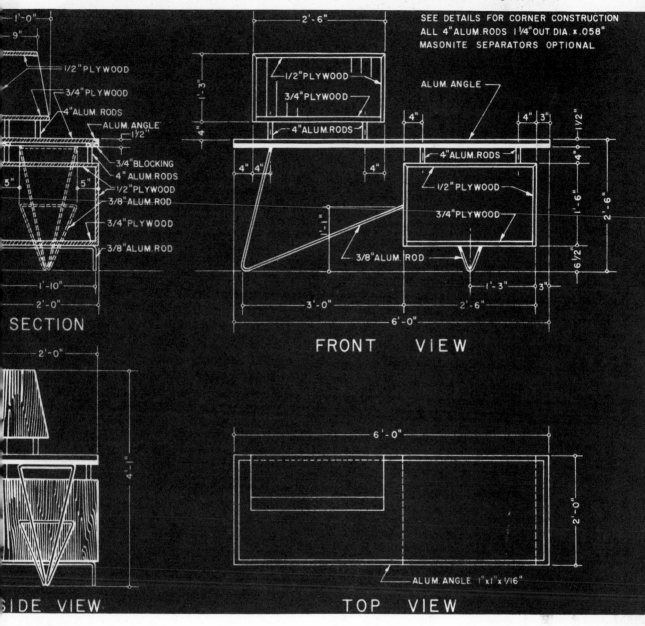

As the aluminum angle (1 x 1 x $\frac{1}{16}$ inch) can be purchased in 6-foot lengths, just carefully miter both ends of two 6-foot lengths to cover front and back edges. Then drill holes and secure the angles to the desk top with wood screws. The ends of the desk top are covered in the same manner. Saw the two end pieces to exactly match the mitered ends of the long side pieces.

THE BOXES

You'll need two thicknesses of plywood: ½-inch stock for the top, two sides, and back of each box, and ¾-inch stock for the bottom. Cut your pieces to the correct over-all dimensions; then, tilt either the

arbor or the table on your saw 45° and saw the end of each board for a miter joint. The joints shown here are the key-and-slot type. Other joints can be used of course. The boards are then glued and clamped together. After the glue has dried, plane the front edges of the boxes carefully.

Note that the top and bottom boards of the upper box have been sawed to admit removable masonite separators. This must be done of course before glueing and clamping the box together.

The bottom box, as shown here, is finished quite simply on the inside. You may wish to add shelves or separators. These can be made of solid stock, plywood,

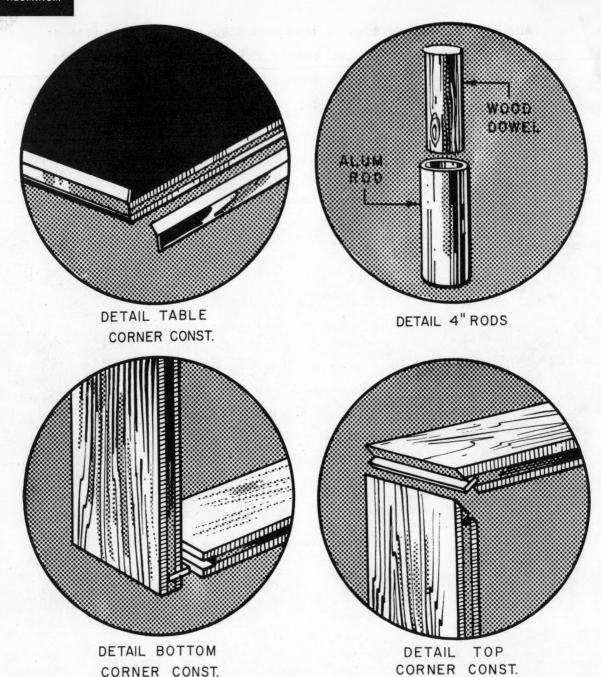

DETAIL TABLE
CORNER CONST.

DETAIL 4" RODS

WOOD DOWEL

ALUM ROD

DETAIL BOTTOM
CORNER CONST.

DETAIL TOP
CORNER CONST.

or even plastic. Many other changes can also be made to suit the decor and the taste of the individual craftsman.

A heavier and even stronger construction can be obtained if the bottom box is lined with either another piece of veneered wood or solid stock. If such a liner is used it may prove more effective to substitute machine screws for wood screws where the formed aluminum-rod legs are fastened to the box. The nuts and washers on the inside of the box could be adequately covered with the liner.

Glass or plastic sliding doors can also be installed if grooves are sawed in the front edges of the box.

SUPPORTS

There are eight of these supports which separate the desk top from the two box structures. Each length of aluminum has inside it a large maple dowel rod. The dowel rod should extend at least ¼ inch up and down into dowel holes bored in the facing wood surfaces. This will give you a greater gluing area and add rigidity to the desk. Screws should also be used in the ends of the dowel supports, securing them from above and below. Be sure to drill large enough pilot holes for these screws.

An alternate method of fastening these supports between the desk top and the

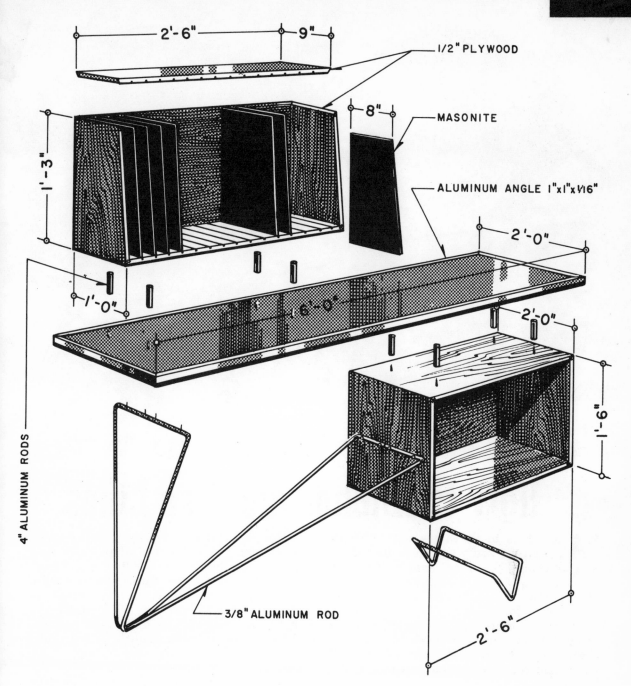

1/2" PLYWOOD

2'-6" 9"

MASONITE

8"

1'-3"

ALUMINUM ANGLE 1"x1"x1/16"

2'-0"

1'-0"

6'-0"

2'-0"

1'-6"

4" ALUMINUM RODS

3/8" ALUMINUM ROD

2'-6"

boxes is to use carriage bolts or other long metal fasteners. If such fasteners are used, the head should be hidden. On the top box this means that a hole must be counterdrilled for each head deep enough to allow a wooden plug to be inserted over it. On the bottom box, the bolt heads can be hidden by drilling the bolt holes only through the frame or blocking which runs underneath the desk top.

ALUMINUM ROD LEGS

These legs are ⅜-inch round stock and can be formed easily on a piece of pipe held in a vise. Since the rods are purchased in 8-foot lengths, the legs are made in two matching pieces. After forming, place in position against the desk and mark for screw attachment. Centerpunch carefully before drilling holes. Mark the desk and drill pilot holes before screwing rods in place.

The shorter leg under the lower box of the desk can be formed from a 6-foot length of aluminum rod.

FINISHING NOTES

The aluminum can be brightened and finished with fine steel wool.

The finishing of the wood, of course, is a matter of taste and of making the desk fit into the decor of a room. •

How to Anchor and Use Lines

"A ROPE is to tie things with." That's an oft-quoted youngster's definition, and it should be good enough for any pleasure boatman, provided he knows how "to tie things," what rope is needed and how to care for it.

A boat left to its own devices is a restless thing. Without rope you can't moor or anchor, tow a water skier, haul a bucket of water aboard, or toss a line to a man overboard.

Another saying applies to the mariner: "It takes a fluke to stay put." Anchors, like fire extinguishers, all too often are not given much thought until they are needed in an emergency.

The vital link between your boat and the bottom is rope. Rope, when cut into specified lengths and used aboard a boat, is generally called line. The pleasure boatman has a choice of four basic varieties of rope from which to make up lines. These are Manila, nylon, dacron and polyethylene. The choice of the lines should depend on the job each is expected to perform.

All rope is cordage whether constructed of natural or synthetic fibers or, in some instances, wire.

Manila, which is made from natural plant fibers, is a general all-purpose rope and can be used wherever line is required. Typical good-quality, three-strand Manila of ¼-inch diameter has a breaking strength of approximately 600 pounds; $\frac{5}{16}$-inch, 1000 pounds; ⅜-inch, 1350 pounds; $\frac{7}{16}$-inch, 1750 pounds; ½-inch, 2650 pounds; ⅝-inch, 4400 pounds, and ¾-inch, 5400 pounds.

Working strength of any rope should be figured at 20 per cent of its breaking strength. Therefore, the working strength of $\frac{5}{16}$-inch Manila is approximately 200 pounds. Since Manila generally costs less than half as much as nylon and approximately one quarter as much as dacron, pleasure boatmen frequently select Manila for reasons of economy. If Manila is kept clean and dried before storing, it will offer a long and satisfactory life. It is lightweight, flexible, easy to handle, doesn't kink and coils readily.

Nylon is a synthetic yarn rope with breaking and working strength approximately three times that of Manila. It offers a number of advantages over Manila, but also has disadvantages. Nylon has high

This boating clown is heaving the anchor out as though he were doing the hammer throw. The line easily could tangle around his ankles and pull him overboard or, at best, it will snarl up into a bird's nest.

Left: The proper way to put down your anchor is shown here. Lower it gently over the side, keeping the line free of your legs while you pay it out from a neat coil on the deck to prevent tangling.

In this case, the sailorette has made use of three lines in tying up between two finger piers. The bow is secured by one line which runs port and starboard from the cleat; two lines, one each side, hold the stern.

elasticity. Stretched, it quickly recovers its original length and will recover repeatedly within short time intervals. This ability to stretch and absorb shock makes nylon desirable as mooring or anchor line, for moored or anchored boats are often kept in motion by wave action. Nylon resists rot, decay and fungus growth and is superior in abrasion resistance to Manila. It may be stored wet and can be washed with a detergent solution without damage.

In contrast to Manila, nylon is difficult to splice and its fresh-cut ends will fray unless they are seized (wrapped with small line) or fused by applying heat. One common method to prevent nylon from losing its lay (that is, untwisting into a fluffy mass of hard-to-handle filaments) is to hold the end in a match flame until the filaments melt. They fuse together as they cool.

Dacron has approximately twice the breaking and working strength of Manila, has far greater stability than nylon. It is silky smooth to the touch, making it desirable to handle. However, since it offers a minimum of stretch, it is not recommended for use as anchor or mooring lines. It is favored for running rigging on sailing craft where stretch is not wanted. On racing yachts, linen lines are most highly regarded for halyards and sheets.

Polyethylene has approximately the same strength as nylon and no more elasticity than Manila. It is recommended for use wherever floating rope is desirable. Polyethylene is lightweight, soft and very flexible. This, combined with its flotation characteristic, makes it a top choice for water ski towlines, dinghy painters, and ring buoy or throwing lines.

As a generality, boats of under 20 feet should carry a 100-foot length of anchor line in ½-inch Manila or ⅜-inch nylon. Boats 20 to 25 feet in length should be equipped with both a lightweight service anchor and a heavy storm anchor. For the light anchor, 100 feet of ½-inch Manila or ⅜-inch nylon will be satisfactory. The heavy anchor calls for 150 feet of ⅝-inch Manila or ½-inch nylon. Boats of 25 to 30 feet should carry 100 feet of line for the light anchor, either in ⅝-inch Manila or ½-inch nylon. The heavy anchor should be fitted with 175 feet of ¾-inch Manila or $\frac{9}{16}$-inch nylon. Boats of 30 to 45 feet in length should carry 150 feet of light anchor line of ¾-inch Manila or $\frac{9}{16}$-inch nylon. The storm anchor should have 200 feet of 1-inch Manila or ¾-inch nylon.

Small power craft up to about 18 feet in length may be satisfactorily moored with two lines, each approximately equal in length to the boat's overall length. These

When someone falls overboard, a life preserver should be thrown to him—but don't secure life preservers to your boat with lines. A separate line should be used for pulling in the person.

If the sailor who has gone overboard knows his lines, he can tie a line athwartships, make up a foot stirrup in an end and pull himself over the gunwale without fear of capsizing the boat.

are secured to the bow and stern cleats, run off at about a 45° angle to the center line of the boat, and made fast to the dock. However, if your boating is done in waters where there is a considerable range in tide, a pair of spring lines are often required in addition to bow and stern lines. Spring lines prevent the boat from moving forward or astern and yet allow freedom for rise and fall.

Boats over 25 feet in length should carry a minimum of four mooring lines. This permits two-directional tie-ups at bow and stern in finger piers or provides for spring lines when mooring only to one side of a dock.

It's nearly impossible to take an active part in any form of pleasure boating without being required to know your ropes, how and where to use them and how to take care of them.

Someone once said, "Give a man enough rope and he'll hang himself." He obviously wasn't thinking of a boatman. Though there have been hangings at sea, mutiny on pleasure boats is a rarity and capital punishment for a mutinous crew of passengers is frowned upon.

Give a seaman enough rope of the right kind and if it's used properly it will add to pleasure and safety of crew and craft. A competent boatman is quickly distinguished from a landlubber by a knowledge of marlinspike seamanship, which entails a knowledge of ropes and skill in working with them.

Several times each year you should inspect all of your lines. Rope is deteriorated by mechanical action, surface wear, internal friction, biological action, bacteria and mold, or boring marine organisms. Don't check only for exterior wear; look below the surface, for the exterior appearance of lines may be deceptive. Twist open sections of the line and check for broken inner

fibers due to mechanical or biological action. Manila lines will wear out from the inside. Synthetic fiber rope surface filaments, when abraded, form a protective fuzz that shields the inner fibers. You are often dependent for your own or your craft's safety on the soundness of your lines. A weak line is often worse than none at all, so replace all damaged and worn lines as soon as they are detected and be sure that your supply of lines is sufficient.

Here are some hints on the care of your lines:

Whenever you beach a boat and put out a line to secure it from drifting, the line should be rinsed carefully before further use. Otherwise, grit, dirt or sand may work between the strands and cut the line's fibers.

Care should be taken not to store lines near storage batteries, for acid from the electrolyte or acid fumes can damage the fibers.

Chaffing gear (sections of old sheeting, canvas, burlap or any acid- or alkaline-free rags) should be wrapped around lines where they pass over the sheer rail or through chocks. Sections of split garden or fire hose make excellent chaffing gear.

Pulley sheaves and chocks that are too small for the diameter of lines increase wear and friction. When in doubt, it is better to use oversize rather than undersize sheaves and chocks.

Knots and kinks tend to shear rope fibers when lines are under strain. Remember that when using rope as a sling, for lashing or turning sharp corners, an excessively heavy strain is placed on the outer fibers of the rope and you should never exceed working loads of more than one fifth the breaking strength of line, giving additional safety allowance for rope that is worn or weakened.

Whenever possible, always use a splice

This craft is being tied up at a place where considerable tide variation is expected. Note spring lines which run fore and aft; others at bow and stern.

instead of a knot, for the shearing tendency of knots may weaken a rope by as much as 50 per cent, while splices will often offer as much as 90 per cent of the breaking strength of the rope.

Manufacturers always coil rope in the same manner. Right-laid rope is always uncoiled in a counterclockwise direction. In uncoiling rope, lay the coil flat with the inside end at the bottom. Then draw the inside end up through the coil. New lines often are difficult to handle as they have a tendency to kink. I recommend securing the end of a new line to the stern of your boat (once under way so the line won't tangle in your prop) and allow the line to trail behind your boat for 10 or 15 minutes. Stop your engine before pulling in the rope, again to prevent prop snagging. You'll find that the permanent wave set into the line when it was coiled will be freed and the line will be pliable for use.

Care in mooring will save you embarrassment and may often prevent extensive damage. I learned how not to moor a boat by goofing badly. My lesson occurred during a fishing junket on the Gulf Coast of Florida.

The Everglades coastline just north of Cape Sable is broken by dozens of rivers and inlets that reach back into the mangrove jungles where tarpon and snook are often as commonplace as goldfish in 5 and 10¢ store aquariums. The fishing party I was with selected one of these narrow inlets, Graveyard Creek, as our headquarters. Our campsite's only claim to fame was that it was the breeding area for the hungriest mosquitoes east of New Guinea. The fish, by contrast, were apparently better fed than pet cats at a creamery.

We had planned to stay at Graveyard Creek for three days. My lack of attention to proper mooring techniques nearly made our stay permanent. We had arrived in two

outboard runabouts. When we killed the motors, we heard mosquitoes singing like banshees and there was no question that they were out for blood. To preserve as much fuel as possible, we tossed all of our fishing gear into the boat and shifted food, spare fuel and camping equipment into the other. I hastily tethered our supply boat to a branch overhanging the creek bank. Thoughtlessly, I allowed only three feet of slack in the line.

Shortly after dawn the next morning we returned hungry, tired, bitten and fishless.

When making fast to a dock cleat, take the half hitch with the free part of the line as shown. By doing so, you may then release the line even with a considerable strain on the standing part.

When you tow another craft, you will find that there is less tendency for it to yaw and cause steering difficulties with the towing craft if you rig up a bridle across the stern as shown here.

Two half hitches are useful in making the end of a rope fast around its own standing part. End B is passed under the ring and under and over the line's standing part twice.

Below: One of the most useful and widely-known sailor knots is the bowline. It is used if you require a loop that will not slip, jam or fail and is easily untied, even if soaked.

STEP 1   STEP 2   FINISHED KNOT

The tide had fallen and risen during our absence. The sight that greeted us was a shocker. Our moored outboard hull, once laden with supplies was upside down. The motor was hopelessly soaked. Tools had been dumped along with food, spare fuel, clothing and practically everything we owned other than rods, reels and tackle.

I had taken the precaution to tilt up and secure the outboard motor, expecting the boat to be supported on the creek bottom at low tide. It had, but I hadn't figured on the steep angle of a bank that sloped at about a 45° angle. When the tide had run out, the boat simply dangled at the end of its short mooring line. As the tide turned and ran in again, the boat had filled with water almost to the steering wheel before it became buoyant. Then, as its artificial flotation gradually gave it lift, the sweep of the incoming current rocked the nearly foundered hull, causing it to become un-balanced. Finally, it simply rolled. Through sheer luck, we located two spare fuel tanks with closed vents about a quarter of a mile upstream.

The lesson is obvious. Though I hadn't, every boatman should carefully check water conditions where he plans to moor or anchor, know what tide may be expected, and sound the bottom.

Care and thoughtfulness in properly securing a boat can save the embarrassment of having a boat stray off on its own or suffer damage due to banging or chaffing.

When beaching a boat, it is always tempting to run the bow up onto the shore. This technique begs for wear and tear. Where no waves and tide are present, drop an anchor astern and secure a bowline to an object ashore. This will prevent the boat from turning broadside and drifting onto the beach. Where waves prevail, moor the boat with a bow anchor to prevent shipping water over the stern.

Five basic knots will serve for most mooring situations: the square or reef knot, used to secure two ropes of the same size; the sheet, weaver's knot or becket bend, three names for the same means of tying two lines of different diameter; the bowline, used to create a nonslipping loop at one end of a line; the clove hitch, used to tie temporarily to a bollard or piling; and two half hitches, used for the same purpose.

The half hitch method is commonly used to secure lines to cleats. The free end of the line should be passed around the front of the cleat, that is that part of a cleat farthest from the secured part of the line. The standing or free part should then continue around the rear of the cleat, passing over the secured line. A half hitch is placed over the forward end of the cleat, then another half hitch over the rear of the cleat. The important feature is to see that the section of line leading to the free or standing end of the rope is always on the bottom of the loop.

At some time you may be called on to take another craft in tow. Rather than pull the entire load from a single stern cleat on your boat, I recommend rigging a bridle with the line secured to both stern quarters. In heavy going, you may find that the weight of the tow limits the maneuverability of your hull. If it is possible to rig the lines farther forward, you will improve your boat's maneuvering ability.

If you take an outboard boat in tow, have the towed boat's operator tilt his motor or motors free from the water so as to reduce drag. Should the towed boat yaw back and forth, have its operator shift movable weight aft as far as possible.

In following seas, be sure the towline is sufficiently long so that the craft under tow doesn't override the crest of a wave while you are in its trough. In such a case, the towed craft may surfboard down the slope and strike your boat, broach or capsize. Adjust the length of towlines in conformance with the distance between one or more waves. Since the distance between wave crests and wave troughs will remain quite constant, strain on the towline will be at a minimum with both the towed and the towing boat ascending and descending the waves simultaneously.

Pay close attention to the freeboard of the boat being towed. If it has shipped water, it will be unstable and, should you tow at a high rate of speed, you may pull the towed boat's bow under. You must also pay close attention to the safety of your own boat, so that the stern is not dragged under. This is of particular importance if you are towing with an outboard with a shallow, 15-inch rather than a 20-inch transom—or with an outboard not fitted with a self-draining well.

You may find that in extremely rough weather it is better to delay returning to the nearest mooring. Instead, it may be more prudent to head directly into the sea, maintaining only enough headway to keep excessive slack out of the towline and to prevent your boat and the towed craft from pounding.

An additional line dragged aft of the towed craft will reduce its tendency to yaw. In extreme cases, add a sea anchor to the end of the line dragging behind the boat in distress.

Don't tow a disabled craft into a crowded anchorage where wind, tide or current may cause the towed boat to collide with others.

SQUARE KNOT

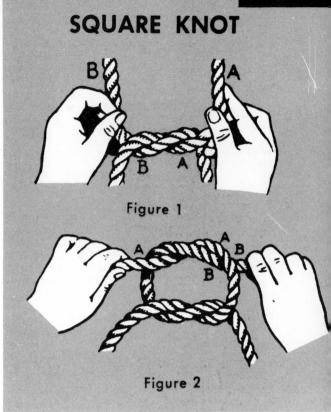

Figure 1

Figure 2

The square knot, as pictured here, is useful to reef or furl sails, and it can be shaken apart. (1) End A is passed over and under B. (2) B is passed over and under A and ends are tightened.

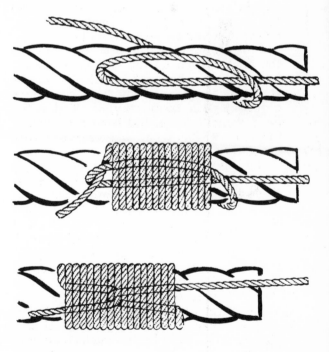

Raveled lines are unsightly. To whip them, use heavy linen fish line. Wind the line tightly as shown for a distance at least equal to the diameter of the rope; then pull the ends and cut.

Right: A fisherman's bend is used to join two light lines. It consists of two overhand knots, each tied in one line and tightened down on the adjacent one.

STEP 1

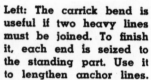

STEP 2

Left: The carrick bend is useful if two heavy lines must be joined. To finish it, each end is seized to the standing part. Use it to lengthen anchor lines.

Left: The clove hitch is used in fastening a line around an object. If used at the end of a line, adding a half hitch or two is a good idea.

Instead, have the disabled boat drop anchor. Then remove its passengers if necessary.

Hardware on some production boats is made up of cheap castings which may snap under stress. If you have any reason to be doubtful as to the strength of towing bits or eyes, or if you do not feel that the fittings are sufficiently secured, exercise extreme caution. Move all of your passengers to a protected area in a cabin or up on a foredeck. With smaller, open craft, have them get down on the floorboards. A broken towing line—or worse yet, a line with a piece of broken hardware secured to it—may under certain conditions be as lethal as a bullwhip or a missile.

A heavy stone tied to a crude rope was the anchor used by the earliest boatmen, but it took a heap of muscle to handle stone anchors large enough to keep even a dugout canoe from straying. Today, the dead-weight anchor has been replaced by far more efficient and lighter types with a hooking action.

One major anchor manufacturer claims that if a lightweight anchor had been designed centuries ago, the entire history of the world might have been changed! This sounds like an extravagant statement, but it's true that the Greeks, Romans, Spanish and English might all have handled their ships differently in exploration, trade and battle if they could have made their rigs stay still when they wished it. The technique of island jumping and amphibious landings used during World War II was made possible only by the modern anchor. Our Navy was able to put and hold ships in any desired location.

The size of the anchor you need for your boat will depend on many factors: the type of bottom on which the anchor will be dropped; wind velocity; exposure of the mooring location; the hull form, size and weight; and the scope (length of the anchor line in relation to water depth). The riding anchor line, incidentally, is called the anchor rode by the salty set.

Since only the hull size, weight and form can be securely determined in advance, the following generalities should serve as a guide in selecting an anchor:

Weight alone has little to do with an anchor's efficiency. That the design is important is apparent when it's realized that a concrete block will hold little more than its own weight. A mushroom-type anchor will hold only about twice its weight, while the modern lightweight patent anchor with pivoting flukes can hold up to 1000 times its weight.

A small outboard utility of under 15 feet can be anchored safely under most circumstances with a four-pound patent anchor. A 15- to 20-foot outboard will require an 8- to 12-pounder. The heavier the boat the heavier the anchor.

A lightweight 25-foot cruiser, either outboard or inboard, should be safe from straying with a 12- to 15-pound anchor, while a 30- to 35-footer will ride out a heavy blow with a patent hook of 20 to 25 pounds.

The anchor line should be long enough and heavy enough so that it will cushion sudden shock loads due to wave action. It should lead nearly horizontally away from the anchor, that is, parallel to the bottom, even when it is under strain.

As a general rule of thumb, the anchor line should be about seven times as long as the depth of the water.

If you've ever had a power failure in bad weather, and had nothing to hold you off a lee shore but your ground tackle, you'll

MAKING FAST TO A CLEAT

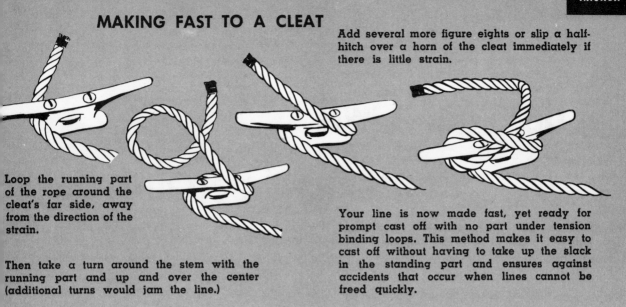

Add several more figure eights or slip a half-hitch over a horn of the cleat immediately if there is little strain.

Loop the running part of the rope around the cleat's far side, away from the direction of the strain.

Then take a turn around the stem with the running part and up and over the center (additional turns would jam the line.)

Your line is now made fast, yet ready for prompt cast off with no part under tension binding loops. This method makes it easy to cast off without having to take up the slack in the standing part and ensures against accidents that occur when lines cannot be freed quickly.

appreciate the importance of a good anchor and line. It's at such a time that you're most likely to remember the boatman's prayer, "Oh, Lord, Thy sea is so great and my boat is so small." Aside from choosing a seaworthy boat, one of the most effective ways to assure your safety and that of your equipment in the event of a breakdown is to be certain that you carry suitable anchors and enough good line so that your boat will hold and ride out any blow.

Every boat should carry two anchors. One, the lighter, should be stowed in such a way that it can be broken out and dropped at an instant's notice in an emergency and be readily available at all times for anchoring under normal conditions. The other will serve as a spare and may come in handy if you are forced to anchor where there is danger of yawing and swinging about under varying wind conditions where such a shift may endanger your boat.

Anchors, like engines, should be matched to the boat they will be expected to hold to the bottom, the scope, current drag and wave and wind action. The design of the anchor used will also provide a variance.

Odd as it may seem, wind on a cold, dry day will exert more drag or force against an anchored boat than will wind of the same velocity on a warm, humid day. This accounts in part for the greater severity of winter seas and also should serve as a warning that boats left at anchor in the winter may require more scope than they do at the same anchorage in summer.

Your marine dealer can help you choose an anchor of recommended size and type for the design and length of the boat you have, as well as for the operating conditions you will meet locally.

There are a number of tips that will help

simplify your anchoring problems and develop your anchoring technique. Keep in mind that the design of your boat will affect its action at anchor. A shallow draft, planing-type hull will react more quickly to shifts in wind and is more prone to swing at anchor than a deep-draft powerboat or a deep-keel sailboat. A deep-keel boat will react faster to changes in current.

In a crowded anchorage, make allowance for the variance of different hulls to wind and current shifts. You may find, for example, that you cannot use the recommended average scope of 7 to 1 and may have to shorten to as much as 4 to 1. The shorter scope will naturally greatly lessen your anchor's holding power. One trick you may use is to secure a weight approximately halfway down the anchor rode. This, in essence, will reduce the angle of line pull in reference to the bottom and reduce the chance of dragging anchor in the event it starts to blow. The weight is called a sentinel.

Don't overlook the effect of tide. If you're in an area, for example, with a six-foot tide and anchor in ten feet of water with 80 feet of line, your scope is 8 to 1. However, if the tide rises six feet, the scope is shortened to 5 to 1, which may be dangerous under certain conditions.

A helpful indication of whether you have sufficient scope is to watch the reaction of waves on the rode. If an upward pull appears to be exerted as the bow rises, you have insufficient line out and should be wary of dragging anchor.

Always select two ranges (landmarks or navigational aids) to fix your position. Watch these ranges for signs of dragging. The bearings also may serve to aid you in recovering your anchor if the line should part. ●

Be Your Own Antenna Specialist

Most antenna problems can be solved with everyday tools

by Art Margolis

Antenna problems in suburbia are minimized by the wide open spaces; metropolitan troubles are complex.

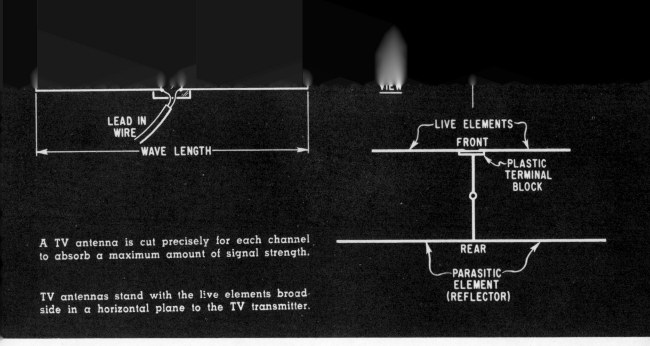

LEAD IN WIRE

—WAVE LENGTH—

A TV antenna is cut precisely for each channel to absorb a maximum amount of signal strength.

TV antennas stand with the live elements broadside in a horizontal plane to the TV transmitter.

LIVE ELEMENTS
FRONT
PLASTIC TERMINAL BLOCK
REAR
PARASITIC ELEMENT (REFLECTOR)

I WOULD say the only requirements anyone needs to handle 95 per cent of home antenna problems are normal handyman house tools, ability and a drop or two of steeplejack blood.

One word of caution at this point. Working on a roof can be dangerous. You must observe strict safety first. Falls are the largest form of home accidents. When you are on a roof, and I don't mean to be facetious, take every precaution so you won't fall off.

A second danger on roofs is the wires. Some carry lethal electricity, others might trip you. If you do go on your roof be sure it is in bright daylight so you can see and steer clear of all wires.

A third danger to watch out for is dilapidated masonry. Before you attach any mounts to any masonry be sure it is strong enough to hold it. I hope I came across on these very important points.

Once you have the roof situation under control, the rest is purely mechanical. Antenna considerations break down into three categories. Installation, maintenance, and troubleshooting. To handle these three antenna areas of endeavor, it would be wise to understand the answers to the . . .

Ten Most Asked Antenna Questions:

Question 1. Why do we need TV antennas when we do not need radio antennas?

Answer 1. Nobody ever said we do not need radio antennas. In every radio there is an antenna or else it couldn't operate. However, due to the long experience of radio, developments have been able to squeeze the antenna down to a tiny size.

TV on the other hand is comparatively new and while tremendous strides have been made in antenna developments, little shrinking of the antenna has taken place.

The reason is the high frequencies that TV operates at in comparison to radio. These high frequencies are much more susceptible to losses of strength. They won't travel easily through structures and have a limited "line of sight" range. In order for you to grab yourself a workable portion of these electromagnetic energies it is advantageous to have an antenna cut to absorb the wave lengths, outdoors and up high.

Question 2. How does a TV antenna work?

Answer 2. A TV antenna with its stick appearance is in reality a complete tuned circuit just like a combination of coils, resistors and condensers. The right TV antenna is tuned to the TV frequencies.

The tuning is performed by cutting the metallic sticks to match a particular half wave length. Channel two's wave length is 200.2 inches while channel thirteen's is 54 inches with the in between channels being in between. (See Antenna Length Chart.)

The line or driven element (the one that is attached to the lead in wire) is thus cut at half wave lengths.

Practically speaking, in a good signal area the actual length is not really critical. So antennas are cut on or around the channel three length requirement. (The lower channel is picked because smaller wave lengths can be absorbed easily by a larger length, while larger wave lengths cannot be absorbed as easily by the smaller piece of metal.)

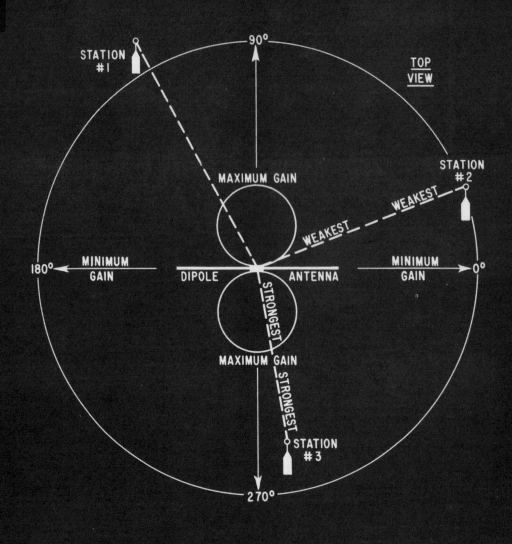

Question 3. How can one tell which way a TV antenna is pointing?

Answer 3. There are two considerations in determining the direction an antenna is looking just as there are two considerations in determining the direction you are looking while you are wearing your polarized sun glasses.

You know that light travels in all planes 360° around. When you don the glasses they obliterate all glare from above and below and the only light that passes through them is on a horizontal plane. If you should lie on your side you would be rotating the polarized glass and then the only light that passed through the glasses would be on a vertical plane.

In addition to the polarization the other consideration is actual nautical direction, north, south, east or west.

Since TV waves are of the same nature as light waves the antenna direction is considered in both polarized and nautical terms.

Radio waves are propagated in a vertical polarized fashion—TV waves in a horizontal fashion. Radio antennas are straight up and down. TV antennas stand arms outstretched, the line elements broadside to the transmitter.

Question 4. Why are there so many different kinds of antennas?

Answer 4. Because there are so many different reception situations. An antenna is chosen for a particular situation according to its basic reception "pattern".

The pattern shows the way the antenna absorbs the signal. Let's examine the four basic TV antennas.

1. The Single Dipole—A single driven element, a dipole produces this pattern. A dipole is two metal sticks that are physically held together by a plastic terminal block that insulates each arm from the other. The lead in wire is attached to the block. One side of the wire is attached to the block. One side of the wire touching the right element and the other side of the

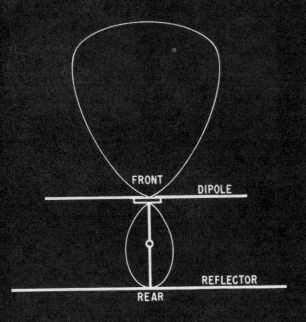

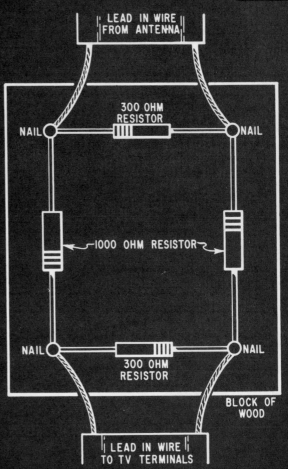

Dipole and reflector pattern. Addition of reflector reduces the rear entrance pickup, narrows pattern.

Dipole pattern. The more area in the figure eight the signal path can cover, the stronger a signal.

Attenuator pad is constructed with four resistors, wood and nails. Signal is reduced through it.

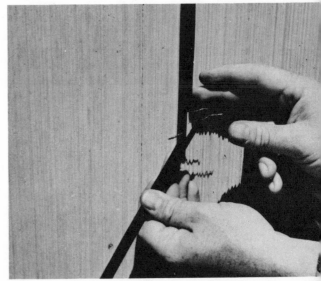

Cut lead-in wire. Spacing must be preserved and staggered to avoid losses. The two ends should fit.

Wind the bare wires together tightly; let them stick out from insulation. Solder them if possible.

wire touching the other element involved.

If the TV transmitter is spewing waves anywhere between 120° to 60° or 240° to 300° the antenna will absorb to its maximum. If the TV rays lob in anywhere else in the circumference the antenna will absorb less and less till it responds at an absolute minimum at 0° and 180°, the ends of the antenna.

Obviously then, for best reception you must aim the dipoles broadside at the transmitter. If there is more than one station you must compromise your aiming of the fixed antenna for best reception from the multiple stations.

2. Dipole and Reflector—a single driven element plus one parasitic element, a parasitic element being one that is not attached to the lead in wire. The driven element could be a single dipole, a folded dipole, a conical or one of a few other variations.

The addition of the parasite called a re-

flector, makes the antenna higher in gain and more directional. The reflector sits broadside behind the dipole as they look at the transmitter. The pattern is narrowed and rear entrance pickup is reduced drastically. For all practical purposes you can consider the reflector like a mirror. It bounces back signal to the dipole and bounces off any signal trying to come in the rear entrance. The best reception is obtained by carefully aiming the antenna's front door, the dipole, at the transmitters.

3. Dipole, Reflector and Director—a single driven element plus two parasitic elements. In addition to the reflector behind the dipole, a director is in front of dipole. With this additional parasite the gain is increased even more and the directivity of the antenna is made more critical. You must be a sharp-shooter aiming this type antenna.

4. Multiple Dipoles and Multiple Para-

Trim off excess but be sure to leave enough windings to insure a very strong windproof connection.

Wind electrical tape in overlapping layers over the joint for weatherproofing and extra strength.

A good splice is hardly noticeable. If done properly, it will cure snow and related TV troubles.

Super antenna installed has 28 elements. Follow the lead in. You'll count 9 dipoles, 19 parasites.

sitic Elements, Super Antennas. There are many antennas on the market that have many reflectors, directors, and driven elements. They are listed by their mileage: 100 mile, 150 mile, etc. They are expensive. Their advantage: highest gain possible plus extraordinary directivity. With the right setup you can pick up stations from far away.

Question 5. What good is a motorized antenna?

Answer 5. In some cases no good. In other situations invaluable. In my area between New York and Philadelphia a careful selection of motor and high gain antenna results in receiving every channel from 2 through 13.

The motor is for use with an antenna such as described in type number four. With the motor you can aim the antenna bull's-eye at a transmitter. Then when you change channel aim the aerial at your new selection. This is the worth of the motor.

Question 6. Why is the lead in wire flat?

Answer 6. Just as the antenna is a tuned circuit, so the lead in wire must also possess the same characteristics. The main characteristic is called "impedance". The impedance of an antenna ideally is 300 ohms. The input of the TV set also is 300 ohms. To match the antenna into the TV, the lead in wire must also be 300 ohms. If it's not some of the hard gained signal strength is lost.

If you think of the antenna as a funnel on the roof and the TV set as a rain barrel, the lead in wire can be thought of as the hose connecting the two. It's obvious if the hose fittings are not correct you'll lose rain water. Similarly you'll lose signal if you do not match impedance.

To obtain a 300 ohm impedance in the wire, the copper must be separated by exactly the distance 300 ohm wire is spaced

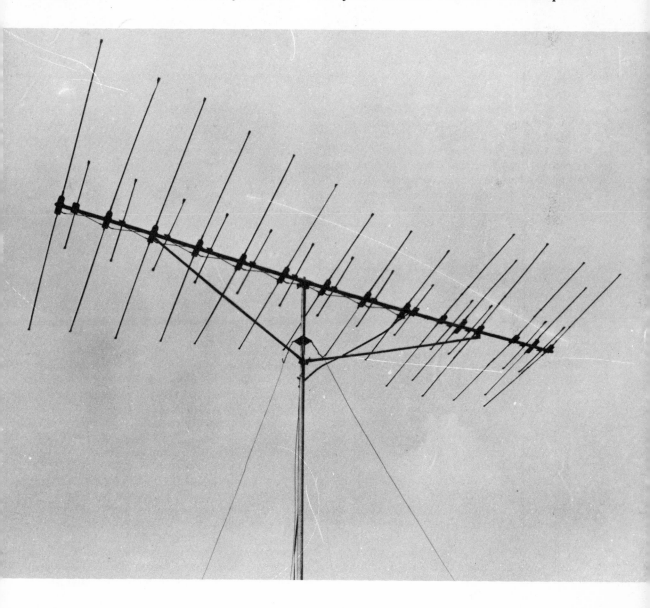

Arrester is best mounted close to antenna. Mount on the mast, wall, window sill or the water pipes.

A mast standoff is attached, and the lightning arrester wire is drawn through it and tightened.

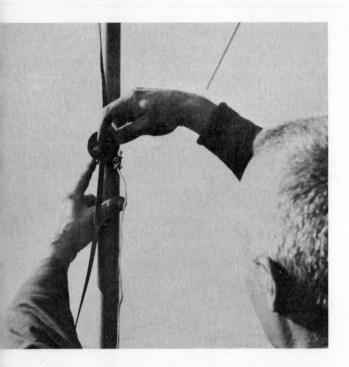

by flat plastic insulation. Remember this.

Question 7. Why use the standoff insulators?

Answer 7. In order to maintain the 300 ohms throughout the length of transmission wire it must receive special care. The wire can't touch or come close to any metal. If it does the impedance will change at this point. At an "impedance bump" some of the waves are bounced back like a mirror reflection. These reflections cancel out some of the signal strength and also enter the TV at the wrong time causing ghost images.

Question 8. Why are some antennas stacked one on top of another?

Answer 8. Two advantages are obtained by stacking one antenna head above another. One, there is increased gain for there are two heads working instead of one. Two, while there is increased gain in the horizontal plane effectively, there is less pickup in the vertical plane. Airplane flutter and most interference travel in the vertical plane. Stacking reduces these unwanted interferences.

Question 9. What are the prime factors to obtain best reception?

Answer 9. The factors are all in a mathematical formula but they are simple. There are seven of them.

1. The HEIGHT of the transmitter.
2. The geographical ELEVATION of the transmitter.
3. The DISTANCE between the transmitter and your TV antenna.
4. The WATTS of power the transmitter is permitted to radiate.
5. The heights of any geographical shadows between the transmitter and your antenna. This includes hills, forests, and buildings.
6. The distances of these shadows in respect to your antenna and the transmitter.
7. The HEIGHT that you install your antenna.

Question 10. What is this thing called signal strength?

Answer 10. Nobody really knows! It can be described somewhat. It can be produced, charted, used and its results felt strongly. It is the same thing as light only it has a lower frequency. We can't see it because our eyes are tuned only for light frequencies. It travels at 186,000 miles per second, which from the transmitter to your antenna means instantly. Anyway, don't worry about it. You can install, maintain, and repair your antenna system without knowing.

Antenna Troubles and Repairs: Antenna troubles are usually the result of wear and tear due to the weather. The wire breaks, the antenna breaks, the connections corrode, the mast bends, the standoffs deteriorate, the mounts weaken, etc. However, the trouble shows up on your TV screen by means of a visual symptom just as in-

Heavy duty lightning arrester wire is drawn to ground through standoff insulators; twin lead also.

Special copper ground rod is taken to out of way place and pounded into ground, leaving 3 inches.

ternal TV troubles indicate their presence.

Once you have ascertained that the trouble is in the antenna system via the rabbit ears test you are ready to troubleshoot. There are nine general types of symptoms.

Snowy Picture: The picture becomes snowy when you lose signal strength. The snow is static that you see. Usual troubles are breaks in the lead in wire. The break can occur at the antenna head connection anywhere along the lead in wires length, at TV input connection and on rare occasions on the piece of lead in wire that connects the antenna TV terminals and the tuner. The job, find the break and splice it. Or if the wire is old and worn replace the entire length.

Weaves and Ghosts: The picture will become distorted in this fashion if your antenna is not pointed correctly at the transmitter. This can happen if it blows around a bit or even if a new building is erected between you and the transmitter. To correct you must reorient your antenna. The best procedure for orientation is one person on the roof and one by the TV.

The one on the roof slowly rotates the antenna. The person by the set yells up the quality of the picture. At best picture setting the antenna should be tightened up permanently.

Flashing: Your picture will flash and break up into all forms of wild disturb-

Final touches on installation are made by connecting ground wire tightly to copper ground rod.

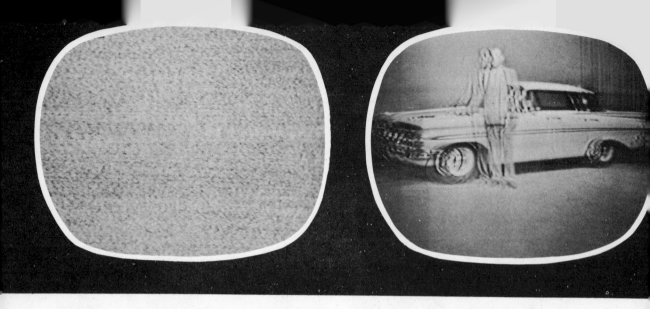

A snowy picture with or without a program happens if the lead-in breaks. Find break and splice it.

Ghosts appear in picture when the antenna is not pointed correctly. Reorientation should be big help.

When lead-in wire flaps in the wind, your picture can bob up and down. Snug wire to remedy.

There is always increasing interference. A new type antenna will do much to exclude the trouble.

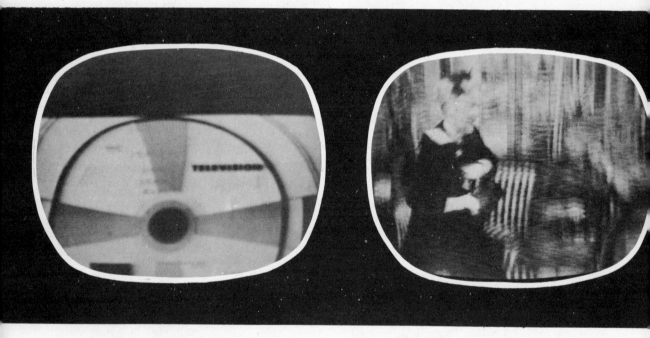

ances if you develop a loose length of lead in wire and the wind causes it to fray or break. Then as the wind continues to buffet the wire the screen symptoms will appear. The cure for this trouble is, replace or splice the lead in wire and snug it down so it won't move in the wind.

Bouncing Pic: The picture will bob up and down seasickwise if your lead in wire gets loose and flaps against some metal such as the TV mast or rain guttering. The cure, snug down with new standoffs till the wire is tight and won't move in the wind.

Excessive Interference: The TV screen will receive excessive interference if you have a simple type antenna in a bad signal area. The weak aerial permits all of the unwanted signal to enter the TV along with the desired signal. The best way to reduce interference is install a stacked, motorized, high gain, highly directional antenna, in place of the simpler types.

Loss of Fine Detail: Loss of fine detail is actually ghost images almost but not quite correctly on top of normal signal. You lose the picture detail because of incorrect lead in wire installation. The lead in wire is too near or mounted right on top of some metal causing impedance bumps or standing waves. The cure, reroute such lead in wire and liberally use standoffs at

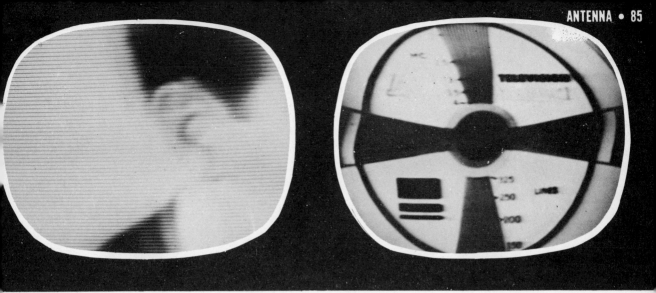

Closeup photo shows ghost on top of normal picture. More standoffs will bring back the fine detail.

A signal that is too strong causes excess contrast and bends. A pad will cut down strength.

If your picture should wash out or turn negative due to your neighbor's TV, reorient it or relocate.

This antenna length chart should give you an accurate notion of how long dipole should be cut.

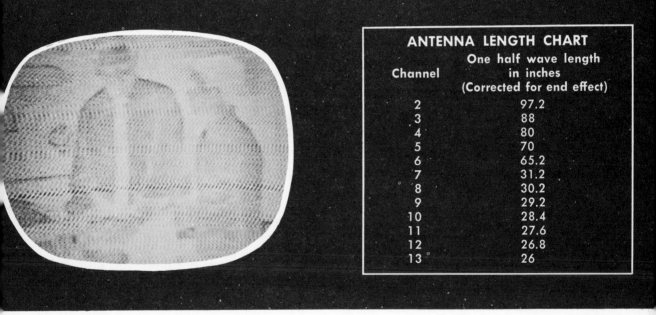

ANTENNA LENGTH CHART	
Channel	One half wave length in inches (Corrected for end effect)
2	97.2
3	88
4	80
5	70
6	65.2
7	31.2
8	30.2
9	29.2
10	28.4
11	27.6
12	26.8
13	26

any possible impedance bump or area.

Overloading: There is such a thing as the TV signal being too strong. That occurs by use of high gain antenna systems in strong signal areas. For instance, the faraway stations come in excellently but the nearby stations are too contrasty and have the bends. The cure is to reduce or attenuate the local stations' strength. This is done by means of a "pad" as illustrated. The pad is switched in for the local stations and switched out for distant TV viewing.

Interaction Between Two TV's: If you discover that your neighbor turns on his TV, you are picking up radiation from his TV. There is only one way to attempt

a cure. You must get your antenna as far away from his antenna as possible. In addition to relocation, reorientation might also be necessary. As a last resort try relocating or reorienting your neighbor's antenna.

Perfect Picture: It is very possible that you have antenna trouble but it doesn't show up on the screen. You usually find out about it when your neighbor calls. "Your aerial fell down!" The way to circumvent trouble is to examine your antenna system after major storms or at least every six months. At this time exercise normal maintenance as indicated by worn or broken materials in your installation. •

It's easy to disassemble fractional horsepower motors for inspection, cleaning or repair. In most cases you just remove nuts from the ends of the long screws through frame, pull out the screws themselves.

The Important Motors

What goes on inside a motor? Here's how they work and what usually goes wrong

MOST of the fractional horsepower motors found in household appliances, ranging from about 1/8 to 1/2 H.P., are of the "split-phase" type. A variation is the "capacitor-start" type generally found in refrigerators and ironers, but the same physical construction is used as in the split-phase variety.

Inside the case of the motor are two interwoven "stator" coils of enameled wire of different diameters. The thinner wire is on the starting winding; the heavier on the running winding. When the motor is at rest, the windings are connected in parallel. One end of one winding is connected permanently to one end of the other winding, and this junction represents one terminal of the motor. The other two ends are connected by a simple single-pole spring switch mounted in one of the end bells; this juncture is the other terminal.

The rotor has no outside connections of any kind. On the end of the shaft nearest the stator switch, however, is a pair of spring-loaded weights. These are collapsed when the motor is at rest. When the line switch is turned on, alternating current flows through both windings causing twisting magnetic fields to be set up around them and through the rotor which is in close proximity. The rotor is dragged around by the magnetic fields and builds up speed rapidly, provided it is not overloaded by the mechanism it is supposed to spin. In a second or two the centrifugal force of the rotation pushes the weights outward against the fixed switch causing it to open and to remove the starting winding from the power line. The motor now operates only with the single running winding.

In the capacitor motor, a large fixed capacitor (or "condenser"), very much like the ones found in radio and television sets, is connected between the free ends of the two windings. This improves the initial

End bells pull off readily and rotor (1) slips out. Stator windings are inside center frame (2). Switch for starting winding (4) is on inner side of one end bell (3). At left, pencil points to centrifugal throw-out that opens the starting switch.

Terminals are usually screw-type binding posts behind small cover plate in same end bell that has starting switch mounted on it. With some motors, direction of rotation can be changed by switching position of one lead on terminal block.

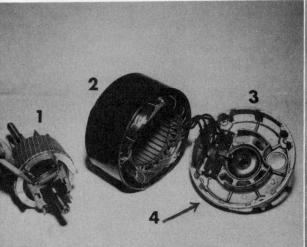
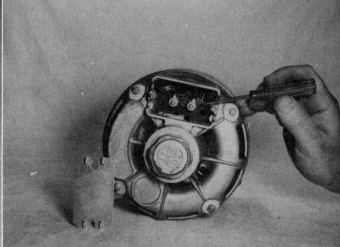

starting twist or torque without increasing the starting current. Otherwise, the throw-out action is the same as with the split-phase type.

The starting winding is alive only momentarily and does not have a chance to heat up. For this reason it can safely be wound of thinner wire than that used for long periods of running. However (and this is a *big* however), if the switch contacts should fuse together or if too big a load on the motor should keep the rotor from attaining normal speed, the starting winding remains on the line and starts to heat up very rapidly within 15 or 20 seconds. Several things may happen. If the motor has an integral thermal overload protector of the automatic resetting type, it will simply stop before the burn-out point is reached. If the power is still on, the motor will attempt to restart after the overload device has cooled off and re-established the circuit. At this point the heating

cycle will begin again and the motor will kick off again. This sort of spasmodic action is a sure sign of a defective throw-out switch, or, more likely, of a simple overload.

If the machine of which the motor is a part uses an external overload breaker, it will usually be found to be of the manual resetting type. The first overload will snap it open, and it will stay open until you press the reset button down. The machine may struggle to start but, if the trouble persists, it will be turned off again by the breaker.

Some motor-driven machines have no built-in protective devices. If a rotor locks, only the line fuse can save the windings. If the fuse is oversized for the momentarily high starting current of a particular motor, it may not blow at all, and your nose will tell you quickly that insulation and copper are overheating. If you don't get to the switch quickly you can be sure that the winding will pop. •

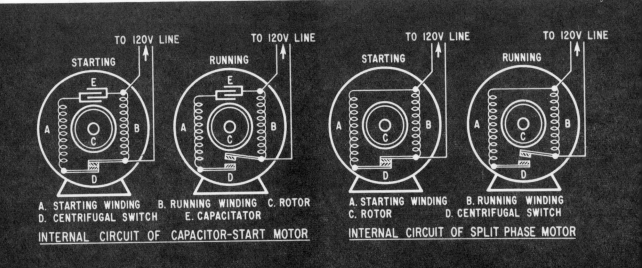

A. STARTING WINDING   B. RUNNING WINDING   C. ROTOR
D. CENTRIFUGAL SWITCH   E. CAPACITATOR
INTERNAL CIRCUIT OF CAPACITOR-START MOTOR

A. STARTING WINDING   B. RUNNING WINDING
C. ROTOR   D. CENTRIFUGAL SWITCH
INTERNAL CIRCUIT OF SPLIT PHASE MOTOR

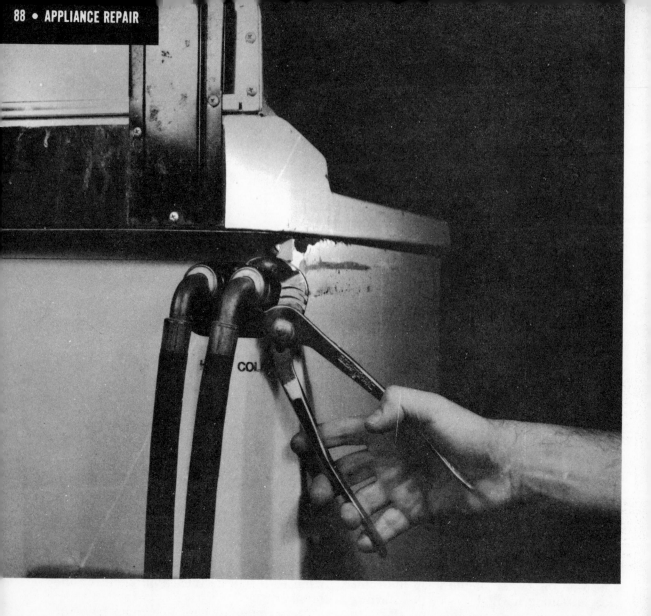

The first step, of course, is to remove the line cord, after which you can uncouple the hot and cold water hoses (for washer). A slip-jaw wrench is the best tool for the job, but gas pliers can be used. There will be some water in the hoses, so have a pail handy into which they can first be drained.

Disassembly

Disassembly is half the job. Find out how to get at the mechanism and take a look

HALF THE TRICK in finding and fixing faults in an appliance is knowing how to take the machine apart so you can get at its innards. With the top cover or back plate off, you can usually spot loose wires, broken belts, leaking valves, etc., in short order.

If you've ever replaced spark plugs, rotated tires or drained the radiator of the family car, you should have little difficulty applying the same wrenches to washers, dryers, broilers, fans and other appliances. You may have to poke around a bit at first to learn which screws hold what parts together, but you can be sure of one thing: Anything that was put together with nuts and bolts can be taken apart. In many cases the fasteners are not even nuts and bolts,

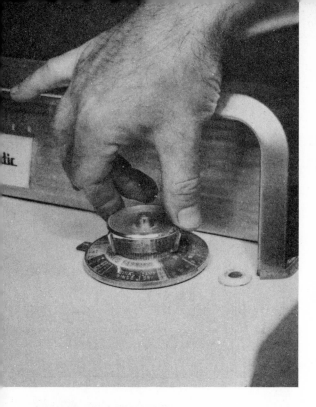

The timer control is turned clockwise for proper cycling of various kinds of clothes, then pulled out slightly to start action. Puzzle: How to remove it? No set screws are in sight. Answer: Twist the knob sharply counterclockwise. It will unscrew readily and separate from dial assembly.

With the knob off, the dial can be removed. It fits over a flattened shaft, and can be simply slipped off. A husky hex-head screw, invisible with the dial in place, now appears in front of the shaft. This is one of the two fasteners that hold the entire top of the washing machine in place.

On the left side of the washing machine is a decorative name plate similar in design to the control dial. This has no mechanical function, but does serve to hide the other hex-head screw that holds the top to the machine. In disassembly, it is simply pried up with a screw driver as shown.

The hex-head screws can now be removed in order to take the top off the washer. The top can be simply lifted free. Caution should be observed here, however. Lift it carefully and watch for wiring along the back side of the machine. Instructions sheet, if it's available, will be helpful.

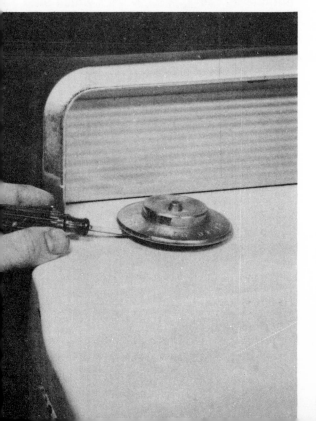

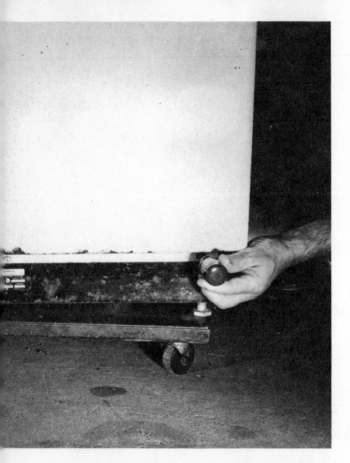

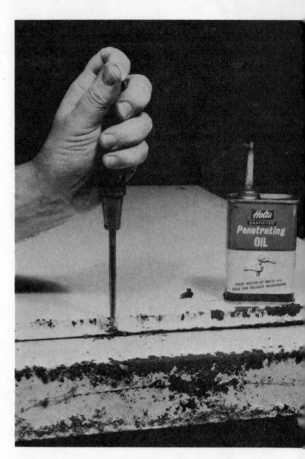

This washer has removable panel in front (some have three-sided cabinet with removable back). Look for self-tapping screws along bottom edge. Machine is resting on a dolly (a square of wood shelving with plate casters in corners) to ease job of moving heavy washer around for inspection.

Damp atmosphere that naturally attends a clothes washer raises havoc with screws and exposed metal surfaces. A few drops of "liquid wrench" penetrating oil will help to loosen stubborn fasteners, making it easy to remove them. Machine has been turned on side to make screws accessible.

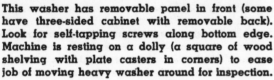

With the bottom screws removed, the front panel of washer lifts off spring hooks at the top. Entire inside "works" of machine are now accessible.

but merely self-tapping screws which form their own "nuts" in the bottom layer of a sandwich of two or more pieces of sheet metal.

Actually, the best time to acquaint yourself with the anatomy of an appliance is when it is in normal working order. Then, if something should happen to it, you can attack it with assurance and save a lot of time and fumbling.

It is helpful, of course, to have an instruction sheet or service manual for a machine but, since these are generally not easy to obtain, you often have to proceed by inspection and touch. Almost immediately you may encounter a puzzle in the form of knobs or dials that have no set screws or other visible means of attachment. If a knob appears to be of solid, one-piece construction, grasp it firmly with your fingers and merely *pull* straight out, and to your surprise it will probably come off readily. Examine its center hole and the

Not a television receiver, but the top of a washer stood on end. Look for pull-apart connectors on various leads and make a careful note of color markings on the latter. Soldered connections are almost never found in modern day appliances.

An unexpected but welcome bonus! Removal of the front panel of the washer reveals a clear and highly valuable schematic diagram of the wiring. With this and a volt-ohm-meter, it becomes easy to trace all connections, locate possible troubles.

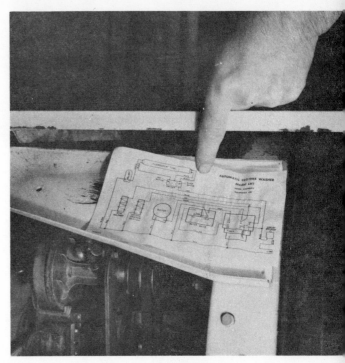

Solderless plug-in connections save manufacturing time, but they are vulnerable to vibration. Machine once failed to operate on spin cycle because this lead had jogged loose from controlling solenoid. All the connector receptacles were squeezed slightly with a pliers to grip more firmly.

This is the timer, the heart of an automatic washer with seven connections to the panel and two more to the timer motor (underneath). Once the tube filled properly with water and then refused to agitate. When the top was pulled off to free the timer, one lead was found to have separated completely from its end plug! Evidently the wire had been pinched a little too much in assembly, and the shaking of the machine finally broke off the few strands that remained.

A very simple reason why this washer stopped working after about six years—the drive belt had finally separated. This is a "normal" failure, and must be expected sooner or later with most machines. Replacement is just a matter of minutes.

shaft from which it came and you will observe that a flattened area on the latter permits the knob to fit only one way while a spring in the hole tightens the assembly. Removal of the controls is the first step in most disassembly operations.

To give you an idea of what to expect, the series of photographs shown here illustrate a typical take-down job on a typical clothes washer. This machine performed honorable service on everything from handkerchiefs to bed sheets, quit a number of times for typical reasons, was repaired each time by the owner and was finally retired after nine years because it was just plain worn out. Since the useful life of most heavy-duty machines is conservatively figured at five years, this washer could be considered a good investment. •

Tools for Testing

Make a small investment in these simple, inexpensive, rugged testing devices. They provide most of the answers when it comes to appliance trouble shooting!

SINCE many of the troubles that develop in electrical appliances are electrical in nature, you will definitely find it advisable to acquire one or two basic test devices. The simplest of all is the "neon tester." This consists merely of a small neon bulb in a protective sleeve or tube with two leads about five inches long fitted with brass tips called "probes." They cost between 50 and 75 cents and are widely sold in hardware, electrical, electronic and home furnishing stores.

The neon tester gives a quick and unmistakable answer to the question, "Is this power outlet or circuit alive?" When the probes are touched to the exposed metal terminals of the circuit or to the "hot" side of the line and to ground, the neon bulb glows red on any voltage between about 60 and 500. Thus, it is usable without adjustment on both 115/230-volt single-phase and 120/208-volt three-phase systems.

By itself the neon tester is capable of revealing trouble in the most unexpected places. For example, when tapped between ground and one side of an apparently good fuse and then the other, it might glow the first time but not the second; this indicates that the fuse is open. A similar check on the two terminals of a switch with the appliance plugged into a live outlet might show very surprisingly that the switch either stays open when it is turned on or stays on when it is supposed to snap off.

For further trouble shooting within an appliance, which should be done with the

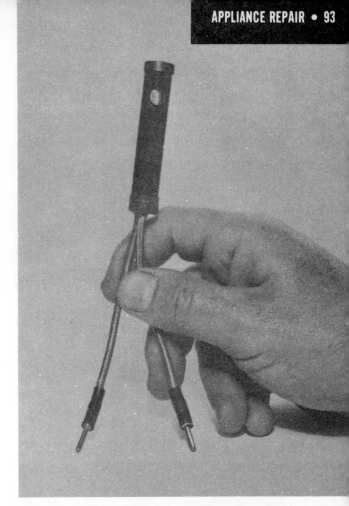

Popular type neon tester sold in hardware, electrical and electronics stores answers question, "Is circuit alive?" Device can be improved as shown in the photo below to minimize the shock hazard.

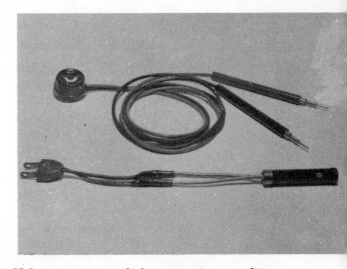

Make neon tester safe by connecting to ordinary AC plug. Buy a pair of flexible test leads with long insulated probes from electronics supply store; connect ends to the receptacle to take the plug.

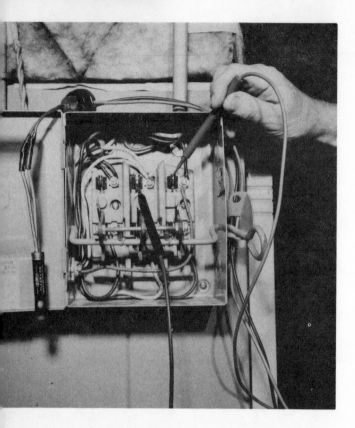

The revamped neon tester is easier to use and, with handles of test leads grasped as shown, shock danger is eliminated. Here it's in use to determine if the circuit to furnace switch is alive.

Knight-Kit VOM is typical of test meters in do-it-yourself form. Assembly is simple nuts-and-bolts job with all components readily accessible for soldering. The model illustrated (less expensive types are also available) sells for about $17, and is manufactured by Allied Radio, Chicago, Ill.

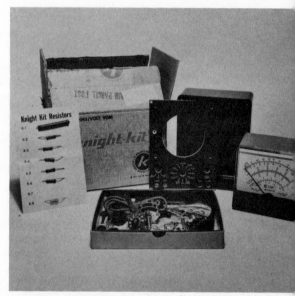

Back view (left) of assembled Knight-Kit VOM. The finger points to single penlite battery which furnishes current for resistance-continuity testing. The battery usually lasts for about a year, and is quickly replaceable; just insert in the spring clips.

power plug pulled out for safety's sake, by far the most versatile instrument is the "volt-ohm-meter," universally called the VOM for short. A VOM differs from a neon tester in that it is a measuring as well as an indicating device. It contains a small, low-voltage battery which provides a safe current for tracing the continuity of wires and connections. "Continuity checking" isolates and identifies probably 90 per cent of all troubles in electrical equipment.

Because they are simple and virtually foolproof, VOM kits for do-it-yourself as-

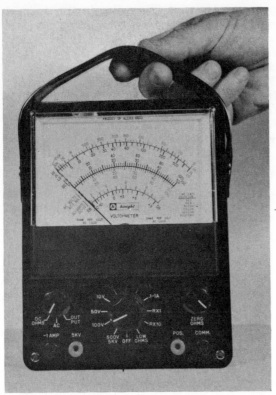

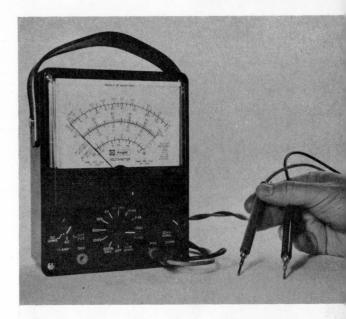

With center knob set for resistance measurement and the probes separated, the meter does not read at all, indicating, correctly, an open circuit.

The finished VOM is compact and portable. The topmost scale on the meter face reads resistance for continuity checking. Other scales read volts and amperes as selected by the center knob. The probes are connected to small jacks at bottom of the panel.

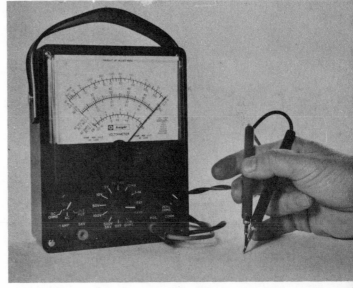

With probes touched together (that is, "short-circuited") meter circuit is completed through the negligible resistance of the test leads, and the needle bounces to right to read zero ohms. Any device having a resistance of more than about ½ ohm or less than one megohm (1,000,000 ohms) produces a definite reading on the meter scale.

sembly are very popular. For an average price of about $17, you can put together in an evening a meter that will last a lifetime (if you don't drop it on a concrete floor!). Such a unit will enable you to make intelligent, definitive checks on practically any device that depends for its operation on moving electrons. This includes everything from hearing aids and pocket radio sets to clocks, fans, toasters, irons, TV sets and hi-fi systems, junior's electric trains, washing machines and even the family car.

The typical VOM shown in the accom-panying pictures, built from a kit, measures both AC and DC voltages as low as 1/10 volt and as high as 5,000 volts in seven ranges selected by a front-panel rotary switch. As an ohmmeter for continuity checking, the VOM has three resistance scales with readings from one to 1,000,000 ohms. The instrument also can measure currents up to a maximum of one ampere. This capability is of no importance in appliance testing, but is useful for checking small dry-battery operated devices.

While the neon tester tells if a power line

is dead or alive, the VOM shows the actual line voltage. This can be extremely important, especially when the figure turns out to be lower than it should be. Many a large appliance works unsatisfactorily only because it does not receive enough juice, and the meter reading is the tip-off in this regard.

The "nominal" voltage for which most appliances are designed is actually a spread between 115 and 120 volts; in the case of some air conditioners and most electric ranges, which can be used only in homes having conventional three-wire service, the values are doubled to between 230 and 240 volts. It is most edifying to measure the voltage at the fuse box, where the lines from the street enter the house, at different hours of the day and especially during hot weather when every air conditioner in the

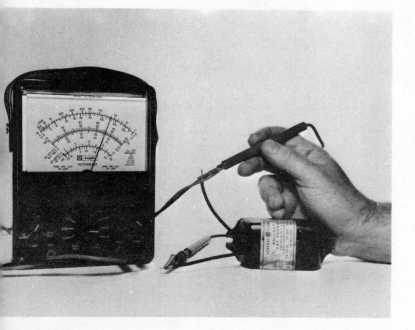

Example of continuity checking: Common fluorescent lamp ballast consists of many turns of wire on an iron core. This one, in good order, measures 55 ohms. If it should develop a complete internal short circuit (not likely) it would read zero. If the winding developed a break (the most usual trouble), no current would pass through it and the meter needle wouldn't budge. Thus, the trouble can be instantly spotted.

Switches rate particular attention because they are subjected to mechanical as well as electrical stress. There are no halfway meter indications for them: when "off," the VOM should show no reading whatsoever; when "on," it should bang over to the zero mark. A high but readable resistance in the "off" position (not common) may be due to accumulation of dirt between the terminals. An unsteady low resistance reading in "on" position (likely in switches breaking heavy currents) is almost invariably due to contact springs being corroded.

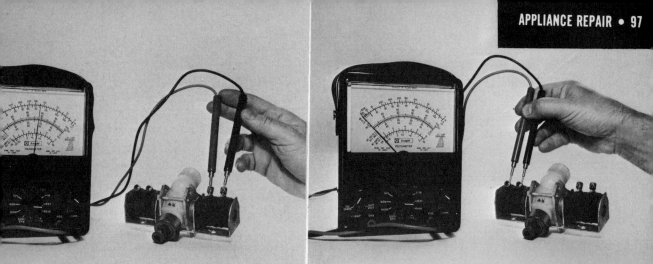

Above is shown the mixing valve of a clothes washer which consists of two solenoids that control the inflow of hot and cold water. A continuity check on the hot coil gave a normal reading of 120 ohms. A check on the cold coil, which should have given an identical reading, showed the winding to be absolutely open. The fact explained why the wash water in the machine's tub was always scalding!

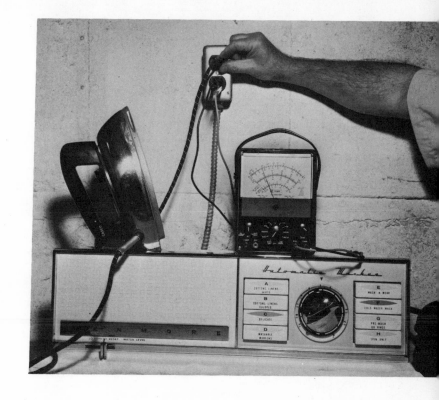

You can readily demonstrate the effect of heavy loads on line voltage by taking an initial reading with an outlet empty and a second one with an iron or toaster plugged in. A slight drop is normal; perhaps two or three volts from 115. If it's much more than that, the lines are too small. While No. 14 wire is satisfactory for most house circuits, No. 12 is much better for toaster or broiler outlets in the kitchen and iron and washer outlets in the home where the laundry is done.

neighborhood is running full blast. There is bound to be some variation from the line's rated figures. However, if the voltage drops from a good value of perhaps 116 on a cool day to 100 on a sultry one, you should notify the local power company. You may be astonished to see how quickly a new and larger distribution transformer is installed on a nearby pole or in an underground vault! The power company isn't being philanthropic; it's only being smart. Low voltage means low current; the combination of the two means low wattage. Low wattage means small bills, to say nothing of customer complaints that might come rolling in. •

Preventive Maintenance

Routine maintenance is important—get the habit of checking appliances regularly

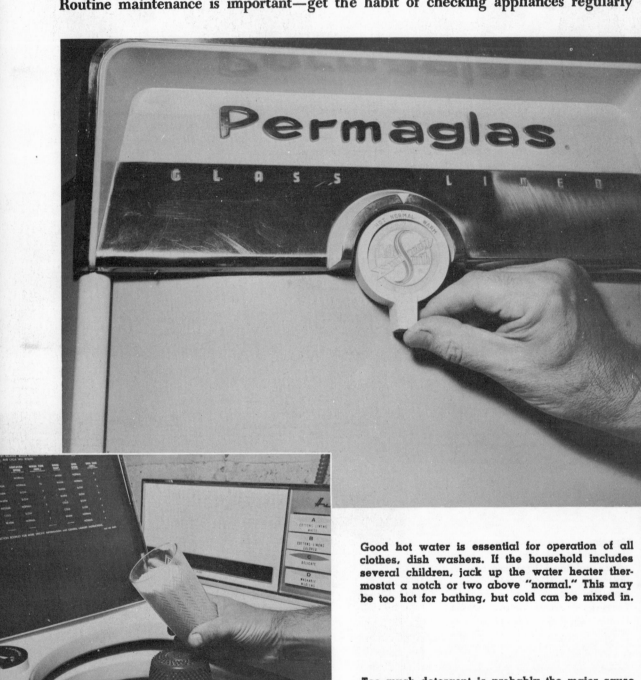

Good hot water is essential for operation of all clothes, dish washers. If the household includes several children, jack up the water heater thermostat a notch or two above "normal." This may be too hot for bathing, but cold can be mixed in.

Too much detergent is probably the major cause of blockage in clothes washers. Many women are fooled by relatively low sudsing action of popular powders; they keep pouring stuff in until a thick foam forms. A glassful is entirely too much.

YOU'VE UNDOUBTEDLY gotten into the habit of checking your tire pressure, the water in the radiator and the oil in the crankcase, and you know that regular attention of this kind assures you trouble-free driving and maximum car life. Extend this same habit of preventive maintenance to your household appliances.

The accompanying photos illustrate just a few of the important points that need emphasis as suggested by the service department of Sears, Roebuck & Co. In poking around your machines you will probably find other elements that can stand occasional cleaning, lubrication or adjustment —simple jobs all. •

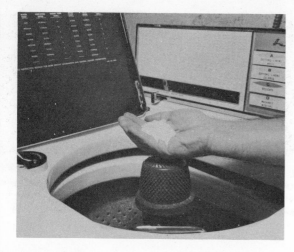

Maximum capacity of common clothes washers is between 7 and 9 pounds, but how many home laundries boast a scale of any sort for actually measuring daily piles like this one? Overloads not only strain the machine dangerously but defeat its purpose: crowded clothes do not wash clean. When in doubt as to how much of a load is too much, play safe and divide it. Two washes are cheaper than headache of stalled drive mechanism.

A surprisingly small quantity of most detergents, like this mere handful, does a thorough washing job even on very dirty clothes despite the fact that it creates little or no suds. Solution flushes out readily without clogging machine. If any bleaching is needed, use a bleach—not more soap.

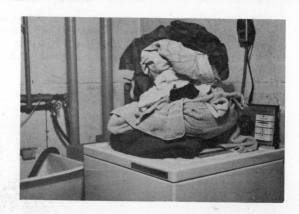

Opening a machine may reveal the existence of unexpected lubrication points such as this one on the drain pump of a washer. Go easy on the oil; three or four drops every three or four months is enough. Some fittings require application of auto-type grease guns. Motor bearings are generally of the "permanently" lubricated type and need no attention during normal life of appliance.

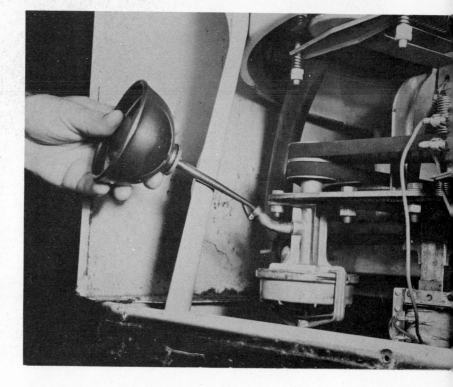

Practically all large machines such as refrigerators, freezers and washers have leveling feet which are adjustable by means of a screwdriver or a wrench. A small spirit level is necessary, and should be used to check both the front and the rear. A properly leveled machine runs smoothly without a shake. This adjustment is also important with refrigerators to make the door swing shut by itself.

Slightest leakage around door gasket of a refrigerator or freezer will cause the cooling unit to run for longer periods than normal. Look for signs of hardening or cracking, the result of frequent slamming of the door. Installing new sealing material around a door is relatively simple.

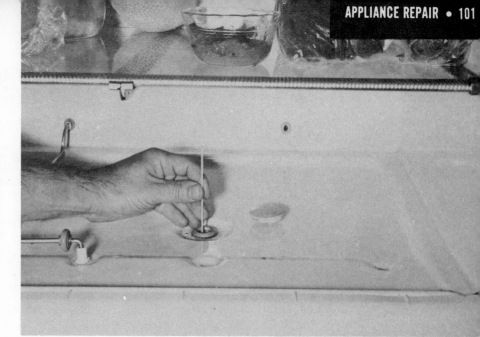

Look for a drain plug on the bottom shelf of a refrigerator. This often becomes clogged with bits of food, and a puddle of water may form around it. Poke the hole clean with a toothpick or a length of wire.

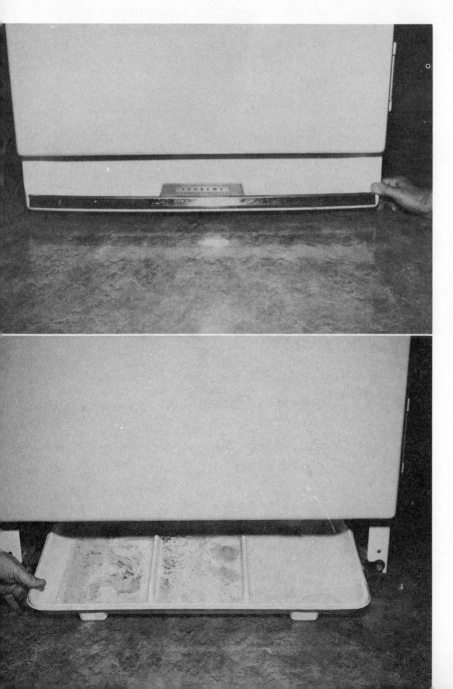

The drain plug has to empty into a receptacle of some sort, usually a shallow pan out of sight behind a panel at the floor line. This lifts or slides off to reveal the drip catcher. The water that accumulates here normally evaporates by itself. However, the pan should be washed now and then to remove any food particles that attract insects.

armchair

These chairs offer proof that well-designed contemporary furniture provides comfort and beauty without fancy frills.

WHAT living room is complete without a few deep, comfortable armchairs? The design shown on these pages shows how you can construct such chairs along modern lines. Admittedly, they bear no resemblance to the overstuffed monstrosities of bygone days, but they still embody the basic characteristics of any armchair: relaxing arm rests and solid comfort.

Assembly: Cut all pieces to exact size given in the diagrams and bill of materials, and bore all ¾-inch holes to accept dowel tenons where indicated.

Screw one seat frame to its arm unit. Notice that the seat frame is attached *inside* of the arm unit. Repeat this operation with the opposite two units; 1¼-inch No. 8 flathead wood screws are used throughout. Observe that although the overall lengths of the three dowel stretchers are identical, 20¼ inches, the tenons on each end of dowels A and C are only ¾ inch long, whereas the tenons on the ends of dowel D are 1½ inches long. This is so because each tenon

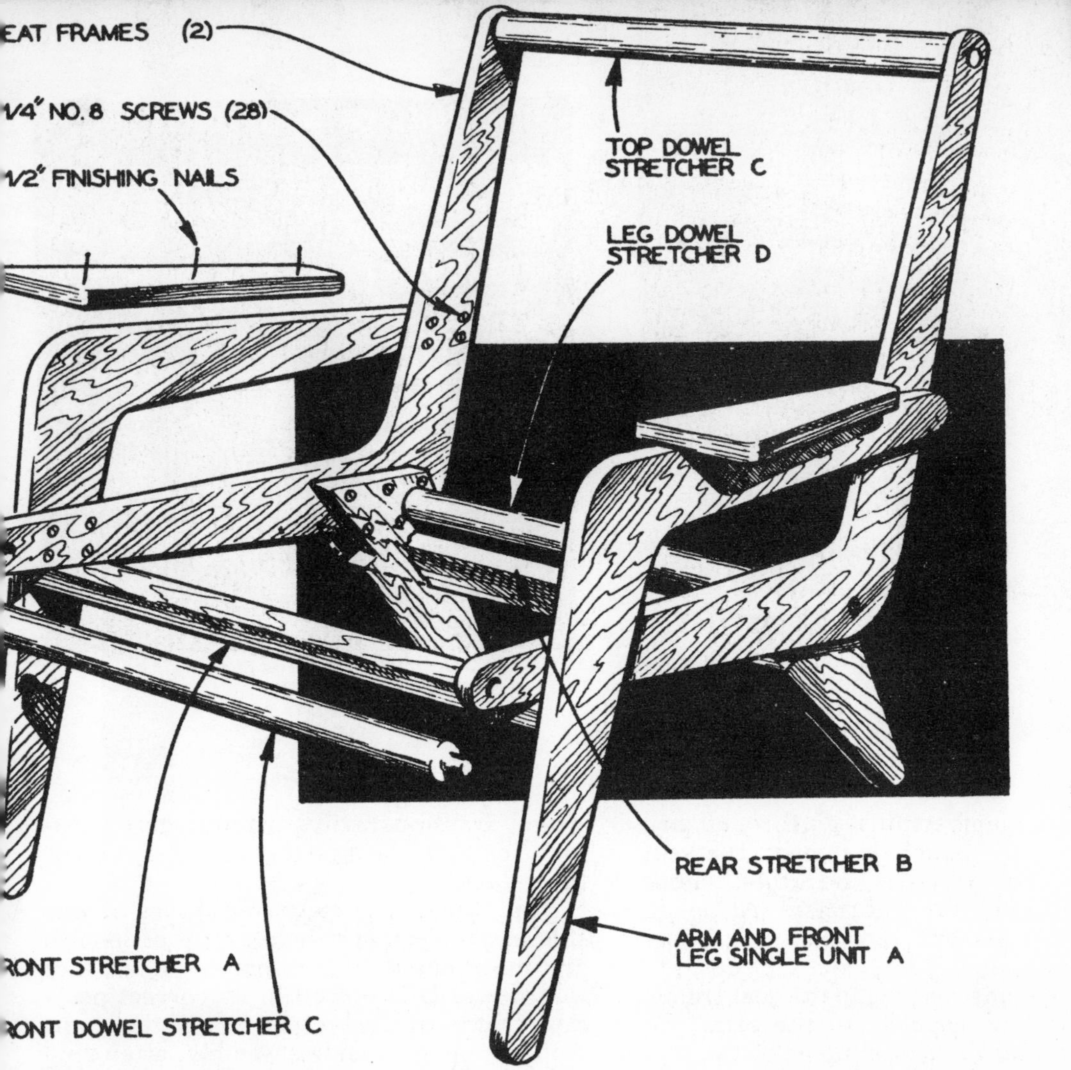

SEAT FRAMES (2)

1/4" NO. 8 SCREWS (28)

1/2" FINISHING NAILS

TOP DOWEL
STRETCHER C

LEG DOWEL
STRETCHER D

REAR STRETCHER B

ARM AND FRONT
LEG SINGLE UNIT A

FRONT STRETCHER A

FRONT DOWEL STRETCHER C

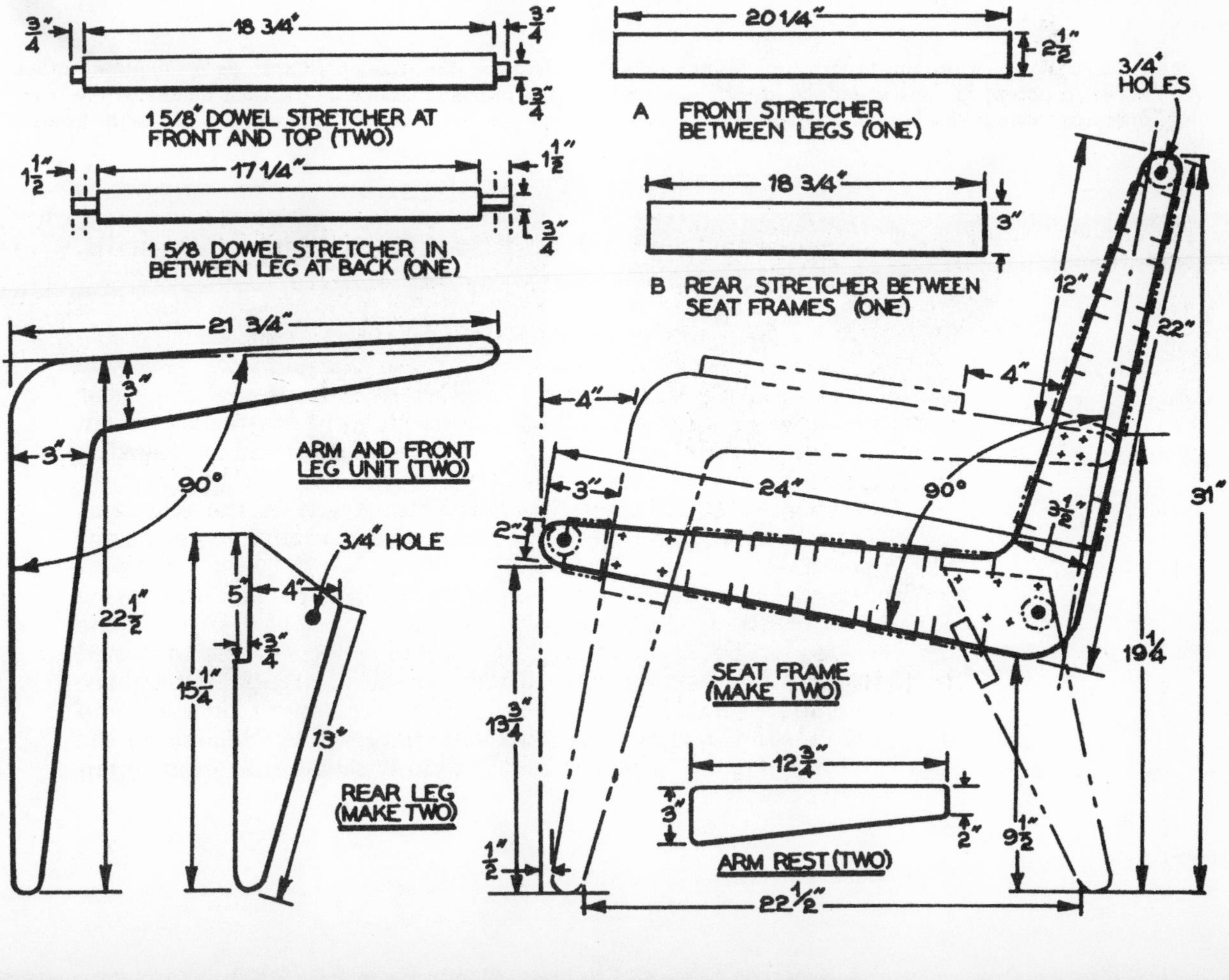

3/4"

18 3/4"

3/4"

3/4"

1 5/8" DOWEL STRETCHER AT
FRONT AND TOP (TWO)

1/2"

17 1/4"

1/2"

3/4"

1 5/8 DOWEL STRETCHER IN
BETWEEN LEG AT BACK (ONE)

20 1/4"

2 1/2"

A   FRONT STRETCHER
BETWEEN LEGS (ONE)

18 3/4"

3"

B   REAR STRETCHER BETWEEN
SEAT FRAMES (ONE)

3/4"
HOLES

12"

22"

4"

31"

19 1/4"

21 3/4"

3"

3"

90°

ARM AND FRONT
LEG UNIT (TWO)

22 1/2"

15 1/4"

5"

4"

3"
3/4"

3/4" HOLE

13"

REAR LEG
(MAKE TWO)

4"

3"

2"

24"

90°

3 1/2"

13 3/4"

1/2"

SEAT FRAME
(MAKE TWO)

12 3/4"

3"

2"

ARM REST (TWO)

9 1/2"

22 1/2"

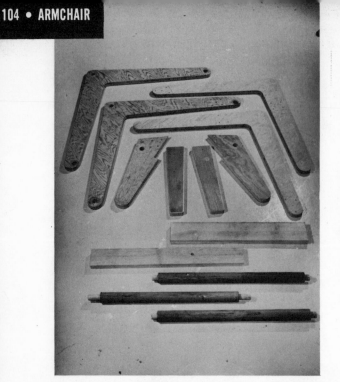

BILL OF MATERIALS

Note: All lumber, unless otherwise specified, is ¾" plywood.

2 Seat Frames, with ¾" holes . . cut as shown
2 Arms (Front Legs) . . . . cut as shown
2 Rear Legs, with ¾" holes . . . cut as shown
1 Front Stretcher . . . . 2½"x20¼"
1 Rear Stretcher . . . . 3"x18¾"
2 Arm Rests . . . . cut as shown
3 Dowel Stretchers,
 1⅝" or 1⅜" . . . . 20¼" overall
30 Flathead Wood Screws . . . . 1¼" No. 8
1½" Finishing Nails . . . . ½ lb.
No. 6 Upholstery Tacks . . . . 1 Box
2" Webbing . . . . 25 Yards

of the latter member must go through *two* thicknesses of ¾-inch plywood: the seat frame and leg, whereas the other tenons go through only one thickness. Although 1⅝-inch dowels are indicated, you may substitute 1⅜-inch round stock, if desired.

Now screw one rear leg to the seat frame, but on the face opposite to the arm. To make sure that the dowel holes of the seat frame and the leg coincide exactly, insert

dowel D temporarily, without glue. Attach the opposite rear leg, using the same procedure.

Apply glue into the tenon holes of one side assembly and to one group of tenons, and insert the dowels in place. Make sure that dowel D is placed in its correct position, that is, at the bottom rear of the chair. Add the opposite side assembly, after gluing holes and tenons.

1. Once elements are cut to size and ¾-inch holes bored to accept the dowel tenons, attach one arm and seat frame with 1¼-inch flathead wood screws.

2. Using the assembled side as a template, attach the opposite assembly. In both instances the arms go on the outside surfaces of the seat frames.

3. Rear leg goes on inside surface of frame. Dowel D is inserted without glue to line up these pieces.

Glue and nail the 2½x20¼-inch front stretcher. Nail through the stretcher into the seat frame, and also through each arm into the stretcher. Now glue and nail the 3x18¾-inch rear stretcher to the recesses of the rear legs. Use two or three 1½-inch finishing nails at each end. At this stage, you are ready to add the arm rests. Glue and nail them to the arms with 1½-inch finishing nails. Notice that the straight edges of both arm rests face the inside of the frame.

This completes assembly. However, to assure good glue joints, tie seat frames together with stout cord, just above the arms. Use a hammer or screwdriver as a tightening device. Allow the glue to dry completely—about eight hours –before removing your cord Don't clutter up the workbench or the floor.

4. Five screws are driven through each rear leg into the seat frame. Save yourself work by boring pilot holes and countersinks where necessary.

5. Repeat operation shown at left, so that both side assemblies are now completed. To combine them, attach glue to tenons and holes of one side.

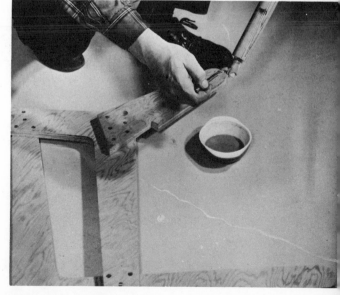

6. After dabbing glue into the holes of one side, insert the dowels into their respective holes. Remember that dowel D goes through the rear legs.

7. Glue opposite tenons and holes, then lift the second side and position the tenons. Be sure that both rear legs face inside during this operation.

To make sure that the dowels will not eventually become loose, drive a single finishing nail into each dowel end, as shown in the photograph on page 105. Sink all visible nailheads into the wood about ⅛ inch, using a nail punch. Fill all holes with a wood composition filler.

Since you won't be able to finish the chair after webbing has been tacked on, it should be finished now. Sand down the entire frame, especially all sharp edges, before applying any type of finish. Paste wax may be successfully employed to finish

chairs; simply rub it on with a cloth, let it dry according to the manufacturer's instructions, then buff. No other finish will be required.

Webbing: After the frame has been painted or varnished, you are ready to web. Cut seven strips 47 inches long for your vertical strips, and fifteen 32-inch pieces for your horizontal strips. Distribute eight of the short strips evenly over the seat area.

The second strip from the front of the seat is tacked to the top of the frame. For the remaining strips, tack one edge to the

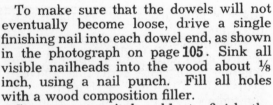

8. The front and rear stretchers are next. Drive two or three 1½-inch finishing nails part way into ends of both pieces to save strain on frame.

9. Front stretcher is nailed into the underside of the seat frames and also through both legs. For extra strength, use glue at these joints.

10. The rear stretcher is inserted into its recesses and is nailed to both legs. This step completes the assembly of your entire armchair frame unit.

11. The 12¾-inch-long arm rests are glued and nailed in place. Be sure tapered ends face back of chair. Sink all nailheads ⅛ inch into wood.

lower edge of the frame. Distribute seven strips over the back. The second and third strips from the bottom are tacked on the top edge of the frame. The rest of the strips are tacked on the outside edge of the frame. Fold the ends of all strips double for extra strength. Stretch your webbing as tightly as possible, cut off excess, leaving enough for a doubled end, and tack to the lower edge of the frame.

For the horizontal webbing, first space the strips evenly, then fold the ends and

tack your seven long strips to the underside of the top dowel C. Interweave these strips with the attached horizontal pieces. Double the ends and tack to the bottom dowel C. Do not pull the long strips too tightly, as this creates an uncomfortable bulge. New webbing may stretch; to tighten, restretch cross strips on seat only.

Either plastic or cloth webbing may be employed. Since both types are available in many shades, you can easily choose one to complement your present color scheme.

12. Before glue has dried, drive single finishing nail into ends of all dowels to assure a good bond.

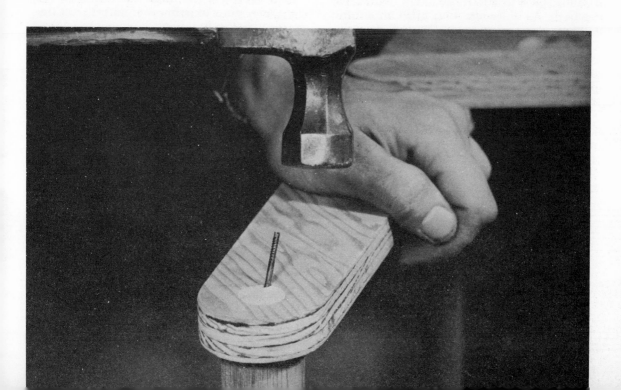

Expand Your Attic

By Henry Clark

HAS your family grown beyond the limits of your house? A simple solution to this dilemma is to look to your attic for space to add those extra bedrooms and bath. As it stands, your attic area may strike you as a puny space for such growth. If so, just visualize a full rear shed dormer, complete with two or three brand new windows. It can give you about 50% more cubic content and make a second floor living area a reality.

Don't be dazed by the terrifying prospect of ripping open your roof to the elements and flooding your home with rain water as you struggle to complete what seems a Herculean task. Exposing your attic interior isn't necessary with the unique method described here, and the job itself can be completed by you alone over relatively few weekends of work.

The secret is to build the dormer roof right over your existing roof and rip out the present roof only when the dormer is completely boxed in. Thus you may extend the period of work indefinitely and never subject your home interior to weather damage.

Before plunging into this money-saving project, save yourself the stray chance of a headache by checking your local building codes to see if a building permit is required (the cost is insignificant). Also there may be a few minimum requirements as to spacing between studs, rafters and joists.

Now do a little preliminary common-

Typical dormer structure begins with erection of studs. Remove or chop hole through eave boards to expose the wall plate upon which studs will bear.

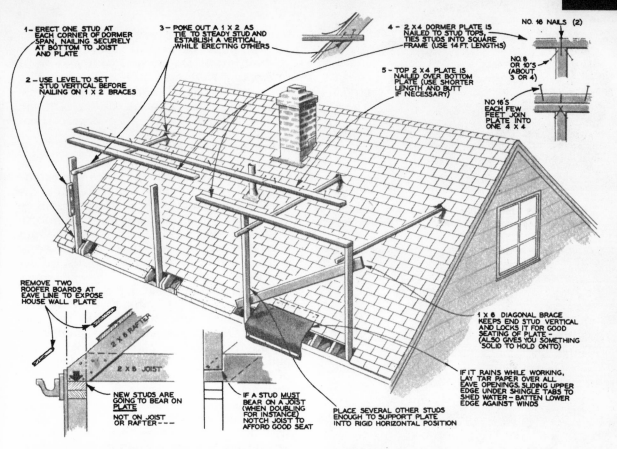

1 – ERECT ONE STUD AT EACH CORNER OF DORMER SPAN, NAILING SECURELY AT BOTTOM TO JOIST AND PLATE

2 – USE LEVEL TO SET STUD VERTICAL BEFORE NAILING ON 1 X 2 BRACES

3 – POKE OUT A 1 X 2 AS TIE TO STEADY STUD AND ESTABLISH A VERTICAL, WHILE ERECTING OTHERS

4 – 2 X 4 DORMER PLATE IS NAILED TO STUD TOPS, TIES STUDS INTO SQUARE FRAME (USE 14 FT. LENGTHS)

5 – TOP 2 X 4 PLATE IS NAILED OVER BOTTOM PLATE (USE SHORTER LENGTH AND BUTT IF NECESSARY)

NO. 16 NAILS (2)

NO. 8 OR 10'S (ABOUT 3 OR 4)

NO 16'S EACH FEW FEET JOIN PLATE INTO ONE 4 X 4

REMOVE TWO ROOFER BOARDS AT EAVE LINE TO EXPOSE HOUSE WALL PLATE

2 X 6 RAFTER

2 X 8 JOIST

NEW STUDS ARE GOING TO BEAR ON PLATE

NOT ON JOIST OR RAFTER – – –

IF A STUD MUST BEAR ON A JOIST (WHEN DOUBLING FOR INSTANCE) NOTCH JOIST TO AFFORD GOOD SEAT

PLACE SEVERAL OTHER STUDS ENOUGH TO SUPPORT PLATE INTO RIGID HORIZONTAL POSITION

1 X 6 DIAGONAL BRACE KEEPS END STUD VERTICAL AND LOCKS IT FOR GOOD SEATING OF PLATE – (ALSO GIVES YOU SOMETHING SOLID TO HOLD ONTO)

IF IT RAINS WHILE WORKING, LAY TAR PAPER OVER ALL EAVE OPENINGS, SLIDING UPPER EDGE UNDER SHINGLE TABS TO SHED WATER – BATTEN LOWER EDGE AGAINST WINDS

STEP 1   OPENING EAVE BOARDS FOR LOCATING STUDS TO FORM DORMER GENERAL FRAME

Create a second floor living area by building a full shed dormer on your roof with this unique method.

sense paper work. The photographs and sketches in this article illustrate every basic building step you need to know. But exact dimensions for height, width, depth and styling must necessarily depend on the individual home. A number of actual houses are used in the photos to show varieties of procedure and finishing techniques. Plan the size of your dormer, the number of windows you want, the type of finishing to match the present exterior and a dormer roof pitch that will blend architecturally with the house.

To start actual work, remove the first and second eave boards, which will reveal the plate bearing on the wall studs below. At each intersection of a joist and this plate

A single 2x4-in. plate is nailed to initial studs. Double plate later. Use 1x2-in. braces to hold studs in true vertical. Check each with a level.

End rafters and gable plates follow erection of initial studs and stud plate. See details below.

Gable plate is attached at interior end to an existing rafter and beveled to match roof pitch.

Make opening through ridge boards to expose the ridge pole to which the end rafters are attached.

you will spike your new 2x4 dormer studs. At this point be careful to avoid an important pitfall. Do not nail your new studs to existing rafters as these will eventually be torn out from inside. Nail only to the plate and joists. Examine the top lefthand photograph on page 113 for correct procedure.

Put up just a few studs at first to form a support for your new dormer plate. Use 1x2-in. ties to support the studs and establish a vertical. Install the plate atop the studs as illustrated. We might presumably erect all studs at once, but this would form a dangerously heavy structure without adequate support. At this point we merely want to form a basic frame of studs, rafters and gable plates.

With stud plates placed, measure, cut and nail in place the two gable plates that form a horizontal directly beneath the end rafters. One end of each gable plate rests on the front dormer plate, while the other end is secured to an existing inside rafter of the house. Note that this is the only instance we will attach a dormer member to an existing rafter, since these particular bearing rafters for the two gable plates will not eventually be removed. See the second photo from the top on this page to note inside attachment of the gable plate.

When the gable plates have been spiked in place, remove the two top ridge boards and install the two end rafters to the ridge pole and dormer plate. First measure properly for span and cut accurate angles at the rafter ends for secure seating on the plate and ridge pole. These will form patterns for all your rafters so cut them carefully. We presume, of course, that the house ridge pole is straight. If not, it will necessitate shortening or lengthening the new rafters accordingly.

You now have a basic frame upon which you may install all remaining studs and rafters. It is perhaps best to cut and place all rafters first since it is desirable to close in a shelter for the old roof as soon as possible. Note that all rafters placed between the two end rafters must be nailed to the plate and ridge pole only. Do *not* nail to existing rafters, as these will be ripped out later. See the bottom photo on this page to see rafter attachment to the ridge pole.

So far we have our old roof intact but considerably punctured in a number of places. Let us suppose storm clouds are gathering and you don't plan to work on your new dormer for a few days. Merely

Left, close-up of end rafter spiked to the ridge pole. Bevel ends to seat accurately against pole.

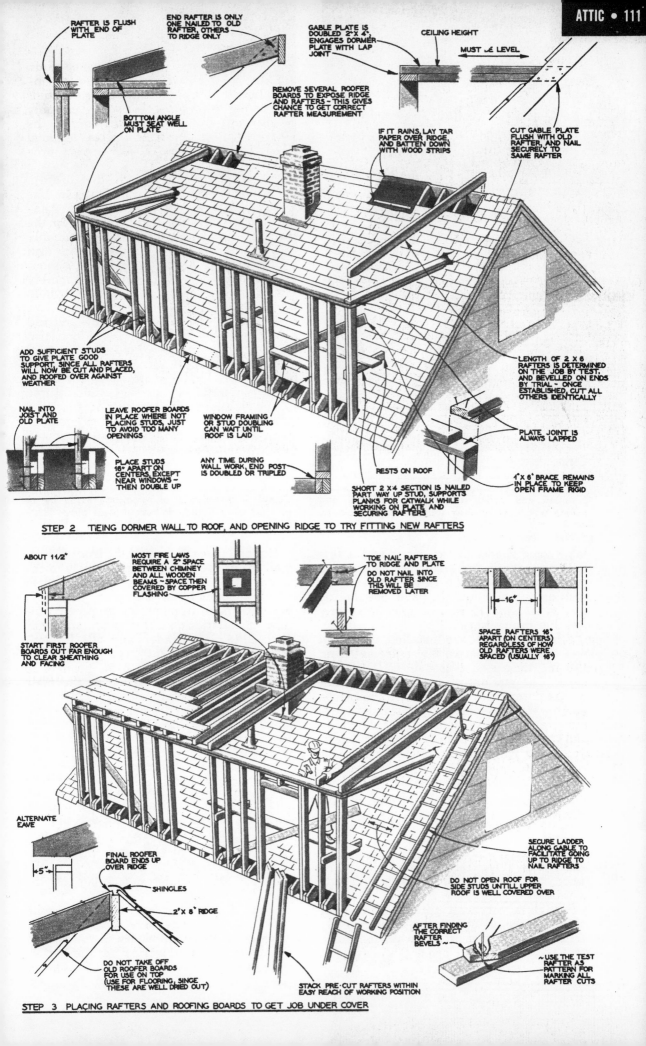

RAFTER IS FLUSH WITH END OF PLATE

END RAFTER IS ONLY ONE NAILED TO OLD RAFTER, OTHERS TO RIDGE ONLY

BOTTOM ANGLE MUST SEAT WELL ON PLATE

GABLE PLATE IS DOUBLED 2" X 4", ENGAGES DORMER PLATE WITH LAP JOINT

CEILING HEIGHT

MUST BE LEVEL

REMOVE SEVERAL ROOFER BOARDS TO EXPOSE RIDGE AND RAFTERS - THIS GIVES CHANCE TO GET CORRECT RAFTER MEASUREMENT

IF IT RAINS, LAY TAR PAPER OVER RIDGE, AND BATTEN DOWN WITH WOOD STRIPS

CUT GABLE PLATE FLUSH WITH OLD RAFTER, AND NAIL SECURELY TO SAME RAFTER

ADD SUFFICIENT STUDS TO GIVE PLATE GOOD SUPPORT, SINCE ALL RAFTERS WILL NOW BE CUT AND PLACED, AND ROOFED OVER AGAINST WEATHER

NAIL INTO JOIST AND OLD PLATE

LEAVE ROOFER BOARDS IN PLACE WHERE NOT PLACING STUDS, JUST TO AVOID TOO MANY OPENINGS

WINDOW FRAMING OR STUD DOUBLING CAN WAIT UNTIL ROOF IS LAID

LENGTH OF 2 X 6 RAFTERS IS DETERMINED ON THE JOB BY TEST, AND BEVELLED ON ENDS BY TRIAL - ONCE ESTABLISHED, CUT ALL OTHERS IDENTICALLY

PLATE JOINT IS ALWAYS LAPPED

PLACE STUDS 16" APART ON CENTERS, EXCEPT NEAR WINDOWS - THEN DOUBLE UP

ANY TIME DURING WALL WORK, END POST IS DOUBLED OR TRIPLED

RESTS ON ROOF

SHORT 2 X 4 SECTION IS NAILED PART WAY UP STUD, SUPPORTS PLANKS FOR CATWALK WHILE WORKING ON PLATE AND SECURING RAFTERS

4" X 6" BRACE REMAINS IN PLACE TO KEEP OPEN FRAME RIGID

STEP 2   TIEING DORMER WALL TO ROOF, AND OPENING RIDGE TO TRY FITTING NEW RAFTERS

ABOUT 11/2"

MOST FIRE LAWS REQUIRE A 2" SPACE BETWEEN CHIMNEY AND ALL WOODEN BEAMS - SPACE THEN COVERED BY COPPER FLASHING

'TOE NAIL' RAFTERS TO RIDGE AND PLATE

DO NOT NAIL INTO OLD RAFTER SINCE THIS WILL BE REMOVED LATER

16"

START FIRST ROOFER BOARDS OUT FAR ENOUGH TO CLEAR SHEATHING AND FACING

SPACE RAFTERS 16" APART (ON CENTERS) REGARDLESS OF HOW OLD RAFTERS WERE SPACED (USUALLY 16")

ALTERNATE EAVE

5"

FINAL ROOFER BOARD ENDS UP OVER RIDGE

SHINGLES

2" X 8" RIDGE

DO NOT TAKE OFF OLD ROOFER BOARDS FOR USE ON TOP (USE FOR FLOORING, SINCE THESE ARE WELL DRIED OUT)

STACK PRE-CUT RAFTERS WITHIN EASY REACH OF WORKING POSITION

SECURE LADDER ALONG GABLE TO FACILITATE GOING UP TO RIDGE TO NAIL RAFTERS

DO NOT OPEN ROOF FOR SIDE STUDS UNTILL UPPER ROOF IS WELL COVERED OVER

AFTER FINDING THE CORRECT RAFTER BEVELS ~

~ USE THE TEST RAFTER AS PATTERN FOR MARKING ALL RAFTER CUTS

STEP 3 PLACING RAFTERS AND ROOFING BOARDS TO GET JOB UNDER COVER

Installed end rafter and gable plate. Fit end rafters with care as they form pattern for others.

Complete installation of remaining studs by removing eave boards to reveal wall plate, joists.

take some sheets of tar paper and a few battening strips and cover the rafter gaps you've made near the ridge pole and the stud holes made near the eave. See the top photos on page 113 for examples of stormy weather precautions.

When all rafters are installed, place and nail the roofer boards. These are cut from 1x6-in. tongue-and-groove or shiplap stock. The amount of overhang you want on the dormer eave will dictate the placement of the first roofer board. It must overhang rafter ends enough to clear sheathing and the facing board. Let the roofer boards lie at odd lengths beyond the end rafters and then trim evenly when all are in place. Secure each board with two No. 8 nails in every rafter. Continue to place and nail boards clear to the ridge.

Upon completion, immediately apply asphalt felt of 15-lb. weight (tar paper) over the entire dormer roof, overlapping generously. It is excellent insurance against wood rot and a well rewarded investment.

Shingling can wait till the remainder of the dormer structure is completely sheathed. Also, we do not want too much roof weight until all bearing studs are in place.

Cut and place the rest of the front dormer wall studs, securing as previously mentioned. Double all studs that will bear window assemblies. Be sure you have accurate measurements of proposed window installations at this point and then proceed to place headers and sills. If openings are to be long for large picture windows, use 2x6-in. or 2x8-in. headers to support the rafters bearing on the plate directly above such headers.

Studding for the dormer sides is the next step. Saw away the old roof directly between two rafters where the dormer side wall will enter the attic. Then erect the vertical side studs between the gable plate and a plate installed along a double joist in the floor of the attic. These studs will butt against the existing rafter holding the gable plate and will be nailed to it. As pointed out previously, this rafter remains permanently in place and forms an untouched natural gable at each end of the house. This completes framing of the dormer "cheeks."

Now sheath the face and sides with 1x6-in. tongue-and-groove boards, shiplap stock or composition panels, as you choose. Whatever you use, work from the bottom up and secure firmly with No. 8 nails. As

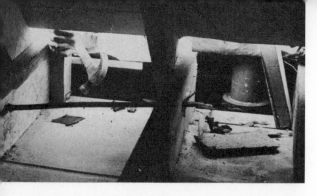

Detail of stud attachment seen from inside. Nail stud to plate and joists, not to existing rafters.

Prepare for rain at any time during construction by battening down tar paper over roof openings.

Stormy weather precautions include covering eave openings well as they receive the most watershed.

Below, framing nears completion. For large window openings use 2x6-in. or 2x8-in. stock for headers to give rigid support to dormer rafters bearing on plate above them.

with the dormer roof, apply tar paper over all sheathing.

Shingle the roof and sides to taste. Butt asphalt rectangles are as durable as anything but slate. Work from the eave up, doubling the first course to hide open slits. Flashing around the chimney and extended vents is usually copper.

With the exterior complete or nearly so, you may plan a period of inside work and get your first glimpse of the added area you have created. Start knocking out the old roof and you can begin to see the space you've wanted for new bedrooms.

You may have some use for this old lumber, so work carefully in removing the old rafters. Saw as close to the eave as you can and try prying the remainder away from the ridge pole.

However, before doing so, note a vitally important precautionary measure. Do *not* remove any rafters until you have erected a group of 4x4-in. temporary supporting studs to hold up the ridge pole in the center of the attic. Space each about ten feet apart. Leave these in place until you have placed attic ceiling joists between the dormer plate and the opposing rafters on the untouched side of the roof. These joists will act as ties or trusses. Still further, leave the supports in place until you have erected one or more bearing partitions inside the attic area to form separate rooms. Be sure these bearing partitions rest on or near a bearing wall on the first floor of the house. Only then is it really safe to remove these temporary studs from beneath the ridge pole.

If you want a wall parallel to the floor joists, double the joist it rests on. Double the top and bottom plates of all bearing wall studs. Try to place a bearing wall as near to the center of the attic as possible to more surely guarantee support for the ridge pole. If you have some spare pieces of 2x4-in. lumber, give the dormer roof added support by installing short lengths of studding between the dormer ceiling joists and the dormer rafters. The pitch of the dormer roof will naturally be shallower than that of the regular house roof and this will be added support against the weight of snow if you are situated in a northern area.

Your dormer is now virtually finished. The installation of electrical outlets, plumbing, etc., is another project and you had best consult your local building codes

Note doubled 2x6s for long span window frame. A 1x6 tops plate in this case for special ceiling.

Securing remaining rafters which have been pre-cut to match end rafters. Spike firmly to plate.

Fire codes usually require 2-in. gap between a chimney and wood. Cover the gap with flashing.

Roofer boards are cut from 1x6-in. tongue-and-groove or shiplap stock. Secure with No. 8 nails.

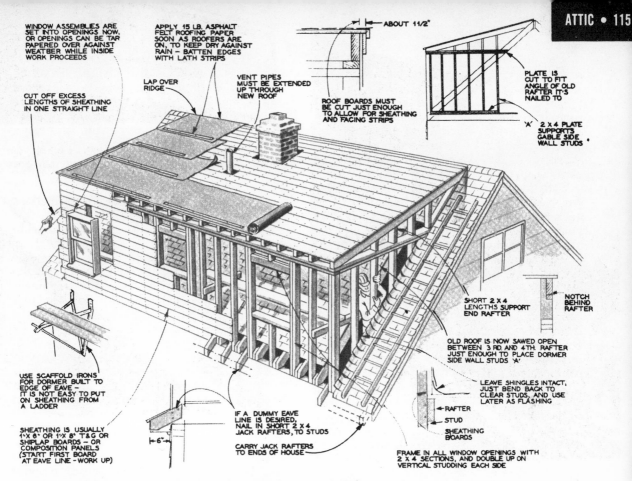

WINDOW ASSEMBLIES ARE SET INTO OPENINGS NOW, OR OPENINGS CAN BE TAR PAPERED OVER AGAINST WEATHER WHILE INSIDE WORK PROCEEDS

CUT OFF EXCESS LENGTHS OF SHEATHING IN ONE STRAIGHT LINE

LAP OVER RIDGE

APPLY 15 LB. ASPHALT FELT ROOFING PAPER SOON AS ROOFERS ARE ON, TO KEEP DRY AGAINST RAIN - BATTEN EDGES WITH LATH STRIPS

VENT PIPES MUST BE EXTENDED UP THROUGH NEW ROOF

ABOUT 1½"

ROOF BOARDS MUST BE CUT JUST ENOUGH TO ALLOW FOR SHEATHING AND FACING STRIPS

PLATE IS CUT TO FIT ANGLE OF OLD RAFTER IT'S NAILED TO

'A' 2 X 4 PLATE SUPPORTS GABLE SIDE WALL STUDS

SHORT 2 X 4 LENGTHS SUPPORT END RAFTER

NOTCH BEHIND RAFTER

USE SCAFFOLD IRONS FOR DORMER BUILT TO EDGE OF EAVE - IT IS NOT EASY TO PUT ON SHEATHING FROM A LADDER

SHEATHING IS USUALLY 1'X 6' OR 1'X 8' T&G OR SHIPLAP BOARDS - OR COMPOSITION PANELS (START FIRST BOARD AT EAVE LINE - WORK UP)

6"

IF A DUMMY EAVE LINE IS DESIRED, NAIL IN SHORT 2 X 4 JACK RAFTERS, TO STUDS

CARRY JACK RAFTERS TO ENDS OF HOUSE

OLD ROOF IS NOW SAWED OPEN BETWEEN 3 RD. AND 4TH. RAFTER JUST ENOUGH TO PLACE DORMER SIDE WALL STUDS 'A'

LEAVE SHINGLES INTACT, JUST BEND BACK TO CLEAR STUDS, AND USE LATER AS FLASHING

RAFTER

STUD

SHEATHING BOARDS

FRAME IN ALL WINDOW OPENINGS WITH 2 X 4 SECTIONS, AND DOUBLE UP ON VERTICAL STUDDING EACH SIDE

STEP 4 WEATHERPROOF ROOF, APPLY SHEATHING, FRAME IN DORMER SIDES

Close-up of new roofer boards nearing ridge pole. Note old roofers beneath plus old and new rafters.

View from on top of old roof and under new roof shows gable plate and side studding of dormer.

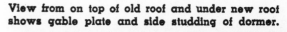

With roofer boards on, cover entire roof with asphalt felt of 15-lb. weight to avoid wood rot.

Photo taken during an actual blizzard shows how method described here protects the home interior.

Cover sheathing completely with asphalt felt paper. Note flashing where dormer wall joins roof.

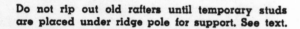

Sheathing material is optional. Use 1x6-in. tongue-and-groove, shiplap stock or a composition panel.

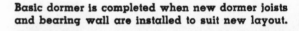

Interior view clearly shows enormous space gain. Note old rafters stripped of shingles, sheathing.

Do not rip out old rafters until temporary studs are placed under ridge pole for support. See text.

Basic dormer is completed when new dormer joists and bearing wall are installed to suit new layout.

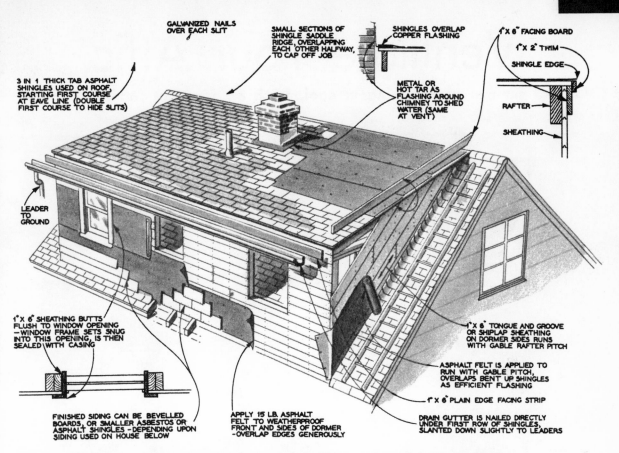

GALVANIZED NAILS OVER EACH SLIT

SMALL SECTIONS OF SHINGLE SADDLE RIDGE, OVERLAPPING EACH OTHER HALFWAY, TO CAP OFF JOB

SHINGLES OVERLAP COPPER FLASHING

1"X 6" FACING BOARD

1"X 2" TRIM

SHINGLE EDGE

METAL OR HOT TAR AS FLASHING AROUND CHIMNEY TO SHED WATER (SAME AT VENT)

RAFTER

SHEATHING

3 IN 1 THICK TAB ASPHALT SHINGLES USED ON ROOF, STARTING FIRST COURSE AT EAVE LINE (DOUBLE FIRST COURSE TO HIDE SLITS)

LEADER TO GROUND

1"X 6" SHEATHING BUTTS FLUSH TO WINDOW OPENING —WINDOW FRAME SETS SNUG INTO THIS OPENING, IS THEN SEALED WITH CASING

1"X 6" TONGUE AND GROOVE OR SHIPLAP SHEATHING ON DORMER SIDES RUNS WITH GABLE RAFTER PITCH

ASPHALT FELT IS APPLIED TO RUN WITH GABLE PITCH, OVERLAPS BENT UP SHINGLES AS EFFICIENT FLASHING

1"X 6" PLAIN EDGE FACING STRIP

DRAIN GUTTER IS NAILED DIRECTLY UNDER FIRST ROW OF SHINGLES, SLANTED DOWN SLIGHTLY TO LEADERS

FINISHED SIDING CAN BE BEVELLED BOARDS, OR SMALLER ASBESTOS OR ASPHALT SHINGLES –DEPENDING UPON SIDING USED ON HOUSE BELOW

APPLY 15 LB. ASPHALT FELT TO WEATHERPROOF FRONT AND SIDES OF DORMER –OVERLAP EDGES GENEROUSLY

STEP 5   SHINGLE ROOF, SIDES, INSTALL WINDOWS, FLASHINGS, GUTTERS — THEN REMOVE OLD ROOF INSIDE

before attempting such work or have it done by licensed professionals.

If it is necessary to build your dormer around a chimney, remember that most codes specify a 2-in. gap between the chimney and any framing. So box in the chimney with 2x4s, leaving the required space, and then fill the gap with copper flashing.

Though most front dormers of full length may detract from the architecture of your house, you may add one in addition to the rear dormer and thus nearly double your attic's cubic content. Procedure is basically the same as described here. Build one dormer at a time, however, and do not attempt removing all interior rafters simultaneously. In the case of double dormers, the new attic ceiling joists will extend from one new opposing stud plate to another and form a balanced truss. Be sure adequate bearing walls are erected under these joists.

For space considerations alone, you will find this type of full dormer more advantageous and economical than building twin gable-type dormers which, though they add window area and some space, will still leave completely slanting upstairs ceilings and will not appreciably increase the cubic content of your attic area. •

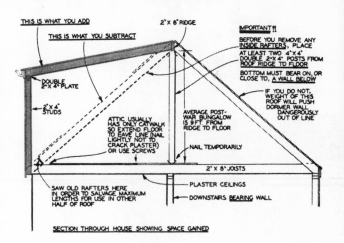

THIS IS WHAT YOU ADD

THIS IS WHAT YOU SUBTRACT

2" X 6" RIDGE

IMPORTANT!!

BEFORE YOU REMOVE ANY INSIDE RAFTERS, PLACE AT LEAST TWO 4"X 4" DOUBLE 2"X 4" POSTS FROM ROOF RIDGE TO FLOOR BOTTOM MUST BEAR ON, OR CLOSE TO, A WALL BELOW

IF YOU DO NOT, WEIGHT OF THIS ROOF WILL PUSH DORMER WALL DANGEROUSLY OUT OF LINE

DOUBLE 2"X 4" PLATE

2"X 4" STUDS

ATTIC USUALLY HAS ONLY CATWALK SO EXTEND FLOOR TO EAVE LINE (NAIL LIGHTLY NOT TO CRACK PLASTER) OR USE SCREWS

AVERAGE POST-WAR BUNGALOW IS 9 FT. FROM RIDGE TO FLOOR

NAIL TEMPORARILY

SAW OLD RAFTERS HERE IN ORDER TO SALVAGE MAXIMUM LENGTHS FOR USE IN OTHER HALF OF ROOF

2" X 8" JOISTS

PLASTER CEILINGS

DOWNSTAIRS BEARING WALL

SECTION THROUGH HOUSE SHOWING SPACE GAINED

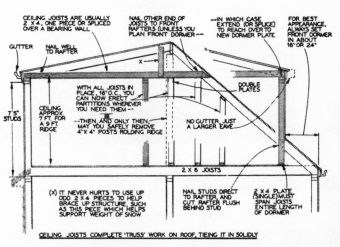

CEILING JOISTS ARE USUALLY 2 X 4, ONE PIECE OR SPLICED OVER A BEARING WALL

NAIL OTHER END OF JOISTS TO FRONT RAFTERS (UNLESS YOU PLAN FRONT DORMER —

—IN WHICH CASE EXTEND (OR SPLICE) TO REACH OVER TO NEW DORMER PLATE

FOR BEST APPEARANCE, ALWAYS SET FRONT DORMER IN ABOUT 18" OR 24"

GUTTER

NAIL WELL TO RAFTER

7'5" STUDS

CEILING APPROX. 7 FT. FOR A 9 FT. RIDGE

WITH ALL JOISTS IN PLACE, 16" O.C., YOU CAN NOW ERECT PARTITIONS WHEREVER YOU NEED THEM —

—THEN, AND ONLY THEN, MAY YOU SAFELY REMOVE 4"X 4" POSTS HOLDING RIDGE

DOUBLE PLATES

NO GUTTER, JUST A LARGER EAVE

X

2 X 8 JOISTS

(X) IT NEVER HURTS TO USE UP ODD 2 X 4 PIECES TO HELP BRACE UP STRUCTURE, SUCH AS THIS PIECE WHICH HELPS SUPPORT WEIGHT OF SNOW

NAIL STUDS DIRECT TO RAFTER, AND CUT RAFTER FLUSH BEHIND STUD

2 X 4 PLATE (SINGLE) MUST SPAN JOISTS ENTIRE LENGTH OF DORMER

CEILING JOISTS COMPLETE 'TRUSS' WORK ON ROOF, TIEING IT IN SOLIDLY

Ventilate Your Attic

On hot summer nights bring in cool, fresh air for your family's comfort

The first step in installing an attic ventilation fan is to mark the intake louver location in the ceiling, preferably in the center of the house. Above this, in the attic, the fan itself will be mounted.

THINKING of cooling your home? One efficient method and a relatively inexpensive one is to install an exhaust fan that will cool the attic and draw air throughout the house.

On a hot summer day, temperature in the attic can be as high as 130 degrees. Even with normal insulation the upstairs rooms can be 102 degrees and downstairs rooms can be 92. Since walls and ceilings absorb and hold heat, even a cool night-time temperature will not effectively reduce inside temperatures fast enough for you to sleep comfortably.

A fan in the attic can make considerable difference. The Lau Blower Co. of Dayton, Ohio, conducted tests which discovered that the 130 degree attic temperature could be lowered 27 degrees, with resultant more comfortable temperatures throughout the house.

The fan system can accomplish other things. It keeps inside air fresher and keeps you cooler by increasing perspiration evaporation; the same way a breeze will cool you.

Two factors will decide what fan size you need to provide adequate cooling.

1. The volume of the house and number of air-changes-per-minute desired. One per minute is recommended throughout most of the U. S. If the area measures 24 x 32 x 8 feet, its volume would be 6144 cubic feet (length x width x height). You know the fan must move 6144 c.f.m. (cubic feet per minute). If you desire to cool only certain rooms in the house (the bedroom, for example) choose a fan with a capacity that is 1.2 times the volume of the rooms, since you will always be drawing some air from the other living quarters.

2. Fan location. Best spot is in the center of the house, in the upstairs ceiling if there are two levels. Air flow to fan must not be restricted. Locating the fan close to a wall or in a corner will reduce its capacity. The fan should be installed a distance of its own diameter from the intake grill. This will permit adequate air flow from all sides.

The fan will be most efficient if there are no obstructions within five feet of the fan

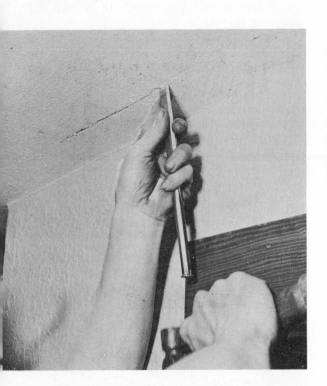

Depending on the size of the intake louver, outline area with a hammer and chisel. You can use this technique either on sheetrock or on plaster.

Clear out the insulation where the fan is to be mounted in the attic. Supporting headers will replace the joist section which must be removed.

Build a platform around fan area for ease of servicing in future. Remove plaster lath by sawing at each end and knock them away from the joists.

After the headers are installed and the opening is cleared away, you can cut off the joist sections. Headers will now support the ceiling load.

outlet. Serious obstructions could even cause the fan motor to burn out.

Provide plenty of exhaust area. Consider the direction of prevailing winds when installing the exhaust grille or openings. Best bet is to have openings on two or more sides of the house to minimize effect of winds.

Here are installation suggestions depending on size and layout of the house.

Single Story Low-Pitched Roof: In ceiling, near as possible to center of house. Install exhaust openings in gable ends or in soffit overhang if house has hip type roof.

House With Attic—No Stairway: Suction box most effective, bringing fan further from the intake louvers and discharging into an unobstructed area of the attic.

Two Story House—Full Attic and Stairway: Suction box over stairway opening to the attic.

Small House With Flat Top: Fan can be installed in a small "penthouse" or in the upper part of a window. Choose window that is located on a side opposite prevailing winds.

Attached Garage: Locate fan at end of garage. Keep garage doors closed, doorway between house and garage open.

General Rule: As warm air rises, best installation of fan is in ceiling or attic wall.

Wherever you put the exhaust grille it should be protected from snow, wind and rain. A porch roof is an excellent place. The exhaust grilles are often placed in the gable ends of the attic. If you install just one, be sure it is in the end away from the prevailing winds. On a flat roof you can install a louvered-wall "penthouse." Louvers can be installed into dormers, or screened openings can be cut into overhanging eaves. Prefabricated louvers are available, so all you need do is cut the opening for them.

The exhaust opening can't be just any size, not for efficient operation anyway. Width and thickness of louvers, size and type of mesh, etc., should be considered since these factors affect the area the exhaust air can move through. Check the accompanying chart for the size opening required for your particular installation.

Certain safety precautions are recommended for the installation of an air exhaust fan.

A frame to support the fan is built of 2x4 stock around the opening and nailed to platform. Size of frame and the opening depend on size of fan.

The fan is now mounted on the platform and centered over the opening; rubber bumpers prevent noisy vibration. Fan shown is the Lau "Rancher."

OPENINGS REQUIRED FOR FAN INSTALLATION

FAN SIZE	22"	24"	30"	36"	42"	48"
Full opening (no screen or hardware cloth)	5.5	6	9	12	18	23
Full opening with 16 mesh screen	11	12	18	26	36	46
Full opening with ½" hardware (cloth)	6.6	7.2	10.8	15.6	21	27
Wood Louvres—no screen or cloth	8	9	13.5	19.5	27	34
Wood Louvres with ½" hardware (cloth)	9.6	10.8	16.2	23.4	32	41
Wood Louvres with 16 mesh screen	16	18	27	39	54	69
Metal Louvres—no screen or cloth	7.2	7.8	11.7	16.9	23	20
Metal Louvres with ½" hardware (cloth)	8.6	9.4	14	20.3	28	36
Metal Louvres with 16 mesh screen	14	16	24	33	47	60

Openings are noted in square feet.

1. Adequate size wire should be run in a separate circuit from the main electrical service entrance panel board to the control switch and fan motor.

2. Local codes and ordinances governing electrical installations must be followed. For this reason, it might be wise to have a licensed electrician do the wiring.

3. It is good practice to install a thermostatic switch in the airstream on the suction side of the fan. This will shut off the fan if a fire in the home causes the temperature to get too high. Only a manual reset type should be used.

4. If a suction box is used in the attic with a fixed grille opening in the ceiling, a fusible link should be inserted in the cord that raises and lowers the trap door. If automatic shutters are used in the ceiling opening, neither the fusible link nor the trap door would be required.

5. The fan motor should be equipped with automatic thermal cutouts to prevent the motor from overheating from any cause and to protect it from burning. A motor so equipped is not a fire hazard. Lau fans are so equipped.

6. It is a good idea to locate the manual fan control switch where it won't be mistaken for a light switch. Inside a closet or high on the wall of a hallway, away from a door, are good locations.

Instructions on how to install specific fans are contained in the cartons housing the fans when they leave the factory. The facts stated above should be taken into consideration, before the actual installation begins, so that the correct fan will be installed in the best spot for free, gentle air circulation throughout the house.

Generally speaking, it is proportionately less expensive to install a fan which will ventilate the entire home than it is to install one which will serve adequately for a few specific rooms. Installation costs change very little according to the size of the fan, and the cost of labor is the largest factor in a fan type cooling system.

Regardless of whether or not the entire house is cooled by use of an attic exhaust fan, the long range upkeep is minor and the electricity used is minimal. When the entire home is fan cooled, the operation will pay for itself in comfort over and over again through the hot summer months of many years. •

Installations of this type should be on its own electric circuit. Wire can be snaked up through wall at service entrance, then across the attic.

A heavy canvas strip, which is supplied with the fan, is wound around the base of the frame and fastened to prevent air leakage from the sides.

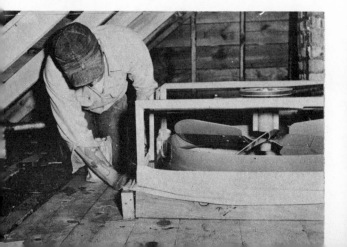

Built-In Attic Closet

FOR this closet, a 24-foot-long side of attic was used. Due to the fact that the opposite wall had to be matched on the outside, construction methods remained the same to a point. However, while the built-in drawer construction dealt with double vertical partitions which formed 4-inch thick pockets the doors could fold into to provide clear passage to the drawers, this was not necessary with the built-in clothes closet.

Single ¾-inch plywood verticals were mounted 9 feet from each end leaving approximately a 6-foot area in the center. This gave the wall a three-part closet which could be nicely divided for the storage of presently used and/or off-season storage.

The metal clothes rack, which is revolutionary, added much to the function and ease of living in this attic. Nylon hooks slide in an extruded gold-anodized aluminum bar, which is mounted with brackets. An additional feature of this new product, a Grant No. 600 clothes rack, has snap-in nylon hooks which can be added or taken off as necessary without having to remove the entire clothes rack first.

This particular attic area had, as shown in the photograph, a duct running across for heating the downstairs. The removal of this duct and the re-routing for the downstairs carrier actually served two purposes. First, it cleared the floor of any obstructions and it lent itself to a floor outlet to heat the attic. The doors were again

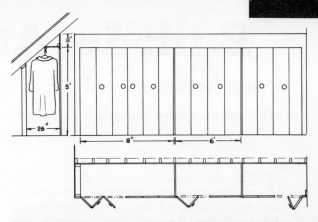

Note lineup of doors and their compartmentation. Because of a difference in space, you may need to change this arrangement a bit.

made of ¾-inch Novoply, mounted with No. 2520 Grant folding door hardware. When the entire front was finished, the entire surface was covered with ¼-inch-thick, prefinished Charter walnut paneling.

Due to the fact that there is a long distance between vertical supports, it was necessary to add on to each pair of folding doors a third door, mounted with piano hinge. These doors, of course, are mounted centrally and are not connected with the folding door track. It is, however, necessary to mount door aligners on the inside of the center doors as well as magnetic catches on the top. Because the piano hinged door is not suspended from the folding door channel, the aligner and magnetic catches hold it. •——*by Bill Baker*

The closet is seen at left with folding doors open beyond planter-room divider of a project that follows. At right, the 24'-long side of the attic that was used for the closet area.

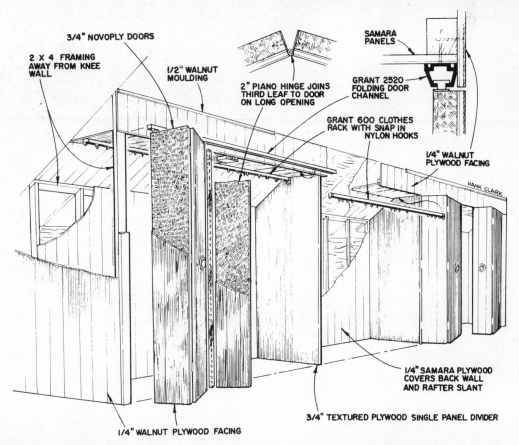

3/4" NOVOPLY DOORS

2 X 4 FRAMING AWAY FROM KNEE WALL

1/2" WALNUT MOULDING

2" PIANO HINGE JOINS THIRD LEAF TO DOOR ON LONG OPENING

SAMARA PANELS

GRANT 2520 FOLDING DOOR CHANNEL

GRANT 600 CLOTHES RACK WITH SNAP IN NYLON HOOKS

1/4" WALNUT PLYWOOD FACING

HANK CLARK

1/4" SAMARA PLYWOOD COVERS BACK WALL AND RAFTER SLANT

3/4" TEXTURED PLYWOOD SINGLE PANEL DIVIDER

1/4" WALNUT PLYWOOD FACING

Built-In Attic Storage

Storage problems became obsolete just as these twelve drawers came off the drawing board. This unit is a veritable wall full of pockets

THIS attic was converted into a bed-room-lounge combination. Extra storage space was necessary for additional items. Since the roof line brought the height on both sides down, a minimum had to be considered for the front of the closet line. In this case it was 6 feet. From this line the closets were 26 inches deep, leaving only crawl space behind them.

As shown in the diagram, once the front line of the closets was established the back was marked, constructed and mounted. Next, the vertical partitions were cut from ¾-inch Novoply, fitted and mounted into place with toenails into the floor and ceiling, making sure all partitions were perfectly square with the back and plumb. Some of the partitions had to be doubled up in order to form 4-inch wide pockets for the folding doors. This is necessary only where sliding shelves or drawers have to by-pass the doors.

Once partitions were installed, they were covered on all sides except the front edge with prefinished ¼-inch Samara paneling to match the back and inside ceiling.

Sliding doors hide away your hoard and make a solid walnut paneled wall. The top shelves add balance.

The drawers were installed next. For this feature, R-Way plastic drawers (which come in sets up to six) were used. The set included metal frames. The drawer fronts were covered with leftover pieces of the prefinished ¾-inch paneling. The units were mounted 4 inches from the front of the closets. On the bottom there is a 4-inch-high front baseboard in line with two side strips on which the drawer units rest. Next, the outside was completed. A 12-inch header is mounted perfectly flush with the front edges of the vertical partitions, snug against the ceiling. A return is mounted to the inside of the header flush with the bottom edge. The return is 6 inches wide and made of ¾-inch Novoply, same as the header.

Then the folding door hardware tracks were mounted to the header (bottom edge). The ¾-inch Novoply doors were cut and fitted into place. When adjusting the doors for proper clearance, follow manufacturer's instructions of the Grant No. 2520 folding door hardware. If a carpet is used, ¾-inch clearance must be allowed. Mount hardware to doors, assemble the door panels and mount them into the tracks, making sure the outside surface is perfectly flush with that of the header.

When all door panels are installed and operating well, close them and surface the outside with prefinished wall panels. Charter walnut was used here, a prefinished walnut paneling with knots. After paneling is complete, mount 3-inch, turned walnut, flush knobs in the center of each door.

NOTE: When mounting paneling, in order to prevent the doors from warping, only spot glue and nail the ¼-inch panels to the Novoply doors. Use a 1-inch No. 18 brad, mostly in the v-grooves if possible. Also, since slanted ceiling was a part of this installation, the header had to be beveled on the back top edge. If this isn't feasible, use ½-inch solid walnut molding to cover the ceiling joint. •——*by Bill Baker*

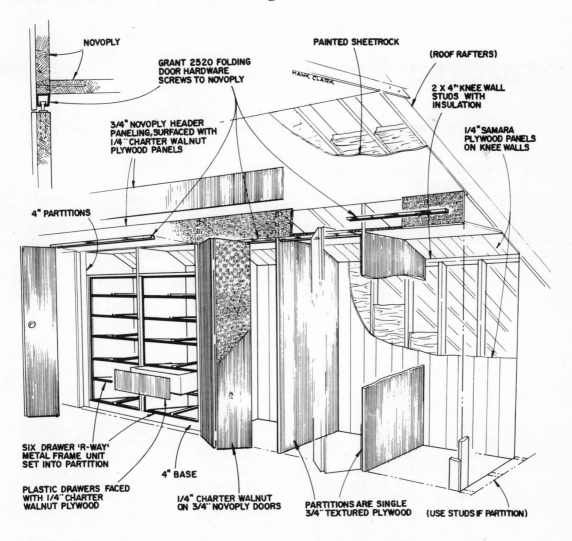

NOVOPLY

GRANT 2520 FOLDING DOOR HARDWARE SCREWS TO NOVOPLY

PAINTED SHEETROCK

(ROOF RAFTERS)

HANK CLARK

2 X 4" KNEE WALL STUDS WITH INSULATION

3/4" NOVOPLY HEADER PANELING, SURFACED WITH 1/4" CHARTER WALNUT PLYWOOD PANELS

1/4" SAMARA PLYWOOD PANELS ON KNEE WALLS

4" PARTITIONS

SIX DRAWER 'R-WAY' METAL FRAME UNIT SET INTO PARTITION

4" BASE

PLASTIC DRAWERS FACED WITH 1/4" CHARTER WALNUT PLYWOOD

1/4" CHARTER WALNUT ON 3/4" NOVOPLY DOORS

PARTITIONS ARE SINGLE 3/4" TEXTURED PLYWOOD

(USE STUDS IF PARTITION)

Be sure air cleaner isn't cramping the automatic choke control.

After flooding, wait; then depress pedal fully to open choke.

Starting your car on a cold wintry morning is not a great problem if you know the fundamentals.

Starting the Car

by Fred Russell   **Mix a few tricks with basic techniques**

HOW TO REMAIN CALM and collected when the engine puts on a mule act is simple enough if you can recall a few tricks mixed with the basic starting techniques. Sometimes this is nothing more complicated than going back into the house for another cup of coffee while the battery recovers sufficiently to crank faster.

Where the car is kept outdoors, or in a damp garage, a normal start often can be had by wiping condensation from the coil, the distributor cap and the tops of the spark plugs. Moisture on exposed ignition parts causes "flashover" of high tension current, and there will be less moisture accumulation if these parts are kept clean. There are spray-on paints to help protect these parts. However, if they have become actually wet from a heavy rain or drifting snow, drying off can be speeded up by spraying on fire extinguisher gas.

Motorists with two cars always have the convenience of hooking up the battery of one to that of the car giving trouble. Batteries should be connected in parallel (positive post of one to positive of the other, and negative to negative) to in-

crease amperage, rather than voltage. You can use a 12-volt battery hooked up in parallel with a 6-volt job, but be careful to have lights and all electrical accessories off during the cranking process. If the engine of the car being cranked uses an alternator instead of a generator be careful, when using extra or spare batteries for cranking, since the alternator can be damaged if the negative post of the battery is not grounded.

Cranking speed is being stressed, here, because it has been proven that an engine will start normally, even at many degrees below zero weather, if the crankshaft can be spun fast enough to build up compression. The trouble is that so often the battery is sapped of its energy in cranking the engine and hasn't enough left over for hot ignition. It takes three ingredients for a start—a rich mixture, good compression and a hot spark.

You can't have the right mixture unless the choke is working properly, so let's keep in mind that this unit usually fails because of a leaky heat tube. Cold air gets into this tube and brings with it moisture

Enriching choke coil adjustment one degree may help you when a cold start has failed to work.

Corrosion in any form cuts down on battery efficiency, so be sure to keep terminals clean.

Spark plugs may need cleaning in winter since more oil is sucked past worn rings on cold days.

Gum solvent applied to choke and fast-idle linkage will help to prevent binding when starting.

from condensation. This corrodes the thermostatic coil which controls the choke valve, thus preventing it from closing. On some of the Rochester carburetors, for General Motors compacts, the choke is designed to pick up clean, heated air to increased its life and reliability. The choke tubes of most cars are easily replaced, and you can buy improved ones that resist leakage. If the choke is suspected of failing to operate, you can take off the air cleaner and close the valve manually. Incidentally, if the engine cranks slowly and you have a can of oil additive handy, pour its contents into the engine to help boost cranking speed.

Before we leave the subject of the battery keep in mind that a 12-volt job can discharge itself more easily than the 6-volt variety if its top is allowed to remain wet or even damp. The higher voltage increases the electrical pressure between battery posts. That means increased inclination to discharge. For any battery, you are assured more cranking stamina if you keep the cell solution level lower in cold weather. Never add water to the cells before garaging the

car. Do the job after the engine has been running and before you plan to give the car a reasonable amount of mileage. Latest in battery aids is a warmer. And don't forget the various discs and aids which check corrosion of battery terminal. Also, it is always effective to use a little petroleum jelly on the tops of the posts and connectors, after cleaning them with ammonia and wiping them dry.

What to do if the engine cranks fast enough but won't go into action calls for some tall thinking. First step is to make sure there's spark. This can be done by taking off a spark plug wire and allowing its tip to come within a fraction of an inch of the engine head while someone turns the ignition-starter key. If spark jumps the gap, ignition to the plugs is good enough. But plug electrodes may be badly fouled with carbon and oil. Reasonable proof of this is steadily increased difficulty starting the engine in the mornings. Burned breaker points, caused by excessively high primary current, will also bring on progressive delay in starting.

In zero weather, check also for ice in the

fuel filter bowl. Hot water poured on the carburetor bowl, fuel line and pump will help get fuel flowing again. But ice in the water pump isn't that easy to lick. Here the engine won't crank. You'll need to have the car towed to a warm place for thawing out.

If you must leave the car out in the cold try to park on a grade at night, blocking the wheels for protection. This offers the prospects of getting the engine started by coasting, unless the car happens to have one of the latest automatic transmissions. With a stick-shift car, switch on the ignition, move the lever to High and coast with the clutch pedal down. When the car is running 15 mph, allow the clutch pedal to come up. There are various rules for coast-starting cars with different types of automatic drives (excepting some which do not permit it at all), but in general the idea is to place the selector lever in Neutral, coast up to 25 mph and then switch on the ignition and move selector lever to Drive. Follow the same procedure for being pushed for a start.

Many drivers foul up starting by flooding the engine. Continued cranking can be a handicap because a cold engine soon robs the battery of power to crank fast enough for good compression. Flooding can be detected by odor of raw gasoline. At this point wait a few minutes and don't crank again until you have pressed the accelerator all the way down. Cranking with wide open throttle will allow the pistons to suck in more air, clearing the cylinders for more normal firing. Continued difficulty may simply mean that the automatic choke needs adjusting toward a richer mixture. But don't move the choke setting more than one degree before testing out results.

It is surprising how much choke trouble is due to the choke lever being cramped by the air cleaner. This big unit, sitting atop the engine, is likely to be shaken into an abnormal position. While the manifold heat control valve doesn't affect starting directly it may contribute to trouble through failure to close when cold. The engine is then slower warming up, may stall more, and thus will foul its plugs.

Generally overlooked is the starting motor itself. Its commutator may be dirty or its brushes badly worn. Be sure to check the battery cable if the car has been kicking around for some years. Another source of trouble is the neutral starting switch on cars with automatic drive. This switch permits current for the starting motor only when the selector lever is in the Neutral or Park positions. Sometimes the switch will fail the first time the driver moves the

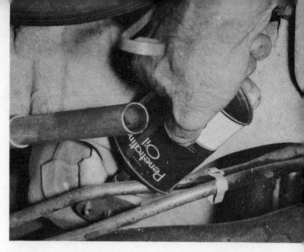

Free the manifold heat-control valve with a good penetrating lubricant to correct choking period.

lever to Neutral or Park but will work if he repeats the process. This is a broad hint that the switch should be replaced.

The modern combination ignition and starting switches also can be troublesome. Here again it pays to repeat the switching-on process. Any smoke at the key is plain warning of trouble. And speaking of switches, don't forget the one for the luggage compartment light. A light that keeps burning all the time will drain your battery. If this switch is suspected, merely remove the light bulb, have the battery fast charged and see if it stays "up."

With a manual-shift car you can help cold starting by holding the clutch pedal down. This relieves the battery and the starting motor the extra job of turning over a lot of gears in cold, congealed lube in the transmission. In most cases one pressing on the accelerator pedal is sufficient to set the fast idle control and choke, but often a couple jabs on the pedal will be needed. To avoid flooding always try the single slow pressing all-the-way-down first. The fast idle control can be kept in prime condition by squirting carburetor cleaning fluid on it occasionally or by using the new Gumout automatic choke cleaner. Never oil these exposed carburetor parts until they have first been cleaned.

If the car is outdoors but still within reach of an electric outlet your problem starting can be solved by use of a headbolt heater. You can vary this with a heater to keep the oil warm. Even an electric light bulb under the hood will help if allowed to burn all night. The particular advantage of a headbolt heater is that when the cooling system is kept hot the engine is ready for action and is not likely to be damaged by use before its oiling system is prepared for normal protection.

The AAA mechanics who answer SOS calls know that many a breakdown is due entirely to a slipping generator belt or a

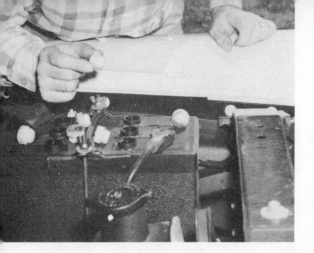

Lowering battery-solution level in cold weather retains more acid, lends extra zip to cranking.

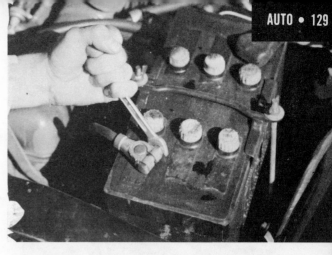

Always keep your battery terminals tight to be sure that you avoid current loss at the posts.

poorly grounded generator regulator. Weak fuel pumps are a common source of trouble. Occasionally ignition timing is found to be too far advanced. Breaker points often are blackened because of oil vapors working up past a worn distributor shaft, especially where there is excessive cranking pressure through clogged vents.

Baffling to millions of motorists is inability to restart a hot engine. They go into a panic, especially if this develops following a stall in traffic. It should help them to know that the most important point in hot starting is to open the throttle wide while cranking. But the accelerator pedal should NOT be pumped. Go down slowly on gas pedal until the throttle is open wide. The idea is to let the engine suck in a leaner mixture to get rid of the over-vaporized mixture in the cylinders and intake.

If the carburetor's needle valve has been held up by a particle of dirt, flooding will develop, and much cranking will be needed to get the valve seating properly again. It may help to tap the inlet area of the carburetor with the handle of a screwdriver.

Very slow cranking of a hot engine often means that varnish deposits have collected on the pistons. These cause binding when heated. You might try additives in the oil, but this remedy is only temporary. The pistons will eventually need to be removed and cleaned with strong solvents. Sometimes it will help to change the oil, using detergent oil for the replacement. If you have already been using detergent oil, try a fresh batch anyway. It may speed hot engine cranking.

Finally, for easier starting, don't forget that a set of hotter spark plugs will help overcome the tendency of a worn engine to foul its plugs. However, the simplest trick of all is giving the car the benefit of more road travel by daylight. It helps keep plugs clean, charges a weak battery, eases valve stickage and burns diluents from the oil. •

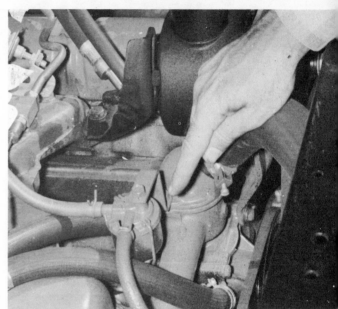

Tardy refilling of the carburetor bowl (indicated) may be traced to a badly functioning fuel pump.

Heating aids are one way to get quicker starts as well as more efficient cold motor operation.

Cooling Systems

by Fred Russell

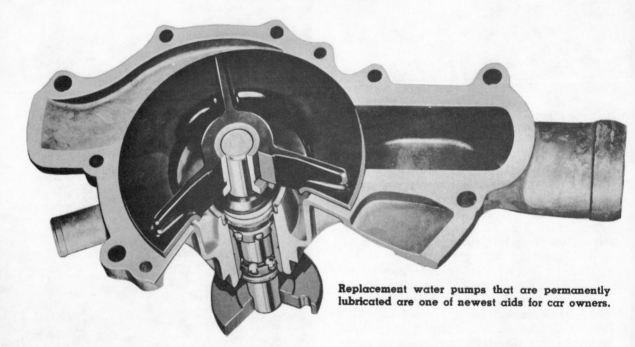

Replacement water pumps that are permanently lubricated are one of newest aids for car owners.

KEEPING COOL under the collar when the thermometer is hovering around ninety in the shade is a lot simpler when you take a broader view of heat in its relation to the efficiency of your car. Too often we are only concerned with engine overheating. Actually heat covers a lot more territory in the car, ranging from the battery to the brakes.

Leakage of lubricants is quite a serious matter in hot weather. Anyone who has ever had rear axle lubricant work past the retainers and into the rear brakes knows what I mean. Because lubricants thin out when heated they naturally seek avenues of escape. Summer is thus likely to be the season when the automatic transmission seals will need replacing, or worn universals will toss off what little grease is still left in them, and when shock absorbers start losing efficiency because their thinned-out oil starts finding an exit.

It is important to carry the solution level of battery cells higher than in cold weather because of increased gassing and risk of a low level encouraging plates to warp. Since the car is likely to be operated for long hours on the open road by daylight there may be overcharging if the generator's regulator isn't on the job. It's thus a matter of wisdom to check the solution level of the battery frequently, being careful not to run the engine or bring a lighted match near the battery when the cell caps are off. Battery gases are explosive. In hot weather it is a good idea to use the starter more often as this will help prevent overcharging.

If a hot engine cranks very slowly, suggesting that the battery is going bad, the chances are that there are "varnish" deposits on the pistons. These are tough forms of gummy deposits which bind when heated. Additives in the engine oil will help some, but usually when varnish becomes a problem the pistons will need to be removed and cleaned with strong solvents.

Whenever using additives make sure that the engine is not loaded with sludge. You can tell about this when draining the oil and poking around the oil drain hole. If there is sludging, better not use additives until you have first taken down the oil pan and manually removed sludge. There will also be sludge deposits in the valve compartment. This, too, can be manually removed. Incidentally, additives may help cool the engine if there is a tendency toward valve stickage. They may, however, cause the engine to run hotter on a hot day because the oil already is thinned out.

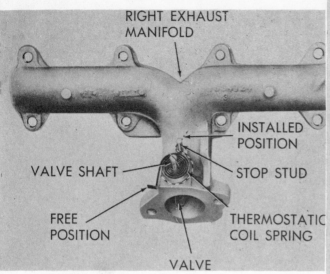

RIGHT EXHAUST MANIFOLD

INSTALLED POSITION

VALVE SHAFT

STOP STUD

FREE POSITION

THERMOSTATIC COIL SPRING

VALVE

If exhaust manifold heat control valve sticks closed, mixture will be preheated and power lost.

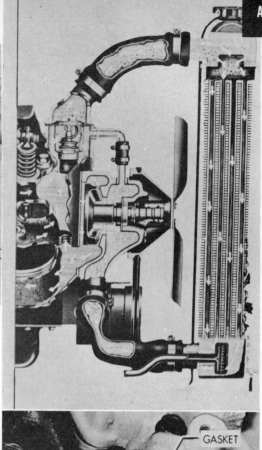

Basic parts of engines cooling system, top right: Radiator, pressure cap, hosing, fan, thermostat, water pump and water circulating jackets in engine block and head. Actual final cooling agent in any system is, of course, the air circulation.

Good oil pressure begins with oil pump efficiency. When servicing, pack pump with jelly to prime.

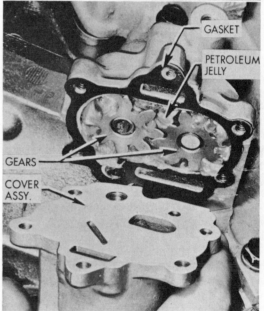

GASKET

PETROLEUM JELLY

GEARS

COVER ASSY.

Brakes can be a problem when the mercury is soaring, but you can prevent trouble by making sure that the system has an approved heavy duty fluid which will not vaporize with heat. Any tendency for the brakes to lose their power when making fast stops in heavy traffic on a hot day is a tip-off that the fluid isn't up to standard. Have it bled off and replaced at once. Such loss of braking power is not to be confused with brake fade which results from overheating the brake drums on downgrades. Here the drums expand away from the brake shoes. Prevention is a matter of using the lower gears for downgrades. In using the brakes on downgrades also remember to be firm on the pedal for brief periods rather than to stretch out the braking. The drums then can cool a bit between applications of the brakes. Drivers of cars with power braking can easily avoid brake fade but they seem to be more inclined to ride the pedal and invite unnecessary trouble.

Many of the automatic transmissions have oil cooling. Oil that circulates through the torque converter and transmission is passed along to an oil cooler built into the bottom of the engine's radiator. Thus if the engine is running too hot the transmission won't operate as well. This applies

Many an overheating engine has responded well to an old-fashioned valve grinding and carbon job.

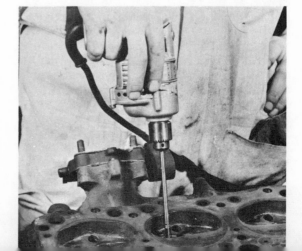

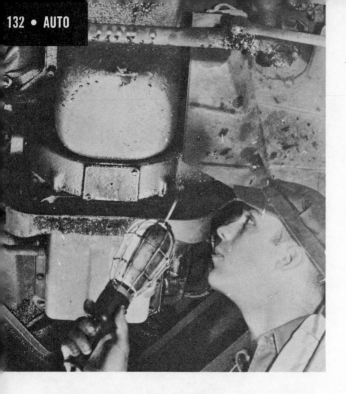

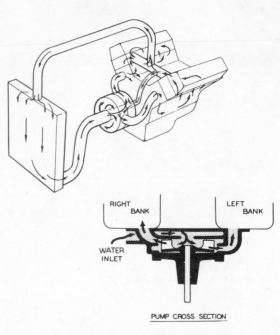

PUMP CROSS SECTION

Often overlooked when seeking cause of engine overheating is a bad oil leak, often at filter.

Shown above: How a single water pump can distribute water to both banks of a V8 type of engine.

even where transmissions are air-cooled. Also remember that if you are driving where the transmission has to make an excessive number of shifts this will be an added load for the engine. That adds up to increased engine operating temperature. Now add some inefficiency in the cooling system, including slight clogging of the radiator core, and the combination can easily result in genuine overheating. You can tell by the rate of temperature rise of the heat indicator whether the trouble is acute or something reflecting general inefficiency.

Let's take the acute situation first. Here the most likely causes of trouble on a hot day are: a slipping fan belt, insufficient oil, overloading, slippage in the automatic transmission (from too low oil level usually), not enough water in the cooling system, or too low octane gasoline. Some very simple things may start the temperature gauge zooming. One is overfilling the radiator at the start. Keep the water level not higher than two inches below the top of the overflow pipe. Make sure that the pressure cap is working properly. Pressure permits a rise in coolant temperature without boiling. Thus unless the pressure cap's release valve is on the job, coolant will more likely go out the overflow as the car nears the top of a long hill where everything is reaching a temperature climax.

A lighter than normal grade oil, or oil that is badly diluted, will start to burn off

rapidly when the engine is working hard in hot weather. As soon as the oil level drops, this process will be greatly accelerated until actual overheating develops with a vengeance. Of course, avoid overfilling, because that causes oil foaming and possible bearing starvation. Too much oil will also foul the spark plugs and cause missing. I stress this partly to draw your attention to the risk in overfilling an automatic transmission. When a tourist thought he was being extra cautious by putting a little more than the required amount of oil into the automatic drive of his car he learned to his sorrow that foaming of the oil caused a lot of it to spew out the filler pipe. Then the transmission started slipping badly. Engine temperature went so high the engine stalled from vapor lock. Motto: caution is dangerous, too.

Slow rising of the temperature gauge can be puzzling. Here you need to experiment a bit. If you find that the engine runs cool enough in cities and towns, but starts rising when you hit the open road, the indications are that the lower hose from the radiator to the block is collapsing. Even slight clogging of the radiator could have this effect, water simply not being able to pass through it fast enough. Often changing car speed will help matters. Every car has a speed at which it runs easier. This will vary not only with its condition, but also with the load carried, head winds or the type of road. It pays to switch to a

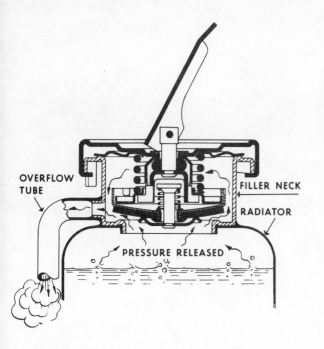

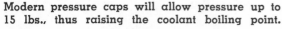

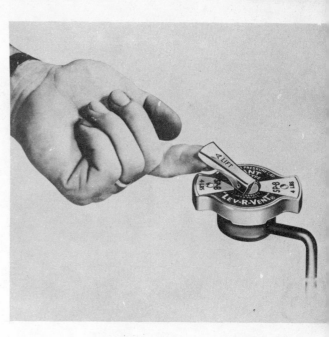

Modern pressure caps will allow pressure up to 15 lbs., thus raising the coolant boiling point.

By lifting this little lever on Lev-R-Vent cap, steam can escape harmlessly out the overflow pipe.

higher octane gasoline if the engine seems to be pinging or laboring.

The new thermostatically controlled motor fan is effective in keeping engines running cooler where cars are equipped with air conditioning. But it is not generally realized by travelers in hot climates that the air conditioner has to work harder when more people are in the car. Since a heavier passenger load also places more load on the engine it would be well to switch off the conditioner when climbing hills. Engine cooling is aided by car heaters since these add to the overall cooling capacity.

Engines frequently run too hot because the exhaust manifold heat control valve is stuck in the position which results on constant preheating of the gas mixture. Make it a habit to keep this important valve free with Gumout automatic choke spray-on solvent. Overheated mixture won't provide sufficient power, and any power loss results in engine heating. There are some special points to consider where engines are 100 per cent air-cooled as in smaller cars.

In the case of Chevrolet Corvair we find a bellows-type thermostat mounted in the exhaust duct at the lower part of the engine. The doors of this duct are controlled by the thermostat so that they start opening at 195 degrees and are fully opened at 210 degrees Fahrenheit. Should the thermostat fail, its bellows return to its normal expanded position, thus allowing the cooling air doors to remain fully open. The blower in this car runs on a sealed, permanently lubricated ball bearing, but is belt driven. Like the water-cooled engine, air cooling is closely related to belt efficiency.

Volkswagen uses a thermostat to regulate air cooling, and a special ring which, if late opening in hot weather, will cause the engine to run a fever. Like Corvair, there also is an engine oil cooler to be considered. With any system, effective oil cooling is obtained by going down long grades in a lower gear, thus speeding up oil circulation. In climbing hills in hot weather it will help keep temperature down if you speed up upon the approach to a hill instead of trying to maintain a steady speed from bottom to top. The latter results in the engine working harder. Taper off on speed toward the top of the hill, and never stop at the top to cool off. Go on down the other side and stop at the bottom if necessary.

Stopping helps cool the tires, improving riding comfort because tires can pick up as much as 7 or 8 pounds pressure in driving. But ease off to a stop, instead of suddenly applying the brakes to halt. Find the shade of a tree if you can. Parking in hot sun reduces gas mileage because of evaporation in the tank. When you try to start a hot engine hold the accelerator pedal all the way down while cranking, and *don't* pump on the pedal. •

Ignition timing should not be attempted until engine reaches a normal operating temperature.

Time for a Tune-Up

Checking with simple tools is easy

Using convenient spray-on degreaser is excellent way to locate parts that need tightening.

YOUR CAR'S power plant should be checked, tightened and adjusted at regular intervals. Otherwise it's bound to choose the most inconvenient time and place to throw a fit and perhaps leave you stranded. All the average home mechanic needs for this job of adjusting is a little information and a few tools.

Something few motorists remember to do is to warm up the engine. This can be done by idling it for about fifteen minutes. Watch it and listen to it during this

warm-up period and you may get some clues as to what adjustments you'll need to make. Note especially if the belts for the fan, generator and power steering pump are squealing. That may indicate that they are loose or in need of a special dressing to quiet them. Sometimes misaligned pulleys will cause belt noise. But before stopping the engine to check the belts in more detail, note if the engine tends to shake too much when its speed is changed. It may be afflicted with loose or worn mounts. Such

Use a gap gauge as shown to check adjusted plugs. Each model car has gap recommended.

Dwell adjustments can be made on the "window" distributor (below) without the removal of the cap.

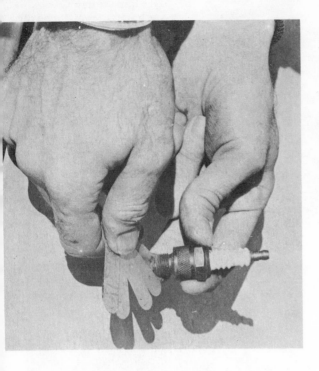

shake, combined with normal vibration, will likely loosen the fuel pump, manifolds, cylinder heads and other parts. A loose air cleaner can be a source of odd noises.

As the engine warms up, the manifold heat control valve should open. It can be adjusted, but in most cases any failure to open is likely due to stickage. Give this valve's shaft a dose of penetrating oil or solvents such as are used to clean carburetors. Listen to the exhaust to spot any oddities in firing that would hint strongly of faulty ignition, bad valving or need for checking the mixture.

Now stop the engine and check out the battery. Twelve-volt batteries often have a weak cell—not so weak that it fails to crank the engine, but weak enough to lower ignition efficiency during cranking so that overchoking, fouling of plugs and sticking valves may result. Take a hydrometer test, of course, but don't be satisfied with this. You will want to check for possible shorts with a voltmeter. Excessively low-tension voltage may exist due to poor connections at the battery, ignition switch or coil. If the points are bad install new ones, preferably the ventilated type with parallel contacts.

Spark plugs are an important feature of any tune up, and a detail often overlooked is cleaning of the threads in the plug holes.

If these are not clean there will be just enough insulation to retard transfer of heat from the plug shell to the engine heat, and the effect of this may be to cause pre-ignition especially at higher speeds and during hill climbing. Today's spark plugs are offered in a variety of heat ranges as well as electrode type. AC, Champion and Auto-Lite continue to use a single center electrode which flashes across to the electrode attached to the plug shell, where many of the others use arrangements designed to provide additional spark routes.

In general, a cold plug is one with a shorter insulator. Heat then travels more quickly from the center electrode to the coolant in the cylinder head. A hotter plug has a longer insulator. If, therefore, your car is used for a great deal of around town driving where the engine seldom gets up to normal operating temperature it may be advisable to switch to the next hotter plug in the heat range. Cars that are operated much of the time on the open road at top legal speeds need cooler plugs. Your filling station, garage or car dealer has a chart which will show the heat range for the make of spark plug used on your car.

Before leaving this important phase of tune up let's list some vital "don't's." They start with the warning not to go longer than 5000 miles without checking the plugs.

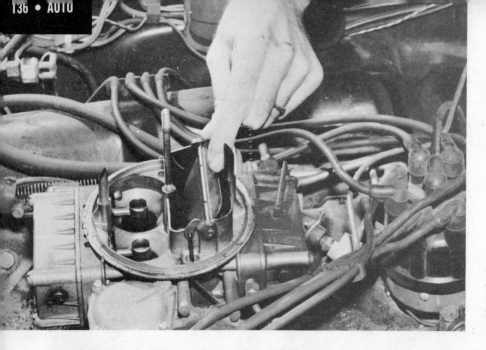

Adjust the carburetor with the engine running. You can have a trouble-making carburetor rebuilt easily.

The manifold heat control valve should be adjusted regularly to prevent it from sticking, not opening.

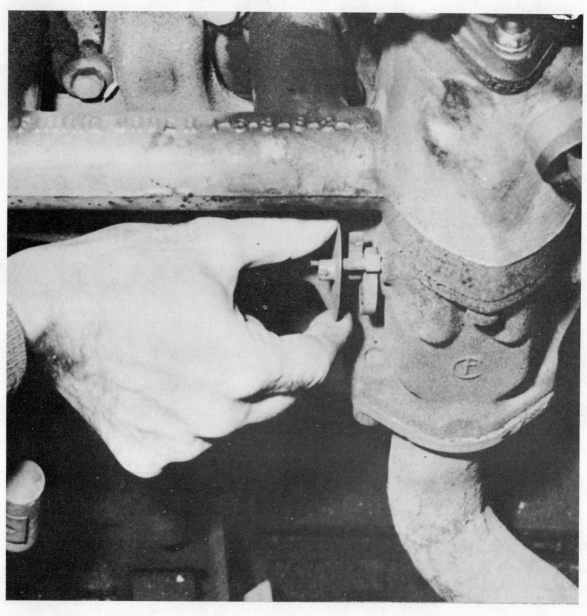

If you blow through the vacuum spark advance line you can often tell if the diaphragm is leaking.

When tuning up, use liquid cleaner to flush out lime, scales and other deposits in radiator.

The battery is checked with a tool which "loads" the terminals and gives a reading on voltmeter.

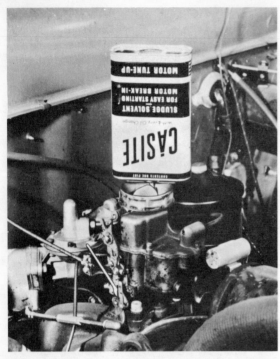

Feeding tune-up oil to the engine via the carburetor (removing air cleaner first) is effective.

The paper air-cleaner elements are cleaned by removing from filter, tapping to dislodge dirt.

The cooling system should be drained by opening the pet cocks on the engine block and on the radiator.

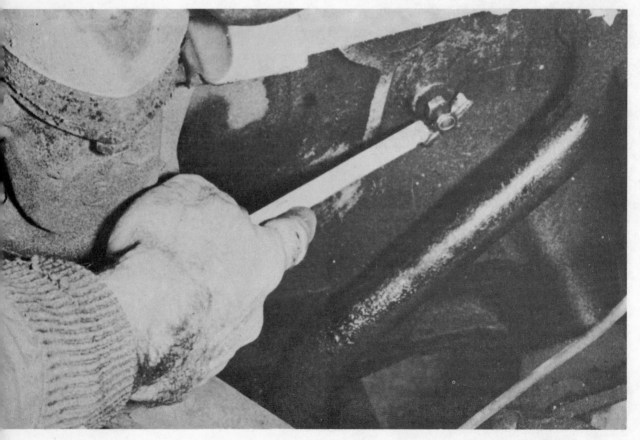

Carbon and oxide deposits are likely to get jammed in the space between the insulator and the shell, and the electrodes themselves will have too much gap because of erosion.

Don't reuse a plug that has a cracked or broken insulator. Burned or worn electrodes should also suggest a replacement. You can take the plugs to the corner filling station where your friends will have a blast type plug cleaner, but it is important not to blast the plugs excessively to clean them. If the plugs are oily they should be dipped in a degreasing solvent and dried with compressed air before cleaning.

Don't use a flat feeler gauge for checking plug gap. Use a round type feeler gauge. Don't bend the center electrode as this might crack the insulator. In bending the side electrode keep the gap closely to the car manufacturer's recommendations for your particular engine model. Don't forget that spark plugs should be checked after the new car has driven a thousand miles.

Don't use worn or oversize wrenches on spark plugs as they may crack the insulator. Care must also be taken when using a socket wrench. Don't replace plugs without carefully cleaning the seat in the head into which the plug fits, and always use a new gasket. Don't forget that the smaller the plug size the less you need to pull on the wrench to compress the gasket and start the plug to its correct tightness.

Lubrication and torqueing of plugs used in aluminum heads is particularly important because of the chance of stripping the threads in the heads. Use light engine oil for such lubrication, install the plugs by hand first and then tighten to factory specifications.

In doing plug work on the engine make sure that no foreign matter drops into the cylinders, for with such high compression even a tiny particle of carbon can cause pinging. Car owners often overlook the importance of making sure the spark plug wires are properly spaced and positioned. Those cars equipped with the Delco-Remy distributor are easily checked for dwell angle (contact point opening) by idling the engine, raising the little "window" in the distributor cap and inserting an Allen wrench to make a last critical adjustment. If you haven't a dwell meter, remember that adjustment is made by turning the screw in (clockwise) until the engine starts to miss, then turn the screw a half-turn out.

Before installing a new condenser check the tension of the breaker arm spring to be sure it meets the specifications for your car. Then don't forget to wipe that film of protective oil from the new points before installation. A very small wipe of Vaseline should, however, be put on the rubbing block of the breaker arm to help quiet its "ride" on the distributor shaft cams and to lessen wear.

Now check the rotor of the distributor to make sure the breaker plate is turning freely. Check the vacuum control which may have a leaky diaphragm. This can be ascertained by removing the vacuum spark advance line and blowing through it.

Carburetor trouble is often due to a too high or too low float level or to failure of the needle valve to shut off the fuel supply when the throttle is closed. Fuel pressure regulators are helpful in such cases. Incidentally, when cleaning out the fuel filter bowl be careful not to leave any lint deposits from the cloth for these can get into the carburetor and unseat the needle valve.

Since most in-line fuel filters have no trap for water in the gas it is well to replace them after a reasonable period of service. Filters swollen with water can cause engine trouble. So can swelling of the flexible fuel line that runs from the main line to the pump. One company found that swelling of this line resulted in a marked reduction in the car's top speed.

One of the common causes of low engine efficiency is incomplete draining of the cooling system. Those drains toward the rear of the motor block must be opened as well as the one at the bottom of the radiator. Also check the pressure cap's two valves to make sure the system really is under specified pressure. If the cap's vacuum valve fails to open when the system cools, air can't enter and the core may be damaged. Make sure the flange of the radiator filler pipe isn't damaged. Use cooling system sealer even if no leakage appears.

Other check points include the oil supply for the power steering pump, hose connections, possible oil leakage around loose valve compartment covers and the oil filter, connections for the power brake booster and the fuel line. There's more about these in other chapters in the book.

While you are at it, of course, clean out the engine's crankcase breathers, including the oil filler pipe. The latter is a press fit into the crankcase and can be withdrawn for removing accumulated grime. A clean air cleaner element is important for top performance and economy. •

In the Renault, with engine in rear, the drive line is eliminated. Power is at the point of application.

Drive Assembly

Connecting systems transmit power from the engine to the wheels

BETWEEN the engine and the car's driving wheels there's an important assemblage of hard working parts which is as vital to performance as the gas in the tank or the steering gear that guides the car. Engineers call it the "power train." It can be concentrated at whichever end of the car carries the engine, as in front drive or rear-engine drive, or it can be spread out as in conventional design where the engine is up front and power is applied to the rear wheels.

Thus Webster was helpful when he defined "train" as a "series of connected wheels or parts in a machine or machinery for transmitting motion or power." Among these parts are the automatic transmission, the propeller shaft with its universal joints, the pinion and ring gears, differential and axles. Of these the automatic transmission has become the most im-

portant unit because it is the most promising.

In fact, engineers are looking forward to the day when the automatic drive will just about be the power train itself. Where the engine is placed in the rear, with rear drive, or up front with drive through the front wheels, we can dispense with the propeller shaft and universals. Latest is combining the automatic drive with the axle and differential. This is called the "transaxle."

Regardless of design, success with the power train depends on proper servicing and handling. Spot checks show that far too many automatics lack the required amount of oil, losses being largely through leakage. Overfilling is a common cause of oil loss because an excess causes foaming, oil then spewing back through the filler pipe. Some of the current automatics are

Even in a conventional chassis the power train
includes an assortment of important components.

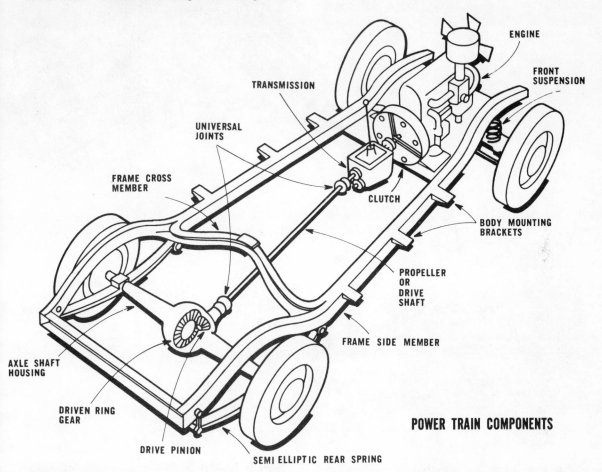

POWER TRAIN COMPONENTS

Labels: ENGINE · FRONT SUSPENSION · TRANSMISSION · UNIVERSAL JOINTS · FRAME CROSS MEMBER · CLUTCH · BODY MOUNTING BRACKETS · PROPELLER OR DRIVE SHAFT · FRAME SIDE MEMBER · AXLE SHAFT HOUSING · DRIVEN RING GEAR · DRIVE PINION · SEMI ELLIPTIC REAR SPRING

smaller, hold less oil. Accurate filling is thus more important. Smart motorists keep a supply of "Type A" transmission oil on hand and add what is needed from time to time. Always run the engine long enough for the transmission to warm up.

Now, let's consider some other points in connection with care of the driveline portion of the power train. If motor mounts are worn or loose there would be far too much engine shake. This affects the transmission indirectly by disturbing the manual control linkage. Here the transmission may not be shifted fully to desired positions, resulting in slippage.

Because an important feature of the power train is smoothness, any trouble in the driveline is certain to handicap things. Frequent troublemaker is the slip sleeve of the propeller shaft. This sleeve serves to compensate for the slight but constant variation in car wheelbase where the driving torque is through the rear springs. This is known as Hotchkiss drive. If the splines of this sleeve are rough, or the unit needs fresh lube, there will be thumping when the transmission is shifting. This is often mistaken for the familiar "clunk" so often heard when cars with automatics are first put into Drive, Reverse or Low, especially when cold. So troublesome has this driveline thump become, one of the suppliers of special parts—Champ Items, Inc., of St. Louis, Missouri—offers a special bearing which can be inserted in the slip sleeve. Naturally, worn universal joints will also lessen smoothness at low car speeds or during speed or gear changes. Another important factor is making sure the driveline is reassembled in proper balance whenever universal joints are taken apart for greasing or replacement.

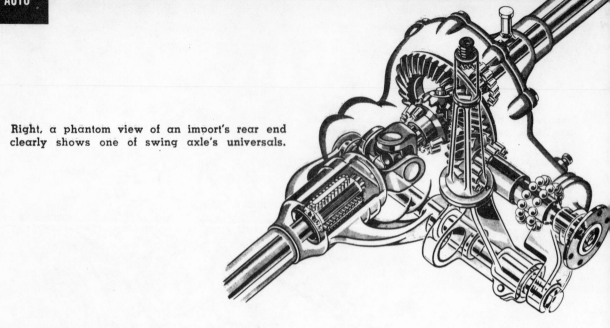

Right, a phantom view of an import's rear end clearly shows one of swing axle's universals.

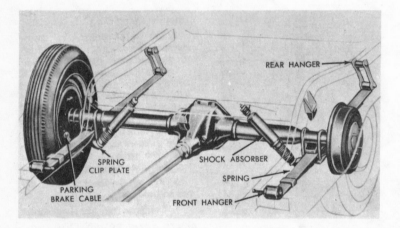

REAR HANGER

SPRING CLIP PLATE

PARKING BRAKE CABLE

SHOCK ABSORBER

SPRING

FRONT HANGER

Falcon's rear suspension assembly shows the importance of spring hangers and clips.

Another problem which has come along in recent years is the use of a driveline split into two propeller shafts, having a center and three exposed universals. They operate at different angles. Here it is recommended that the joints be disassembled, cleaned with a sodium soap and repacked with a fine fiber grease every 20,000 miles. It is also recommended that the slip sleeve be lubricated every 6,000 miles or so. However the center support bearing is self-sealed and needs no attention.

After a replacement of universal joints, or following repacking, any failure to observe the matter of balance and angularity is likely to result in shuddering, especially in the very low speed range with or without an automatic transmission, especially if the car is well loaded. Sometimes this calls for correction by removing a shim under the transmission mounting.

Such shudder with a light passenger load usually means that the front center and rear joint angles are too great. A small shim is added to the transmission support to correct the front angle. The rear joint angle is reduced by adding a shim on each side at the rear upper control arm. The center angle is then decreased automatically.

Most unusual of the drivelines is the one which was introduced with the arrival of Pontiac's Tempest. This is known as a "rope" shaft, and while it is made of triple alloy forged steel, heat treated and shot peened, it actually sags in the middle. However, there is no whipping as might be anticipated. This is, in part, due to the fact that a special torque tube encloses the shaft and is rigidly joined to the engine at the front and the transmission at the rear. This torque tube is also curved, the result being a greatly lessened tunnel in the flooring of the car. We find that this shaft is supported by sealed ball bearing, two assemblies being bolted inside the torque tube.

Cars like the Renault Dauphine, Chev-

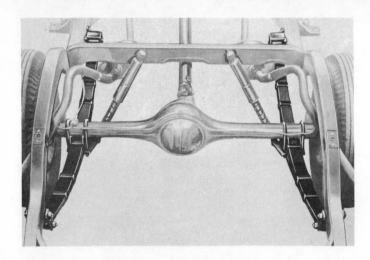

This tipped view of the underneath construction of the Corvair shows how power train is concentrated at rear, and just ahead of the engine.

Closely related to power from the engine to driving wheels is transmission of push, or torque, from rear axle to car's frame and body.

rolet's Corvair and Volkswagen have no propeller shaft problems because the engine is located at the rear. The usual arrangement here is to position the engine to the rear of the rear axle, the transmission being slightly ahead of it. Compact is the word for this sort of drive. But let's leave this for the next chapter which will describe how power finally gets to the driving wheels and what we can do to help keep it flowing smoothly.

To go back to the automatic transmission itself, just a few words about the importance of knowing what your car may need by way of special attention. To drain the V8 Torqueflite automatic, for instance, first remove the transmission oil pan drain plug and plate from the torque converter housing. Then rotate the converter until its drain hole can be reached. After complete draining, put back both drain plugs as well as the converter's plate. Five quarts of transmission fluid are then poured into the transmission through the

oil pan filler tube. About three more quarts of fluid will need to be added as the engine is running, with button control in Neutral, in order to bring the lever to the low mark. Recheck after shifting through all the ranges.

Every 25,000 miles the automatic transmission in the Buick Special should have its oil pan removed and cleaned. The oil strainer should be replaced. Buick stresses the importance of using accurate foot-pound and inch-pound torque wrenches when doing this work. The torque strainer strap bolts, for example, should be exactly tightened to 100 inch-pounds. Over-tightening will cause trouble. The oil-pan-to-case bolt is torqued 15 to 20 foot-pounds.

An oddity in servicing the Buick Flight-Pitch and Triple Turbine transmissions is the need for raising the rear wheels. With the transmission in Drive range and engine idling, add eight quarts of fluid to the four already added to the gearbox proper. •

Emergency Road Repairs

by Fred Russell

Emergency measures that can keep you rolling

Are your brakes dragging? They may be freed by opening clogged vent of the brake master cylinder.

IT IS COMFORTING to know that if you're in trouble with the car there's no need to push the panic button. In most cases a slight change in the car or the way you drive it can get you rolling again.

I am thinking especially of a good friend of mine who, returning home on a cold winter night, discovered that the fuel pump had come loose. One of the bolts was missing and the other would not hold the pump tightly enough. Alone, there on the open

highway, the situation might have been a bit desperate. Having no replacement, or small tools, he nevertheless looked for some way of making temporary repair. He went to the luggage compartment where he immediately noticed a wood wedge which Cadillac supplied for many years to block one of the car's wheels whenever changing tires. This was exactly what he needed to wedge the fuel pump securely in place. When he drove into a filling sta-

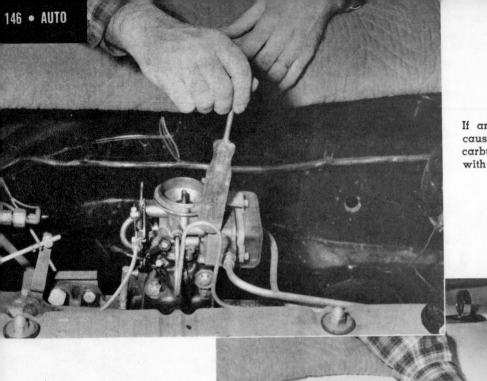

If an unseated needle valve causes a stall, try tapping the carburetor's fuel intake area with a screwdriver handle.

An unseated radiator cap can cause overheating on the highway. Always keep the filler-pipe neck clean.

tion with the news that the fuel pump had failed the attendant thought he was kidding.

On the theory that some of the finest things come in small packages, shrewd motorists are learning how to cure many car ailments by the simplest of remedies. A touch here or there at the right time can put new life in the old bus, make a new one turn in a better score, or save a breakdown. Minor things can cause the most disturbing conditions. Like the car that always shimmied about a week after front-end checking. Finally an observant mechanic noticed that the left front tubeless tire always lost five pounds of air pressure through a slow rim leak. That was just enough to throw the balanced wheels out.

When a stalled engine refused to start, the mechanic who came to the rescue lightly tapped the fuel inlet area of the carburetor with the wood handle of a hammer. Immediately the engine cranked to a start. Dirt had held the needle valve off its seat. A bit of shock at the right spot dislodged it.

I once got rid of severe engine knock by driving fast up a long hill. The result was that some loose carbon in one of the cylinders blew out the exhaust, thereby ending a bad case of pre-ignition.

It is natural to become alarmed when a noise, suggesting front-end looseness, is telegraphed up the steering post. This, however, may be nothing more than a loose front wheel bearing. Clicking in the

It is a good idea to check your tires weekly. Just one low front tire can cause a shimmy at speeds over 35 mph.

If you can remember to clean crankcase vents and oil filler pipe, you can prevent oil fouling pistons and plugs.

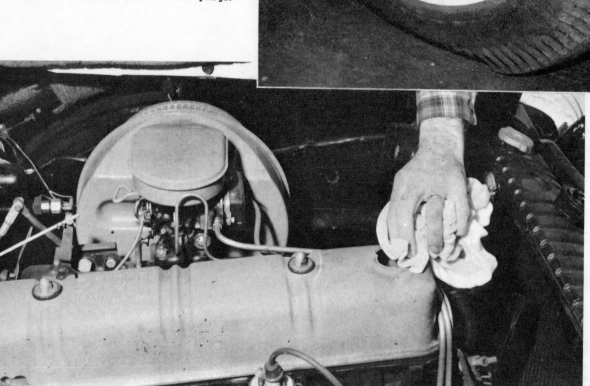

brakes after a major brake overhaul may simply result from failure to smooth out all the drums, after they have been trued. The shoes pull sideways on threads left by the lathe, making an odd click when they snap back.

The car's horns going into action of their own accord need not be cause for concern. Locate the horn relay box and rap it with your fist. Chances are that its points have merely stuck together. This business of rapping is most effective in loosening up a corroded exhaust manifold heat control valve. First flood it with penetrating oil and then, while grasping the valve's counterweight and working it back and forth, tap the end of the shaft lightly with a hammer. Shock helps oil travel along shaft.

Your car has a surprising number of vents which, neglected, can cause a lot of trouble. Brakes will apply themselves and drag you to a halt if the air hole in the master cylinder's filler cap becomes clogged with dirt.

If there's dirt around the filler pipe of the radiator, or if this area is nicked, the pressure cap won't fit tightly. This may cause boiling on a hot day, or if the winter antifreeze is alcohol. Some gas tanks are vented by their cap. This recalls a trick used by one owner to foil car thieves. When he left his car unattended he replaced the cap with one that was purposely unvented. Without air pressure working on the fuel in the tank the engine would soon starve for gas.

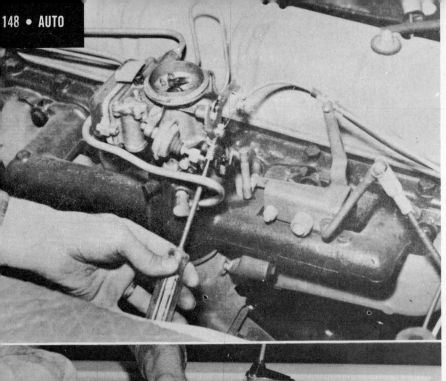

Adjusting the throttle linkage of an automatic transmission will correct shift points to your satisfaction.

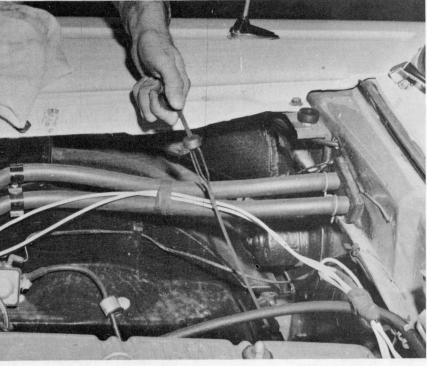

Don't overfill an automatic transmission or you may cause foaming and force oil out through the seals.

A skip in the engine may be the result of oil being forced up past the piston rings when crankcase pressure becomes excessive. Remedy is to clean out the vents, the oil filler pipe and the crankcase ventilators. A clogged air cleaner will make the engine draw in a higher ratio of gasoline to air. This means lower gas mileage.

Power brakes have a filter in the air intake which can cause trouble with the system if it becomes clogged. When rear axle lube works into the rear brakes an experienced mechanic always checks to see if the housing's vent is clogged.

Serving as a brake on the throttle to prevent stalling during sudden deceleration, the dashpot control on some carburetors is one of those little things that can make a big difference. Maybe you have already had occasion to discover the importance of correct adjustment of the throttle linkage control for the automatic transmission. Clunking and incorrect "shift points" often are nothing more serious than a need for checking this linkage. One driver became worried because of clunking during the second to third shift and found that all his mechanic did to correct the condition was to shorten the transmission rear rod a little. Another driver

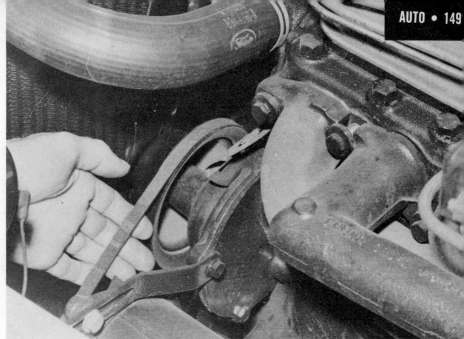

Squealing V-belts may be caused by pulleys which are out of line. Simply align them to stop noises.

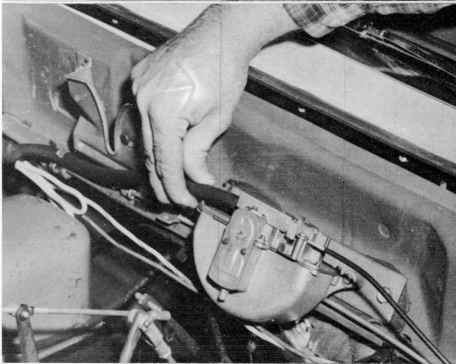

Sluggish windshield wipers are a common problem, often traceable to a poor vacuum hose connection.

thought he was due for a fancy repair bill when he found his automatic transmission was undecided whether to stay in third or to shift to fourth during light throttle operation. This is called "hunting." It was remedied by adjusting for a longer throttle rear rod.

A slipping automatic transmission usually panics most drivers the first time it happens. It's usually caused by low oil level. This condition will stop normal downshifting and generally means erratic shifting. Low oil will make the transmission overheat and in some cases produce a buzzing noise. Slippage can also be due

to an improperly adjusted manual control —a common trouble that is easily fixed.

If your car creeps forward when in reverse, don't run to your psychiatrist. The trouble may be nothing more serious than the need for rechecking the manual control. A low growling often heard when first starting out is produced by cavitation of the cold oil. Just keep going along moderately and the noise will disappear.

The owner of a standard shift car heard noise in the clutch with the pedal up. He figured he was faced with a binding release fork, a loose disc hub or a broken pedal return spring. The trouble was easily cor-

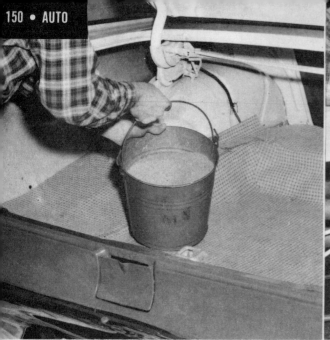

In the winter, carry a bucket of sand in the trunk to use in case you find yourself stuck in a snowbank some blizzardy night.

Are you adding water to the radiator too frequently? Examine your hose connections and check for leaks—and find the answer.

It is often possible to trace malfunctioning stop lights to a loose connection at the switch. Loose wires are easily tightened.

rected by restoring some "play" in the clutch pedal.

Many motorists find it hard to restart the engine after a short period of parking. This is due to a combination of conditions. The engine may be running hotter than normal because of a winter high temperature thermostat or possibly because the owner has covered too much of the radiator with cardboard to get more warmth from the car heater. A hot motor, combined with gummy oil and deposits of "varnish" on the pistons, will cause very slow cranking. Oil additives will help here. A little pa-

tience will go a long way toward preventing the battery from being weakened through futile cranking. Wait five minutes and the engine will likely start again. When you crank under such conditions hold your foot all the way down on the accelerator, but don't pump it.

Sometimes the engine will stall and refuse to start a few minutes after a cold start. This means that the choke valve hasn't opened far enough, and that the mixture is simply much too rich to fire. The situations calls for checking the choke's automatic control. A leaky heat-control tube

A handy item to keep in the truck is an air hose which serves in an emergency to inflate a flat with the air from the spare tire.

Excessive oil consumption may be traced to a gas pump flange which has been loosened by rough driving over bad roads.

probably is the answer, heat not reaching the choke's thermostatic coil quickly.

To get the engine started again just take off the air cleaner and use a screwdriver to hold the choke valve open. Let the engine run until warm and then take out the screwdriver, replace the choke and you won't have any further trouble that day.

An overlooked cause of fan belt noise is misalignment of pulleys. Now that we have belts to drive the water pump, the air conditioner's compressor, the power steering pump, the generator and the fan, pulley alignment is more important than before.

Engine vibration often is due to uneven compression, the annoyance being as bad as shake from a sprung crankshaft, loose fan blades or "missing" spark plugs. Such compression variation should not exceed 10 pounds. Variations may not be due to worn piston rings but simply to poor seating or sticking valves.

So try something simple if your car is not perking properly. There's no use making a Federal case of car trouble that may easily yield to a five-cent idea or a few minutes work. •

Trouble Shooting

Think fast and save that long, long walk to the gas station

MORE than 60 million calls for help are made by car owners annually. But you need not be one of those who are caught on the road—if you have a knack for knowing what to do when the car threatens a breakdown.

Some clever ideas have been used to surmount unusual and seemingly impossible situations. Like the fellow whose engine quit because the distributor's breaker arm spring broke. Reaching into his pocket he produced a rubber band which he carefully used to produce temporary spring action. This he did by slipping one end over the arm and the other over the primary terminal outside the cap. Replacing the cap he started up the engine, drove three miles to a garage.

Not everyone can be so resourceful. Not every broken part lends itself to emergency treatment. But in a surprising number of cases it is not necessary to give up.

I once drove 25 miles without being able to declutch. Stops called for stalling the engine. Starts were made in second gear—the one the car happened to be in when the clutch quit. You may seem to be licked when an automatic transmission starts excessive slippage but sometimes you can keep going to a garage if you wait awhile for the unit to cool off.

A change of speed often works wonders. At fast road speed a soft lower radiator hose will suck inward, thus blocking coolant flow, but if you will drive 30 mph or slower, the engine's temperature will drop. The same situation is found where there's a partially clogged radiator core. It can handle water flow only up to a certain point.

Waiting will often result in a battery recovering enough to crank the engine, especially if temperature is rising. When one motorist's engine broke into a terrific clat-

Is your horn stuck? It may be because of sticking points. Try rapping the horn relay cover to separate them, as shown at the right. It might help.

Struggling with a frozen luggage compartment key? You'll be able to get into the trunk if you heat the key first with a cigarette lighter or matches.

Caught with wet ignition? A quick job of spraying with a carbon tetrachloride fire extinguisher will dry the parts. Carry a small one with you.

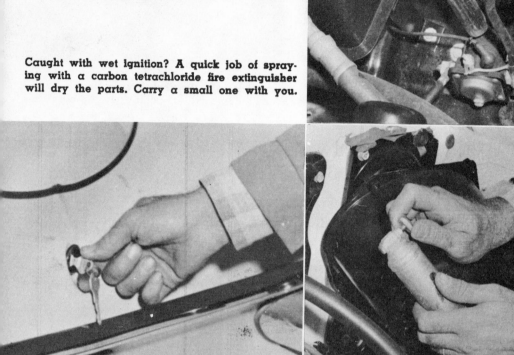

tering of its hydraulic valve lifters he found the engine's oil supply quite low. Obviously what oil remained was too hot and thus too thin. So he waited a half hour for the engine to cool off; then drove five miles to a filling station. The tappets did not make a sound.

If an engine with good spark and a lively battery won't start there's a good chance that the choke isn't working properly. So, take off the air cleaner and hold a block of wood (or anything flat that's handy) over the carburetor's air intake while someone operates the starter. This chokes the engine and will often provide the needed start. You can do the job even without an assistant if you tie a string to the block. This will enable you to pull the block away and check overchoking as soon as the engine starts.

In some cases of car trouble you need to be quick on the trigger rather than

philosophical and .patient. For example, if both of the warning lights (which replace the ammeter and oil pressure gauge on many modern cars) start flickering while the engine is idling during a traffic wait, it's a sign of an impending stall. Gun the engine immediately in order to get more fuel flowing through the needle valve. Similarly if the brakes do not hold well when you first press on the pedal, start pumping immediately. There may be fluid loss or air in the system, and pumping may help. In the case of power brakes a second pressing of the pedal may bring into action more effective assistance (actually atmospheric pressure acting on a piston in a vacuum-exhausted cylinder). And speaking of brakes, if one of the rear wheels start spinning when on ice or hard packed snow, try holding the parking brake partly on. If this brake operates through the rear wheels (rather than on the propeller shaft)

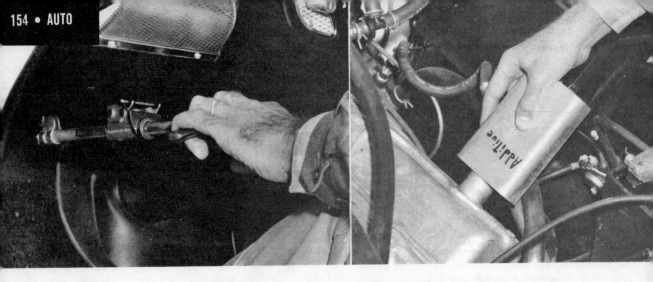

Are your back wheels spinning on ice and snow? Apply hand brake lightly for an easier start.

Valves sticking? Prevent overheating on a hot day by adding can of additive to the crankcase.

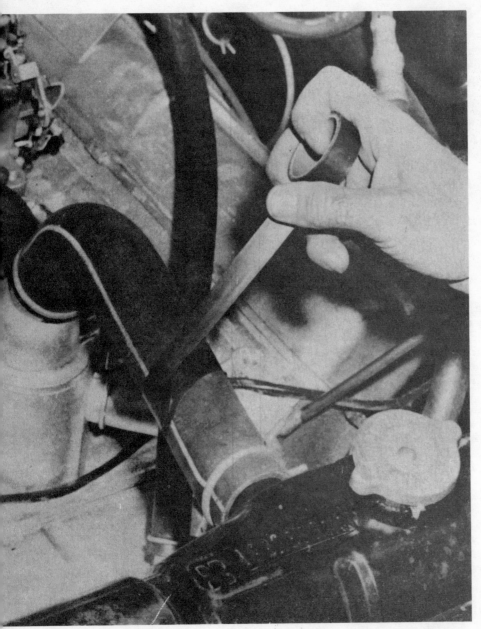

Suspect a leak in radiator hose? Wrap it with tire tape to seal off the drip and drive for repairs.

If jack doesn't fit bumper, roll car on spare tire to raise it, and give some more working room below.

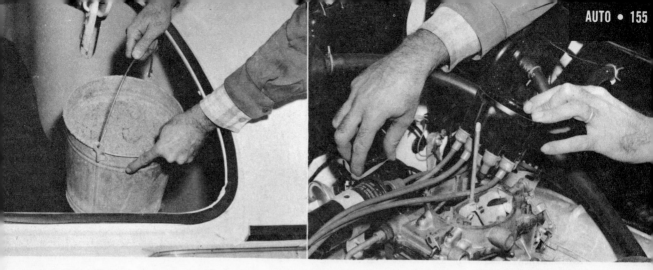

A bucket of sand kept in the luggage compartment will prove invaluable when roads are icy.

In an emergency, a rubber band can be used to replace a spring. It will take you to the station.

a variation in braking power between the two brakes on the driving wheels may be sufficient to retard the spinning wheel and throw some of the power to the opposite wheel. The action is somewhat similar to that of a nonslip differential.

I heard of a resourceful motorist who was caught with brakes that built up pressure and applied themselves until the car came to a halt. This was due to a clogged hole in the filler cap of the master cylinder, and called for bleeding the lines. Not having a bleeder hose, however, was no obstacle to this fellow. Removing the hose from the tire pump which he always carried in the car, he connected an end to one of the front wheel bleeder fittings, after having removed the bleeder screws and loosened the bleeder valve. No fluid came out of the hosing, however, because over the other end he had snapped one of those spring-type clothes pins which he had been using on the vacation trip to hang up wet bathing suits. When he sat at the wheel, and pressed the brake pedal, pressure opened the clothes pin and allowed fluid to escape. But when he removed his foot from the pedal no air was sucked in.

On a trip I began to worry about lack of power on hills and correctly guessed that it was a carburetion condition. Sure enough, lifting the hood revealed the exhaust manifold heat control valve stuck in the closed position. Mixture was simply overheated. Penetrating oil for the valve's shaft would have been the easiest remedy, but there was none in the tool kit. I recalled that it pays to tap the end of the

Having trouble draining engine block? Park car on hill, heading down, and water will drain easily.

Did you forget your key? A jumper wire is handy to have for starting in such embarrassing situations.

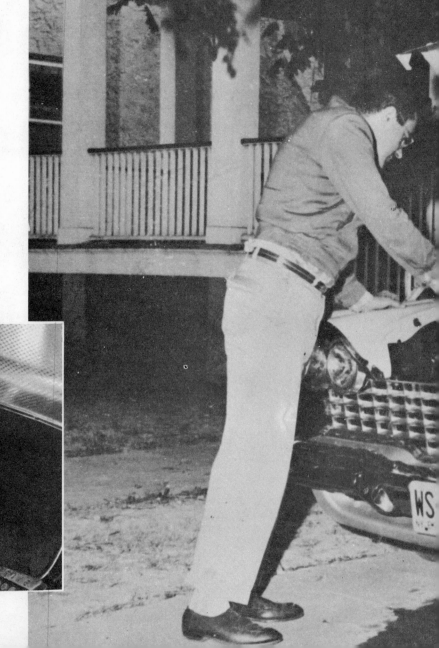

shaft. This I did with the end of a wrench. Almost immediately the valve snapped open. By working it back and forth a number of times I got it free enough to obtain normal action the rest of the day.

Few things are more annoying on a trip than lights that cut capers. Especially likely to give trouble, and blow fuses, are the tail, stop and turn signal lights. This often can be traced to failure to use more caution when packing the car for the trip, connectors for these rear lights being disturbed so that they ground if the male connection is pulled out of the connector.

Just about baffled because the engine of his car would not start, a friend of mine decided to check the engine end of the ground strap. He discovered that it was loose. Thus the engine cranked fast enough, but failed to fire because it didn't have sufficient primary current for hot ignition. Had he not decided to do a bit of checking he would have run down the battery and really been in a jam. Incidentally, very slow cranking with a hot engine usually is a sign of "varnish" on its pistons. This is an especially troublesome kind of deposit which causes binding when parts are heated. It drags on the pistons to a point where you'd suspect a badly run down battery. The immediate answer is simply to wait until the engine cools off.

You can avoid the need for hollering "help" at the first stall if you make it a point to know at least enough about your car that you have a fighting chance of being able to get going under your own steam whenever trouble strikes. •

Completed patio adds a rustic spaciousness to the rear of the house. The playroom (lower section of house in back of patio) is made cooler in the summer and warmer in the winter.

translucent patio awning

By Emil E. Brodbeck

A PATIO adds much to a home. It not only is a place to relax in comfort, but it also improves the property in value and in appearance.

Herein is a patio addition that was designed for maximum comfort, simplicity, appearance and with a view toward minimum upkeep through the years. It covered an area that was a problem to the maintenance of a neat home and something definitely had to be done, especially with a growing family, to have an outdoor area pro-

tected from insects and the summer sun, and a place to relax in the cool of the evening.

As with any construction project, the patio required special planning, especially in regard to materials to be used. The best type of patio flooring for our particular needs had to be considered. Also the type of roof, side covering and wood construction required special attention. Since cost was of utmost importance, it was decided that a cement slab would not do. Instead, it was

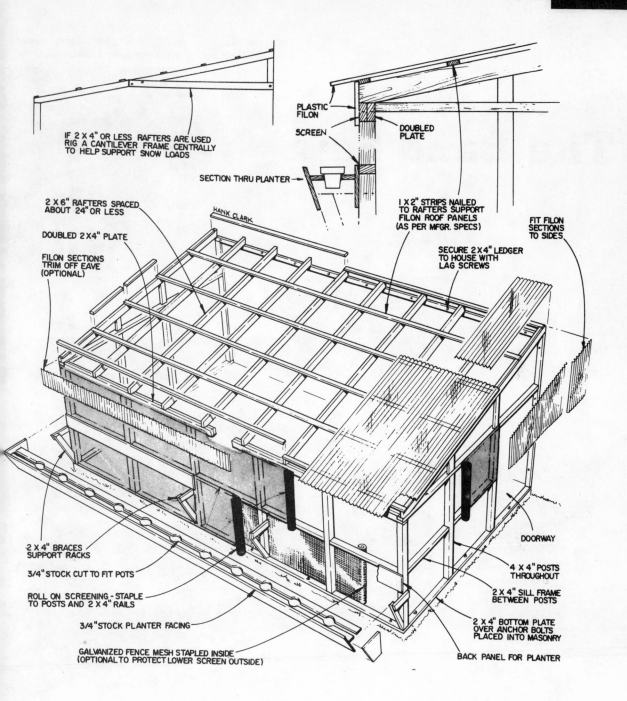

IF 2 X 4" OR LESS RAFTERS ARE USED
RIG A CANTILEVER FRAME CENTRALLY
TO HELP SUPPORT SNOW LOADS

PLASTIC
FILON

SCREEN

DOUBLED
PLATE

SECTION THRU PLANTER →

2 X 6" RAFTERS SPACED
ABOUT 24" OR LESS

HANK CLARK

1 X 2" STRIPS NAILED
TO RAFTERS SUPPORT
FILON ROOF PANELS
(AS PER MFGR. SPECS)

FIT FILON
SECTIONS
TO SIDES

DOUBLED 2 X 4" PLATE

FILON SECTIONS
TRIM OFF EAVE
(OPTIONAL)

SECURE 2 X 4" LEDGER
TO HOUSE WITH
LAG SCREWS

2 X 4" BRACES
SUPPORT RACKS

3/4" STOCK CUT TO FIT POTS

ROLL ON SCREENING - STAPLE
TO POSTS AND 2 X 4" RAILS

3/4" STOCK PLANTER FACING

GALVANIZED FENCE MESH STAPLED INSIDE
(OPTIONAL TO PROTECT LOWER SCREEN OUTSIDE)

DOORWAY

4 X 4" POSTS
THROUGHOUT

2 X 4" SILL FRAME
BETWEEN POSTS

2 X 4" BOTTOM PLATE
OVER ANCHOR BOLTS
PLACED INTO MASONRY

BACK PANEL FOR PLANTER

decided that colored cement blocks set in a layer of sand would be best because it could be kept clean by sweeping with a broom and an occasional spraying with a garden hose.

For a roof we decided to use a forest green translucent plastic since it would transmit light to the playroom that was to be enclosed by the patio. A solid roof would have been costly and would have made the area extremely dark. The plastic paneling we decided to use is called Filon, made of Fiberglas rein-forced with nylon. It never requires painting, is shatterproof, weatherproof and light in weight.

The size of the patio shown in this article may easily be varied. In fact, your choice of style and design may be different. It was not intended that this patio be exactly duplicated, but rather to open up an approach to a way of con-struction that would save you money and time, and yet give you a most durable patio—a home improvement project for the do-it-yourselfer. •

The Band Saw

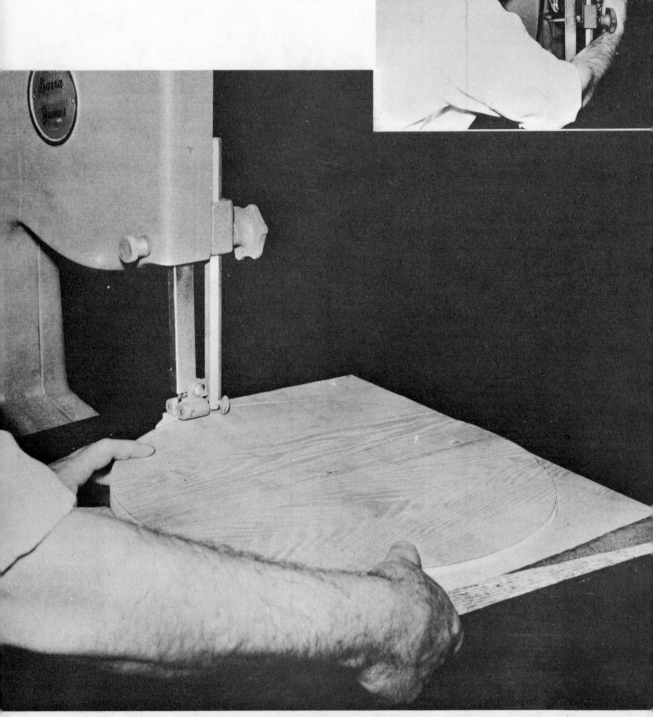

An endless number of jobs can be performed with this tool. This craftsman is cutting out a stool top.

You can check tension of the blade by flexing it. About ¼ inch in a 6-inch span is correct.

Thickness of a tissue between the blade and side guides will provide sufficient blade clearance.

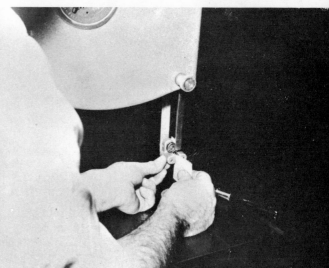

THE band saw, one of the oldest of the woodworking machines, is still basically the same as the one on which William Newberry was granted a patent way back in 1808 in England.

Band saws are now made in many sizes varying from the smallest, such as the little bench models with 9-inch wheels, to the giants used in mills with wheels that are 84 inches and more in diameter. The blades on these large models are as much as 16 inches wide and 50 feet long.

The band mill is used for sawing logs into planks and the band re-saw is used to cut thick stock into thinner boards. A third kind is the band-scroll saw, used for sawing curved or straight work, a combination of both, and on occasion for re-sawing. This third kind is the one illustrated and described in this article. The machine is so named because the cutting blade is actually a narrow, flexible, endless band of steel with teeth on one edge. This blade runs over revolving pulleys or wheels which have rubber tires stretched over their rims.

The size of a conventional band saw is indicated by the diameter of each of its two wheels. For instance, an 18-inch band saw has 18-inch diameter wheels and will cut 18 inches, less the width of the blade guard. In some instances, the size is given as the actual throat opening rather than the wheel size.

Several models of band saws have three, rather than two wheels. This makes possible a much larger throat opening in a smaller, more compact, less expensive machine. A band saw, because it is so well guarded, is one of the safest woodworking

Thickness of writing paper is proper clearance between back of blade and roller guide wheel.

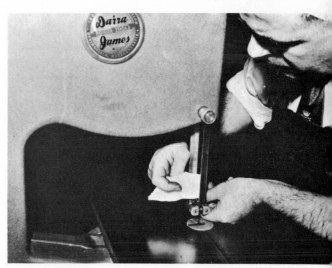

The upper guide assembly containing blade guard should be lowered to clear work by about ¼ inch.

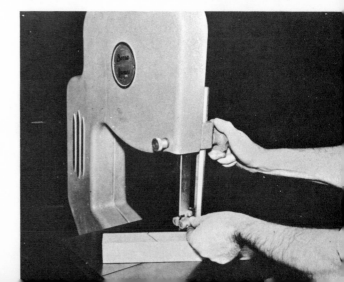

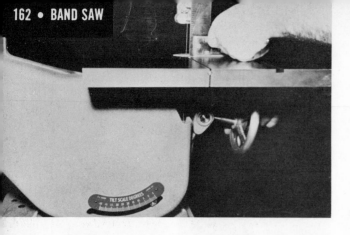

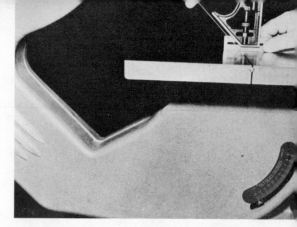

A try square may be used to check the 90-degree accuracy of the blade in relation to the table.

When using either a tilting table or a tilting saw blade at 45 degrees, first check with square.

machines to operate. The doors enclose the blade and wheels. The upper guide assembly contains a blade guard which travels with it when raised or lowered. If used in its correct position, just above the work, the blade is always covered except for that part which does the actual cutting.

Adjustments, while not complicated, must be carefully made in the order given and should never be made while the machine is running. Once made, re-adjustments are seldom necessary while using the same blade. The first of these is to make the blade run in the center of the track by tilting the upper wheel either in or out while turning the machine by hand. Tension is next. On saws that do not have an indicator scale, tension may be judged by pressing on the side of the blade. A flex of about ¼-inch in a 6-inch span is just about correct.

The third step is to adjust the two sets of side guides that are located one above and one below the saw table. The side guide pins should each clear the blade by about the thickness of a thin piece of paper. They should also be positioned 1/16 inch or less back of the gullets of the teeth to avoid any injury to them. The blade should not touch the roller guide wheels, usually located just above and back of the side

guards, except when material is being sawed. A clearance of about the thickness of a piece of writing paper should be sufficient. If permitted to continually touch, the back of the blade will become hardened which will hasten its breakage.

The final check on the saw travel is to run the machine by hand. If all seems correct, and provided the doors are closed, a short trial run should be made under power. The table on most saws may be tilted up to an angle of 45 degrees and returned to a right angle to the blade when it is lowered to an adjustable stop screw. It is advisable to check the accuracy of the setting with a square. At least one band saw available—the one used for this article— has a blade which may be tilted 7 degrees forward and 46 degrees backward while the table remains flat. This angle may even be varied while the saw is in motion to make cuts that are impossible on a conventional saw.

Blades for cutting wood on a small band saw include widths from ⅛ to ¾ inch, and from 3 to 7 teeth per inch. If the selection is limited, a ¼ and ⅜-inch size will prove to be satisfactory for most jobs. Tooth styles are the standard and the buttress (skip tooth). The standard is used for regular woodworking operations and

You can construct a simple rig like the one shown here to hold the blade for sharpening or setting.

To coil blade for storage hold it like this, with teeth pointing away, foot holding bottom of loop.

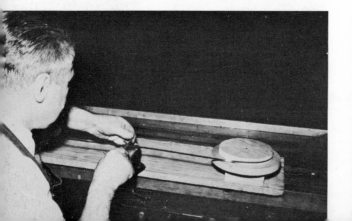

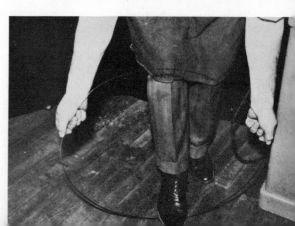

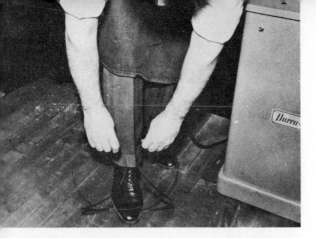

Twisting blade in causes upper loop to fall inside lower. Three loops result by crossing hands.

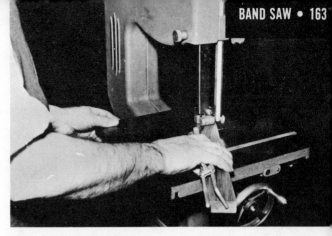

A miter gauge and stop is being used to cut duplicate pieces at 45 degrees on the 90-degree table.

skip tooth for cutting aluminum or brass, plastic, or any other soft material which may plug up the teeth.

A broken blade may be successfully hard soldered or brazed at home but most people prefer to send these jobs out. Even though new blades are inexpensive and dull ones can be sharpened at little cost, some people like to do the job at home. A simple rig may be made with discs to hold the blade in position as one section at a time is clamped in a small vise for either setting or filing. Teeth are set to alternate sides and are filed straight across as on a ripsaw, using a blunt triangular file with rounded edges.

Blades should be coiled for storage. To do this, hold the blade in a vertical position and with the teeth pointed away, stand on the bottom of the loop. Twisting the blade inwards, you will cause the upper section to bend down toward the lower. Next, place this upper loop inside the lower, move the hands until they cross each other, and three loops will be formed on the floor.

On larger blades where five loops may be desired, one of the three loops formed should be pulled out from the others and twisted as before.

Band saw work is very simple, yet proper technique will result in a saving of time and material. First, a blade should be selected that is the widest that will do the job. It may help to know that a ¾-inch blade will cut a 1¾-inch radius and a ¼-inch blade will cut one ¾-inch, but also that it is not wise to run quite this small. The complete cut should be thought out in advance to eliminate the necessity of backing out of long stock. Also, a little advance thinking will prevent sawing a piece in the direction that will cause it to run into the column. Similar planning will show the necessity for making the shortest cuts first. Many cuts that do not involve curves may be made by using a miter gauge or a rip fence. Boards may be ripped with their edges square or they may be beveled or chamfered by tilting the blade or table. They may also be re-sawed after first being sawed from both sides on the circular saw.

Many wood joints can be entirely cut on the band saw even though this operation probably can be done more accurately on the circular saw. These joints include end-lap, middle-lap, cross-lap, and slip joints. Parts of others such as tenons and tails of dovetail joints are also possible. When only one curved piece is to be sawed, the outline may be drawn directly on the wood. If this same outline will be duplicated many times,

Blade is shown tilted to saw plywood board. The laminated edges can be decorative when sanded.

Square stock is shown being ripped at 45 degrees. You can make a fence with C clamps and iron bar.

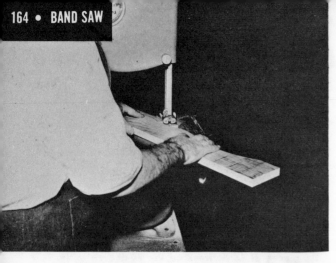

A cornice board is a good example of combination cuts. Proper planning eliminates extra cutting.

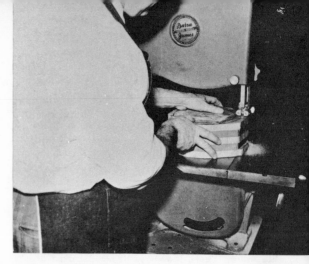

Corners of glued-up stock are being cut off in preparation for later turning on the wood lathe.

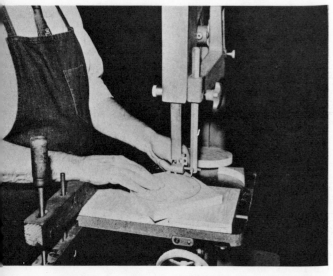

Flexibility of band saw allows you to cut many accurate patterns, just like the one shown here.

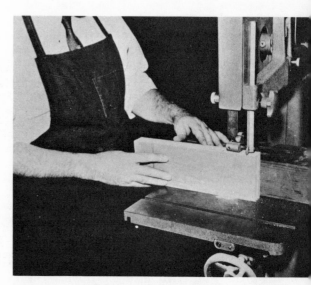

To re-saw a wide board you can make a temporary rip fence. Pivot style guide stops blade leading.

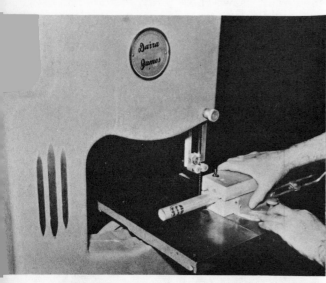

Reynolds aluminum may be cut with a wood blade. Round stock should be clamped to prevent rolling.

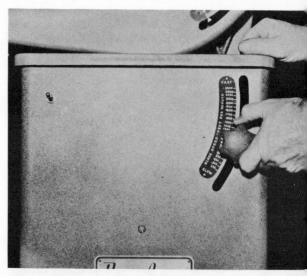

Reduce speed for cutting metal. Use the variable speed drive assembly or external pulley system.

a pattern or template should be made of cardboard, hardboard or metal. When two or more pieces are to be sawed to the same shape, work will be more accurate and time will be saved if they are nailed together and sawed as one unit. The nails should, if possible, be in the waste and so located that they will not interfere with the sawing.

Many jigs may be constructed. Some of these make the work easier and some are necessary to perform certain operations. V blocks in various positions may be used to split round stock, to cut triangular pieces, to cut the corners off a square block that is to be turned, or for making diagonal cuts in the end to receive the live center of work to be turned in the lathe.

Circular discs of any predetermined size may be cut accurately by means of a simple jig made of a board clamped to the table. The pivot point is made with a brad driven through the bottom of the board, located at right angles to the blade and at a distance equal to the radius of the circle. If the disc radius is larger than the table, an extension may be made with boards clamped to the table and built up even with its surface. Other jigs include those for doing multiple sawing by using a pattern, for cutting circular arcs or segments, for cutting either parallel or beveled curves and for trimming the ends of glued-up stock, and for cutting tapers or wedges.

The band saw can be used for cutting metal by changing the blade to one suitable for this work. These blades look like and cut like hack saw blades. The same rules apply in their selection. The teeth should not be too fine on heavy work or they will clog, nor should they be too coarse on thin work or they will strip. A good rule to follow is to use a coarse blade whenever possible but always to make certain that at least two teeth are in contact with the stock at all times.

Three styles of sets obtainable are: "every tooth set," which is similar to that on saws used for wood; "regular," has one unset tooth for each pair that is set; and "wavy," where groups of teeth are formed in waves, first to the right and then to the left. If the number of saw blades must be limited, a group of three regular set, one with 14, one with 18 and one with 24 teeth will do most metal cutting jobs in a home shop. Metals are sawed at a slower speed than wood. If the saw is not equipped with a speed control, you can get around this with a set of pulleys used like back gears, or by the use of separate countershaft, or by a drive from the spindle of a metal cutting lathe. •

Weighted bucket used to pull the miter gauge will provide desired rate of feed when cutting metal.

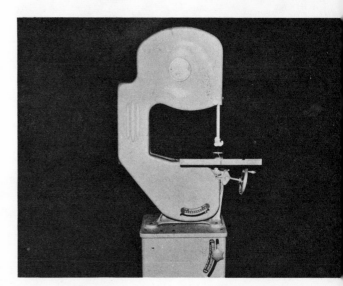

The tilting blade Darra-James 12-inch Model 512 used in illustrations, in 90-degree position.

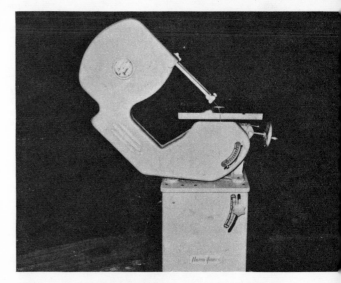

The saw tilts 7 degrees forward, and 46 degrees backward as shown. Its 14x14 table stays flat.

For a liquor cabinet on wheels,
make Bill Baker's compact and convenient

GARDEN BAR CART

Front view of bar cart. Drinking glasses used must be slanted so they slip into, not through, holes.

Side view of bar cart. Entire unit can be made from one piece of plywood, some miscellaneous wood.

BEGIN making your bar cart by tracing the patterns shown in this section. Then cut all the pieces out carefully.

Start assembling as follows: screw "N" onto edge of "Q," holding good side of "N" facing out. Take solid block "A" and insert 4 screws through the inside of "N" and tighten.

Take previous assembly and hold onto inside face of back "O" and flush with top edge, insert two 1½-inch No. 8 flathead screws and tighten.

Turn complete previous assembly upside down, holding flush edges down. Put center shelf "C" onto it with better side down, tight against back, and screw on by starting through the back first and then the other parts.

Turn complete assembly right side up. Set top "B" onto assembly, holding back edge flush with back piece "O," insert 1½-inch No. 8 flathead screws and tighten. Put complete assembly aside.

Take piece "D-1," holding finished side of plywood down, and set piece "D-2" onto it, holding it flush on straight edge and leaving equal margin on the round edge. Nail or screw both pieces tightly together.

Mark ⅜ inch in on long edge (21 inches) of piece "H." Mark one inch in from each end and then in equal spaces for 5 screws. Bore holes for 1½-inch No. 8 flathead screws and countersink on unfinished side of plywood.

Plant previous piece onto straight edge of assembly "D-1" and "D-2," holding it flush with outside edge of smaller circle "D-2" and let it reach to the bottom surface of bottom circle. Insert 1½-inch No. 8 flathead screws and tighten.

Take complete previous assembly, hold it onto bottom surface of center shelf "C" making sure that all front edges of the round portion extend equally. This can be done by nailing a 1x2-inch strip 26 inches long onto front edge' (round portion) of both top and center shelf and using that as a guide for the lower front shelf assembly. Insert 1½-inch No. 8 flathead screws through holes of shelf "C" into piece "H," making sure that "H" will be recessed one inch on each end and tighten. Now line up and square up lower front shelf assembly. Hold it in place and put nail through temporary 1x2-inch guide so that all pieces will stay in place for further assembly.

Turn assembly upside down. Put bottom "K" of cabinet on assembly by propping it up with same guide and holding flush with bottom edge of back "O". Insert 1½-inch No. 8 flathead screws through back into bottom and tighten. This completes the first part of the assembly.

Now cut 10 pieces, 1 inch thick x 3½ inches wide x 7¼ inches long out of solid wood. Dado out both edges and back of each piece. Cut two pieces 1 inch thick x 3¾ inches wide x 7¼ inches long out of solid wood. Dado out one edge and back of each piece; however, on these two pieces, the side that you dado out will be opposite on each piece. On one piece you will plough out from the front of the panel, while on the other piece dado out from the back as you did on one side of each of the previous 10 pieces. Now bevel both front edges of all 12 pieces. The dados or cutouts will be $\frac{9}{16}$ of an inch deep x 1½ inches wide and in the back of each panel ¼ inch deep x 2 inches wide. Mark on all 12 panels, ⅜ inch from each end for two screws. Bore holes, countersink surface for 1½-inch No. 8 flathead screws.

Cut two pieces, 1 inch thick x 3½ inches wide x 16 inches long out of solid wood. Also cut two pieces 1 inch thick x 4 inches wide x 16 inches long out of solid wood. Dado out and bevel edge on all four pieces. On these four pieces, the dados or cutouts will be ½ x ½ inch.

Mark ⅜ inch from bottom of each piece and bore two holes through each piece on this line. Countersink on surface for 1½-inch No. 8 flathead screws.

Mounting Panels

Mount each pair of panels onto cabinet, holding them flush with bottom surface of cabinet bottom and snug against bottom surface of center shelf and flush with the surface of piece "H." Bore two holes for each panel through center shelf and countersink for 1½-inch No. 8 flathead screws. Insert screws and tighten.

Set first short panel approximately in center of round section onto bottom and lower front shelf reinforcement, again holding it snug against lower front shelf and flush with bottom of cabinet. Tack on with two finishing nails to hold piece in place. Now start inserting all the panels to both sides, tacking them on temporarily with finishing nails. After they are all properly fitted in place, insert 1½-inch No. 8 flathead screws through all holes.

Cut two pieces "U," 1 inch thick x 3 inches wide x 24¾ inches long out of solid wood. Bore two holes ⅜ inch from bottom edge of each piece and countersink for 1½-inch No. 8 flathead screws. Insert each piece on back corner of each side of cabinet, holding them flush on bottom and flush with cabinet back and snug against cabinet top and inside of notch of center shelf. Insert two screws on the bottom and two screws through the top and bore additional holes to go into back

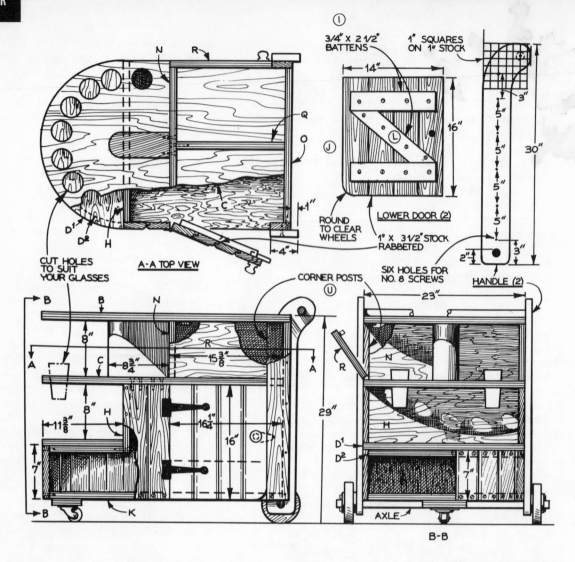

and center shelf and countersink for 1½-inch No. 8 flathead screws.

Fit doors "R" in both top spaces on each side, holding a ¾-inch piano hinge underneath and a piece of cardboard on one side on top. Door edge must be flush with vertical partition "N." Mount piano hinges, doors and touch latch.

Mount handles and wheel supports onto each side of cabinet, holding them flush with inside edge of piece "U" and let bottom one-inch dowel hole just clear. First mount one handle by inserting screws and tightening. Cut one-inch dowel 24 inches long. Sand smooth and insert into hole of fastened handle. Now insert into hole of loose handle and fasten same with screws. Insert one one-inch No. 8 flathead screw through handles into dowel.

Make complete wheel assembly. For the wheels use 1½-inch solid wood and for the little side wheels use ½-inch solid wood. Before putting wheel assembly into handle and wheel support, cut one inch dowel 31½ inches long. Bore one hole six inches from each and through dowel and

countersink for 1½-inch No. 8 flathead screws. Sand six inches of dowel from each end well. Rub large amount of paraffin onto sanded ends. Now insert dowel through bottom holes of handle and wheel support, leaving equal amounts extended on each side.

Once wheels are finished, mount small ½-inch washer-like wheel solidly onto large wheels using glue and finishing nails. Bore a $1\frac{1}{16}$-inch hole through center of complete wheels. Put paraffin inside hole in wheels and on top of small washer-like wheel which faces cabinet. Put wheels on and bore ¼-inch hole on dowel extending beyond wheel. Insert a ¼-inch thick dowel two inches long in axle to hold wheels in place. Insert two 1½-inch No. 8 flathead screws through axle where holes are and fasten against cabinet bottom.

Bore holes and countersink for 1½-inch No. 8 flathead screws. On bottom surface of cabinet bottom in exact center of round portion one inch in from outside edge, mount piece "E" with glue and screws. Now mount a rubber caster onto block.

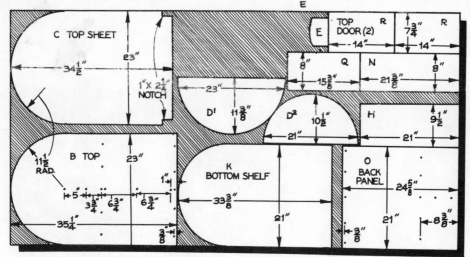

ONE PANEL OF 3/4" X 4 FT. X 8 FT. EXTERIOR PLYWOOD YIELDS ALL MAJOR COMPONENTS

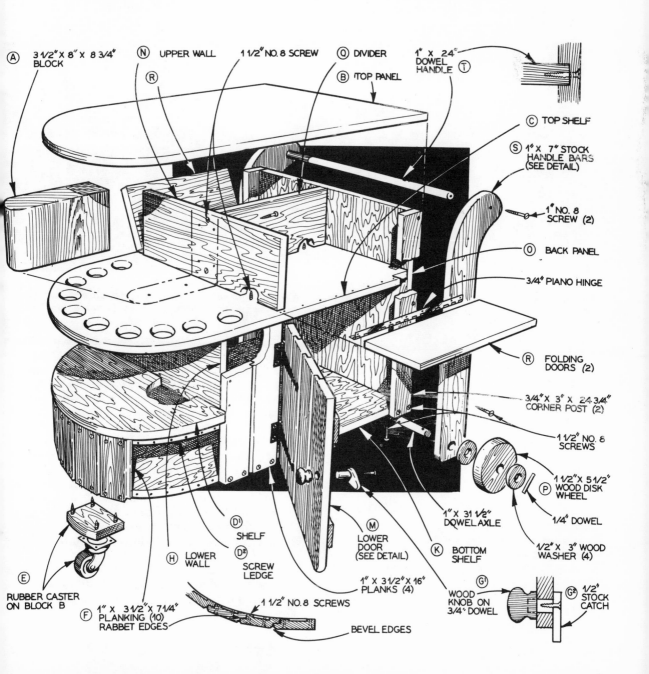

(Left to right) After cutting all pieces, bore holes through shell "C" according to size of glasses to be used. Attach back reinforcing strips "U" to back "O." Assemble "Q" and "N" partitions to block "A."

Fasten assembly "Q-N-A" to back "O" in upside down position on level surface to keep all edges flush. Still in upside down position, attach shelf "C." Now turn assembly right side up and attach top "B."

MATERIAL LIST

1 sheet ¾" plywood, 4' x 8' (outdoor waterproof)

3 boards, 1" x 4" x 8'

1 board, 1" x 8" x 3'

1 board, 1½" x 6" x 12"

1 board, ½" x 3" x 12"

1 board, ¾" x 2½" x 8'

2 hardwood dowels, 1" x 3'

2 pair, ornamental strap hinges, 6" with screws

2 pieces, ¾" piano hinge, 14" long, with ½" screws

1 gross flathead screws, 1½" #8

4 flathead screws, 1" #8   2 touch latches

1 length, ¼" dowel   1 rubber caster

2 pieces, 10" length brass chain, plus 4 pieces ¾"

#6 roundhead screws and washers

Waterproof glue

Make two doors, one *reverse*. Use one-inch thick solid wood for outside panels and ¾-inch thick solid wood for inside supports. Use 1½-inch No. 8 flathead screws for assembling. Bore a ¾-inch hole for doorknob. Put two six-inch ornamental strap hinges 3¼ inches center from top and bottom edges of doors. Mount doors.

Turn doorknob out of solid wood. Bore a ¾-inch hole half way in. Insert a ¾-inch hardwood dowel into knob using glue. Dowel must extend 1⅛ inches. Cut out two door latches ("G-2"). Bore holes for 1-inch No. 8 flathead screws and countersink. Sand extended part of dowel smooth and insert through hole in door. Glue and screw latch into place.

Sand all edges and surfaces using No. 2/0 sandpaper (preferably Garnet paper). The bar cart is now finished. •

Assemble pieces "D-1" and "D-2," holding edges flush at back. Turn assembly upside down and use guide strips for spacing and support as 'H' and "D-1" and "D-2" are mounted. Then attach bottom piece "K."

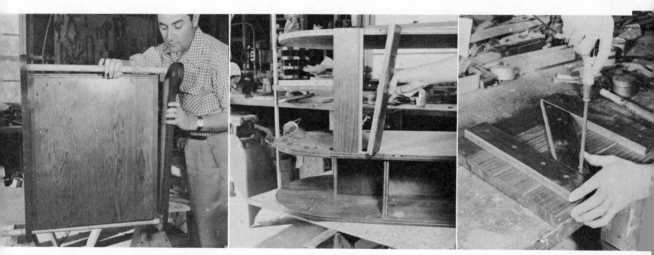

Handle and wheel supports are mounted, holding them flush with front edge of back reinforcing strips "U." Then attach side panels, lower panels, and upper doors. Next step: construction of lower doors.

Outside face of lower door gets ornamental hinges door knob, catch. As lower door is mounted, cart is on level surface so door is flush with bottom of cart. Last job: attach caster on mounting block of front bottom.

Build a Stone Fireplace

An economic double hearth for family outdoor cooking and entertainment

YOU CAN SPELL the beginning and end of many serious fireplace-building projects with just one word: foundation. Unless your structure is to be small, light-weight, on well-drained, frost-free ground, the foundation of your fireplace is as important as all the above-ground structure.

To play it safe we used a reinforced concrete slab. This seemed to offer the layman the best possible and lowest cost foundation that would give the least amount of trouble in the greatest number of climates.

In the selected site, measure off an area with at least a 1-inch border further out than the fireplace base will be on all sides. In the fireplace herein illustrated, the base was 46″ x 46″ so the measured area was no less than 48″ x 48″. At each corner drive a long stake deep into the transcribed area just outside, to hold the form solidly. Using boards of 6-inch width (or more if you like), construct the form for the foundation slab. Take special care in insuring the levelness of the top edges of your form.

Dig the foundation hole to a depth of 19 inches below ground level. Pitch in the direction of the terrain slope to allow drainage in the natural direction. Then fill the first 8 inches with fist-sized rocks. Fill the next 9 inches with smaller stones, cinders or gravel. In most areas it is possible to find stones to fulfill these requirements.

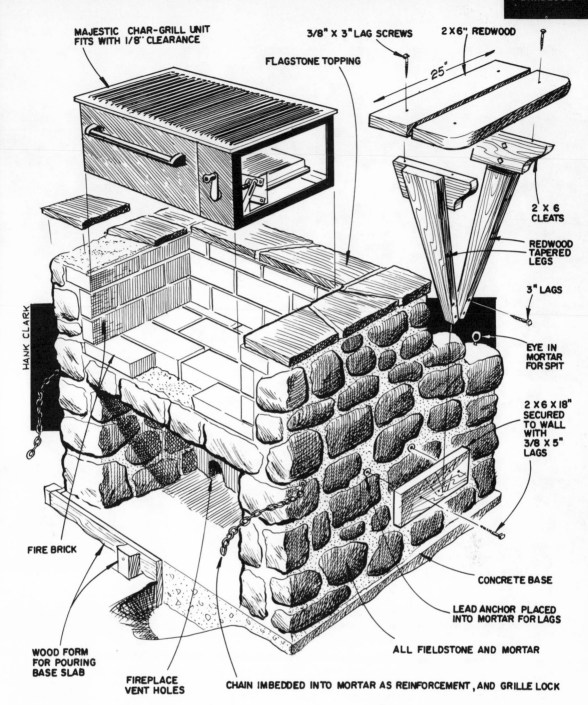

MAJESTIC CHAR-GRILL UNIT FITS WITH 1/8" CLEARANCE

3/8" X 3" LAG SCREWS

2 X 6" REDWOOD

FLAGSTONE TOPPING

25"

2 X 6 CLEATS

REDWOOD TAPERED LEGS

3" LAGS

EYE IN MORTAR FOR SPIT

2 X 6 X 18" SECURED TO WALL WITH 3/8 X 5" LAGS

HANK CLARK

FIRE BRICK

CONCRETE BASE

LEAD ANCHOR PLACED INTO MORTAR FOR LAGS

WOOD FORM FOR POURING BASE SLAB

FIREPLACE VENT HOLES

ALL FIELDSTONE AND MORTAR

CHAIN IMBEDDED INTO MORTAR AS REINFORCEMENT, AND GRILLE LOCK

The last 2 inches are filled with construction sand. Water thoroughly to force sand down among the rocks and stones. Do this several times to force the sand down into the crevasses and cavities. Now fill the form to within 5 inches of the top with more sand and tamp down solidly until well packed. This should bring you up to within 1 inch of the lower edge of the 6-inch wood frame for your concrete.

Before mixing the cement and filling the form to make the slab, here are a few facts about concrete: Concrete is a mixture consisting of a water and cement paste which binds fine and coarse materials, called aggregates, into a rock-like mass. Unless all the aggregates are completely covered with water and cement paste, you will not get a strong concrete. The cement and aggregates are put in a mixing container and water is added as the mixture is turned over. Mixing is continued until the water and cement paste have completely soaked and covered all materials. Be sure to use both clean aggregates and clean water.

To test your mix, take a handful of the mixture, mold it into a ball; if it holds the shape without running or crumpling, you have a good consistency. Crystallization of the cement should start within 45 minutes. Try to make use of your mixture before this time elapses.

Measure and stake out an area 48 inches square. Dig a hole 24 inches deep and fill the first 8 inches with large rocks. The next 9 inches are filled with smaller stones or coarse gravel and then wet down.

Now put some dirt and rock around the outside of the form to strengthen it and to absorb any seepage, and fill the form to within 3 inches of the top. Onto this lay a 4' x 4' piece of galvanized fence wire, for reinforcement, as flat as possible. Then fill to the top of the form. It is best not to eliminate this step, since such reinforcing will double the strength of the slab. Now smooth the slab with a piece of scrap lumber. After "floating" (about 10 to 15 minutes) level with a long 2 x 4, using the smoothest, straightest edge. Be certain this level is longer than the width of your form. Level with a back-and-forth, side-to-side motion. A few hours after the concrete has set, sweep the top of the slab to remove any glaze left from the leveling process.

Cover the slab with wet burlap sacks during the curing period—about a week. Keep bags damp all the time for the best curing and strongest slab. This dampness aids uniform drying. Complete curing takes about 28 days. For the builder this amounts to no fire in the new fireplace for at least a month, and it should be kept dampened for about three weeks. The last week allows slow drying out of the whole structure. A week is sufficient before beginning the stone structure, however.

In buying mortar for the above-ground construction, ask your building supplier to give you a mortar mix designed especially for this type of construction. This contains a lime additive that is recommended for all types of above-ground binding. Use this mortar for the top of your first course of rock, on up. On the bottom, next to the slab, mix your mortar using the same cement as used on the base slab.

To start the base, keeping the form intact if working on the slab before a week has passed, lay a strip of mortar about 15" wide and 1½" thick along the left side of the slab. Be sure the slab has been wet down first and sprinkled lightly with dry cement powder. Then lay a strip of chicken wire, about 4' square, over the newly laid mortar. Pin down the loose end with a rock and lay the first corner stone on top of the chicken wire and mortar bed; work down into the mortar. Lay ½ inch of mortar over the exposed wire around the base of the corner stone and trowel mortar up against the stone, filling all spaces to prevent water seepage, which, when frozen, would crack the structure. Wash the next rock and place it up against the first. Fill in again with mortar and continue to lay stones, maintaining straight line construction.

Once the left wall is finished, begin the right-hand wall in the same manner. Keep about 1 inch in from the edge of the slab. As each wall reaches a height of 19 inches, level it with mortar 1½ inches thick.

The chicken wire covering the base slab will serve to tie the opposite walls together, since cement will be laid over the slab between the two walls. Wet slab before covering with cement and sprinkle with cement powder dampened by a mist from the garden hose. Float cement smooth,

being sure it is snug against the bases of the two walls. When set up, brush lightly to remove the glaze. Allow a minimum of two days, keeping the new work damp with bags or damp straw, for the structure to become firm and strong. During the drying time, build a strong, durable wooden platform to fit between the walls and come up level with the tops of the walls. This must be strong enough to sustain the weight of the mortar and bricks that will form the crossover between and on top of the walls. It will be removed at the completion of the job, of course.

Lay a strip of mortar across the leading edge of the platform, once in place, and imbed the center section of a ten-foot chain in the mortar. This will reinforce the arch and, once again, help to tie the whole fireplace together. Cover the chain with mortar and lay small stones across the top of the arch, on top of the chain. Mortar is then laid over the top and in between the stones, as shown in the photos, to form the leading edge of the fireplace.

The wooden platform should be about 25" deep. Sufficient mortar is mixed to fill in between the two fireplace walls across the top of the platform. First lay newspaper across the top of the wood platform. This is to prevent the mortar from adhering to the wood. Mist spray the leading edge and the tops of the two walls. Sprinkle lightly with cement powder and spray again, being sure to dampen the powder without wetting it so it runs. Immediately fill the tops

After adding 2 inches of sand, pour 3 inches of concrete, lay fence wire, and add last 3 inches.

After floating with a small board, use a smooth 2x4, 4½ feet long to do the final leveling step.

When slab has cured for one week, lay chicken wire over slab and use mortar to bind the first course.

Build wall up 19 inches high, lay 1½ inches of mortar on top. Level and float, then begin right-hand wall.

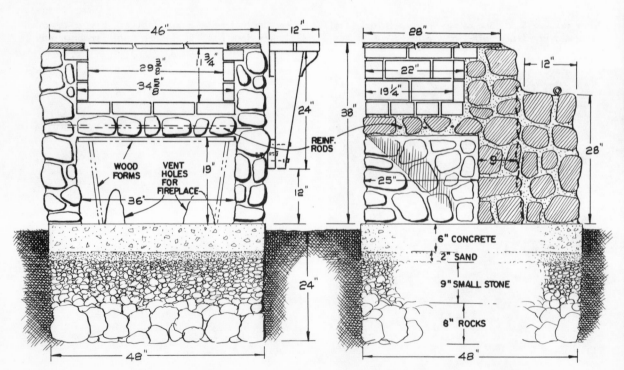

Embed the center section of a 10-foot chain across the front of the fireplace in 1½ inches of mortar. This chain will reinforce and bind the structure together.

of side walls, the leading edge stones and the platform with mortar. Lay 22-inch high, 5-foot long length of border fencing (about 16 gauge, 5-inch mesh, galvanized) to extend beyond the edges of the walls. Push fencing down into the mortar until it tends to stay embedded. Add about 1½ inches more mortar on top of this. Wait about five minutes and float it level. In another 10 minutes float again with a flat board and check the levelness of the whole top. It is important that the whole top be perfectly level.

Place a rock at the right side, wedged into the wire, and on the left as well, to help keep the fencing pulled down into the mortar. Rocks can be removed in about two days when mortar has set. A straight, flat board is temporarily, but very firmly, set on edge across the back of the structure to serve as a guide for firebrick top surface and rear alignment.

Before laying, wash each brick. Firebrick is used exclusively for this part of the operation. First course consists of five bricks laid as shown, about 1½ inches back from the front edge of the fireplace. The first course goes all the way across the structure to within 1 inch of the left and right outside edges of fireplace walls. As each brick is laid in the mortar, put pressure on it and wiggle it a little to create a suction between the brick and the mortar. This also causes the cement-water paste to work up into the pores of the brick and do a better bonding job. Take care to

set the bricks firmly, in a straight line, and level all the way across. Leave about ⅛ inch to ¼ inch all around each brick for mortar. Work mortar down between bricks to a depth of about 1 inch from the top.

Start the second course about 2 inches in from the right end and use four firebricks. Start a third course about 2 inches in from right end of second course and use four bricks. Start fourth course in line with the first course and use four bricks. The fifth course starts 2 inches in from the right end of the fourth course and uses four bricks. This is the floor of your firebox. If there is any pitch at all, a very slight pitch to the front is permissible to aid drainage. Too much will cause the need of extra shimming when the firebox is put in place. *Note:* After regular mortar is forced down between bricks to about 1 inch from the tops of the bricks, mix 50% fireclay with 50% cement powder with a bit of water and fill in the cracks completely. Level off.

A Majestic Masonry Char-Grill was used as the actual grill unit. This is a well-constructed, heavy-duty unit with vented pull-down front doors. Unit has a heavy metal firepan which can be easily lifted out and emptied of ashes. The crank arrangement permits a raising or lowering of the entire firepan. You can vary the intensity of your heat by moving your coals up closer to the grill or farther down from the grill surface. This is an extremely simple means of offering a wide range of heat control.

After laying firebrick as shown in above photo, work mortar down into the spaces between the bricks to 1 inch from top. Fill with fireclay and cement mixture for last inch.

Right-hand photo shows how a 5-foot piece of galvanized wire fencing is laid into mortar on top of the temporary wooden platform between the walls. This doubles strength of slab.

Self-tapping flat head screws were used to form a raised triangle to keep hot pans off the wood.

Lag bolts are tightened while level is used. If necessary, use wood shims to make corrections.

Rear of fireplace is for open wood burning and cooking that requires no special heat control.

In installing any kind of metal in a fireplace you must be sure to allow for metal parts expanding and contracting. The simplest way of allowing sufficient room for this is to cut pieces of corrugated cardboard to the size of the sides and back of the masonry unit you are going to install. Attached to the grill unit the cardboard will act as an adequate spacer, when the unit is placed on top of the firebrick base. Now the sides and back of the firebrick encasement can be installed. Note the drawings for the placement of these bricks. They lie on their sides, not as was done on the base. Mortar is applied to the outer edges of the bricks, leaving the side nearest the metal grill free for a later filling in of the mortar and fireclay mixture. The unit is left in while all construction goes on around it. The fireclay mixture is the last to go in, naturally, after the unit has been removed, for final touchup.

Before cementing up the sides, the overlap of wire fence is cut off with a hack saw as close to the side wall as possible. To show how the rear of the partly completed fireplace should look, this fireplace was finished up to a point where it would be possible to see all of the major steps of construction: *First,* the last course of fire brick will be laid on its side (3rd course up); the two courses laid on edge are shown. Note how firebrick makes a lining inside the outer fireplace wall. *Second,* the firebrick, after being mist sprayed and salted with a straight cement is stuccoed with mortar. More mortar is added as rocks are laid tightly against this section to form the firebrick lining all around. *Third,* the lower portion of the rear fireplace has been started. The center portion of this was started with very large, heavy rocks. This center portion may be joined to the bottom of the firebox area. Note the draft holes at left and right corners of rear fireplace. Rear lower area is built up and joined to the side walls of the fireplace. Also note how mortar was spread over the sides and back to help tie both sides of the structure together.

Excess wire fencing was hooked together and set into the mortar around the corner. This was covered with two inches of mortar all around the side. Then the left side was constructed on top of it.

The top is built up to a height of approximately 37 inches; width runs to 46 inches and depth is 28 inches. The top course of firebrick was laid a half inch back from the lower firebrick wall to allow for easy removal of the cover when the grill is in use. Properly dampened firebrick was then covered with a one-inch layer of mortar, and colorful flagstones were set in place. The spaces between the flagstones were cemented and the whole top was checked and leveled.

The last step involves going over the entire structure with a water and cement powder mixture called grout, filling in cracks, smoothing corners and generally bringing the appearance up to par. Then, after a sufficient drying time, brush the stone with a stiff brush, or use muriatic acid, to remove excess cement.

Before finishing off the rear of the fireplace, set 2 eye bolts in the mortar about 2 inches in from the inside edge of the rear wall. Coil a piece of coat hanger around the base of the bolt. Then the whole piece is put in with mortar, traweled smooth and allowed to set. This arrangement will hold a spit or a rod to hold a kettle.

The redwood table is made from 1¾-inch planking 5½ inches wide by 10 inches long. Vertical supports are 24 inches long.

Cut the base plate first from 2 x 6 stock eighteen inches long. Fasten it to the fireplace with 5-inch lag bolts through previously set lead slugs. Some shaping may be necessary to fit the stone contours. Fasten two 24-inch tapered supports to base plate after drilling ⅜-inch holes to accept 3-inch lag bolts. Shape 2 x 6 cleats with a jig saw and fasten them to vertical supports as shown in drawing. Now place table top planks, 25 inches long, onto the cleats and drill for lags. Glue should be used between all wood parts for greater strength and weatherproof durability. Cut top boards to shape and fasten them in place using a level and wood shims to keep even. Fasten down and add two self tapping screws to the top, forming a triangle with lags and allowing a ¼-inch clearance between the wood and the screw tops for possible hot metal pan placement.

Flagstones finish off the fireplace rear and the small shelf on the left side of the rear fireplace. Any leftover firebrick can be used on the floor of the rear fireplace also and the lower facings in the rear are cemented with a 50% fireclay and 50% cement mixture to protect the firewall.

The Char-Grill unit is intended for charcoal burning, giving the advantages of controlled heat. The rear fireplace is perfect for logs and less formalized back-yard cookery. The two make up all that is needed for outdoor cooking and entertaining, yet, the cost is equivalent to that of just one fireplace. It all adds up to a true bargain for your outdoor pleasure and that of your family. •——*Emil E. Brodbeck*

Most meals prepared in a kitchen can be cooked on this grill. Intensity of heat is varied by moving the coals closer to the grill. On other side is fireplace for logs and more usual type of outdoor cooking.

Large enough for four people seated comfortably, this lightweight, fold-away is the ideal summer companion for a charcoal grill and a pile of hamburgers. It can be tucked away into the trunk of a car, too.

Folding Picnic Table

An easy-to-make outdoor table for the suburban family, designed for the patio or small back yard, and as convenient to store away as a card table

FOR those whose tastes and desires run to the great outdoors but who are hampered by a small area which is anything but suitable for the large cumbersome standard picnic table, this folding one with its unique attached seats and drop leaf extensions goes a long way toward solving the problem. Made from durable pine or cedar and finished in the natural or colored paint this type of table can be moved about with little effort, and when completely folded up can readily be stored in an unused corner of the patio or back yard, or even in the garage.

Fully extended, the area of the top allows four people to sit comfortably and with no danger of getting one's elbow in the neighbor's salad; if unexpected guests drop in, a couple of chairs placed at either end enlarges the serviceability of the project. A unique method of supporting the table extensions is a feature of the table; when the extensions are locked, and held in place, there they stay and eliminate hazards of the soup or salad gracing some dress or trousers. Should the craftsman desire to make the project even more portable, the legs can be shortened and casters added.

Since most of the work is done on the leg assemblies of the table and seats, it is well to get this done first, and best results are obtained in this respect by first making a full-scale layout of the leg assemblies on a separate sheet of material such as Masonite or thin plywood. This will enable the craftsman, by using a protractor or T-bevel, to determine the correct angle of cutting for the individual legs for the table and seats.

After marking to the correct sizes given in the plans, cut one end of all twelve legs, and, by the use of a stop, cut them to the correct sizes desired. As noted in the plans, the top rails of both the table and seats are set in a dado and cut into the upper end of the legs. The cutting of these dadoes is the next step. When these dadoes and those for the bottom rails have been cut, the rails are then attached to the legs. This is where the full-sized layout comes in since it enables the craftsman to assemble the parts accurately and identically. The top rails are secured in positions with glue and two 1¼-inch RH No. 10 steel wood screws driven in from each of the two faces; the bottom rails in much the same

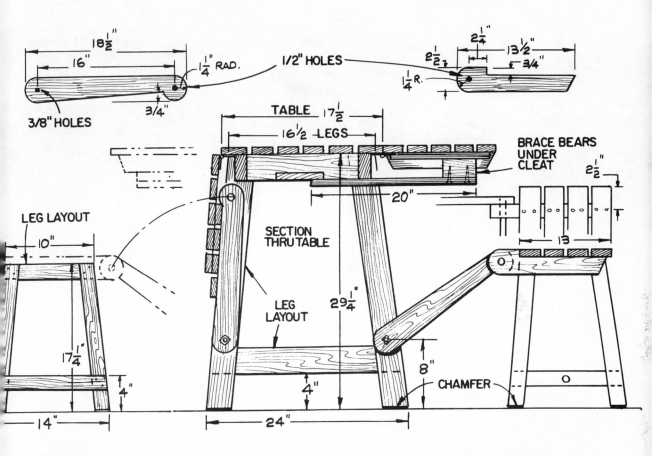

manner except that the screws are entered only through the front.

Side or spacer rails are attached at the top section of the table leg assemblies by means of two ⅜-inch dowels in either end. Between these two spacer rails and in the center between the two legs assemblies two rail supports are attached as shown in the plans, and, on the bottom face of these rails, is attached the extension support. Use 2½-inch finishing nails and glue to attach these three items to one another.

Since a feature of the project is the spaced-slot table and seats, it is well to prepare all the slats necessary for these components at the same time. The plans show that, for the table proper, six slats are required—two of them being 3 inches wide and the remaining four being 2¼ inches in width; for each of the two leafs or extensions five slats 2¼ inches wide are needed, and for each of the two seats four slats 2¼ inches wide are used; making a total of:

13 slats ¾″ x 2¼″ x 40″
2 slats ¾″ x 3″ x 40″
10 slats ¾″ x 2¼″ x 35½″.

All of the 2¼-inch slats used in the top

have three holes bored and countersunk: one in the center and one 2¾ inches from either end; the two 3-inch slats have, in addition to the two holes bored near the ends, three others spaced equidistant between these two and 1 inch from the inner face.

The slats for the extension have three holes bored and countersunk: one also in the center and one 5 inches from either end.

The slats for the seats have three holes bored and countersunk: one in the center and one 2½ inches from either end.

All the above holes are $\frac{5}{32}$ and are countersunk.

Remove the sharp edges from the top surfaces of the slats with a hand plane chamfering $\frac{1}{16}$ inch; sand the ends and chamfer them on the sander. Prepare also the reinforcing cleats under the extensions, and the seat brackets. In the latter item, bore the ¾-inch hole before attaching slats.

The attachment of the slats to the table framework, the seat brackets, and the extension cleats is a relatively simple operation and can be carried out with the required results by making constant use of the square and a spacing strip. In the case of the table frame, this latter has al-

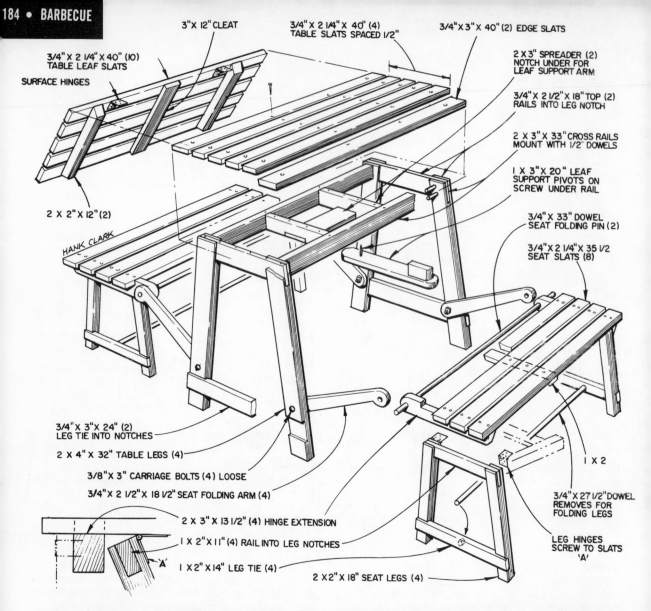

3"X 12" CLEAT

3/4" X 2 1/4" X 40" (4)
TABLE SLATS SPACED 1/2"

3/4"X 3"X 40" (2) EDGE SLATS

3/4" X 2 1/4" X 40" (10)
TABLE LEAF SLATS

SURFACE HINGES

2 X 3" SPREADER (2)
NOTCH UNDER FOR
LEAF SUPPORT ARM

3/4" X 2 1/2" X 18" TOP (2)
RAILS INTO LEG NOTCH

2 X 3" X 33" CROSS RAILS
MOUNT WITH 1/2" DOWELS

1 X 3"X 20" LEAF
SUPPORT PIVOTS ON
SCREW UNDER RAIL

2 X 2"X 12"(2)

3/4" X 33" DOWEL
SEAT FOLDING PIN (2)

3/4" X 2 1/4" X 35 1/2
SEAT SLATS (8)

HANK CLARK

3/4"X 3"X 24" (2)
LEG TIE INTO NOTCHES

2 X 4" X 32" TABLE LEGS (4)

3/8"X 3" CARRIAGE BOLTS (4) LOOSE

3/4"X 2 1/2"X 18 1/2" SEAT FOLDING ARM (4)

2 X 3" X 13 1/2" (4) HINGE EXTENSION

1 X 2"X 11" (4) RAIL INTO LEG NOTCHES

1 X 2"X 14" LEG TIE (4)

2 X 2"X 18" SEAT LEGS (4)

1 X 2

3/4"X 27 1/2"DOWEL
REMOVES FOR
FOLDING LEGS

LEG HINGES
SCREW TO SLATS
'A'

The legs fold toward the center of the bench, leaving the bench unit free to swing in easily.

The side leaf drops down over the folded seat to hold it securely. Other side works the same.

MATERIALS NEEDED

PINE OR CEDAR

2 pieces 1½″ x 3½″ x 32″ (Table Legs)
2 pieces ¾″ x 2¼″ x 18″ (Top Rails)
4 pieces ¾″ x 2½″ x 24″ (Bottom Rails)
2 pieces 1½″ x 2¼″ x 33″ (Cross Rails)
2 pieces 1½″ x 2¼″ x 12½″
  (Rail Spreaders)
2 pieces ¾″ x 3″ x 40″ (Top Slats)
4 pieces ¾″ x 2¼″ x 40″ (Top Slats)
4 pieces 1½″ x 1½″ x 18″ (Seat Legs)
4 pieces ¾″ x 1¾″ x 11″ (Top Rails)
4 pieces ¾″ x 1¾″ x 14″ (Bottom Rails)
2 pieces ¾″ x 1¾″ x 9″
  (Cleats under Slats)
4 pieces 1½″ x 2½″ x 13½″
  (Hinge Extensions)
2 pieces ¾″ x 2½″ x 12″
  (Center Leaf Cleat)
8 pieces ¾″ x 2¼″ x 35½″ (Seat Slats)
4 pieces 1½″ x 1¾″ x 12″
  (Outer Leaf Cleat)
10 pieces ¾″ x 2¼″ x 40″ (Leaf Slats)
4 pieces ¾″ as per plans (Seat Arms)
2 pieces ¾″ x 2½″ x 19½″
  (Leaf Support)

OTHER MATERIALS

2, ¾″ x 33¼″ Dowels
2, ¾″ x 27½″ Dowels
6 pr. 1½″ x 1½″ Surface Hinges
4, ⅜″ x 3″ Carriage Bolts, Nuts,
  Flat Washers
50, 1½″ #10 FH Steel Screws
30, 1¼″ #10 FH Steel Screws

It's easy to build and difficult to break, all of which makes it a necessary item for yardbirds.

ready been squared up when the side rails were attached to the leg assemblies. The one point to remember is the spacing.

The plans indicate that the first slat has an overhang of 2 inches; when this slat has been attached and the overhang checked, it is a simple matter to proceed with the remainder. Similar measurements are given in relation to the seats and extensions.

The plans indicate the manner in which the extension support is attached to the underside of the side rails. Use a 2½-inch No. 10 RH steel screw for this, inserting between the extension support and the edge of the rail a ¼-inch steel flat washer.

For storage, provision is made for the leg assemblies of the seats to fold up under the seats, and this is done by the attachment, to each of the leg assemblies, of a pair of hinges. When in use, and to prevent the leg assemblies from folding in, a length of ¾-inch dowel fits snugly into a hole bored on the inside of the bottom rail of each leg assembly.

In order to make a snug fit and so prevent sloppiness, the ¾-inch dowel at the front of each seat, which passes through the seat bracket, is glued and bradded in place; the end of this dowel protruding ⅝ inch past the outer surface of the bracket.

The extensions or leaves are attached to the outer slats of the table by means of three surface hinges applied underneath, and the extension held in a horizontal position by swinging the support on its swivel screw and bringing the projection directly under the center cleat.

Attachment of the seats to the table legs is done by means of two outer members for each seat—called the seat folding extensions. As the plans indicate, these have a ⅜-inch hole bored in one end and a ¾-inch hole, bored to a depth of ⅝ inch in the other end, and bored in such a manner as to make these members in pairs. Two ⅜ x 3-inch carriage bolts with flat washers between the two members, and flat and lock washers under the nuts, hold these members to the legs. At the other end, projecting ¾-inch dowel is inserted in the ¾-inch hole bored for that purpose, and prevented from slipping off by insertion of a 1¼-inch RH screw.

Folding of the unit begins with the seats. Remove ¾-inch dowel spacer, and fold in and under the two leg assemblies. Lift up the front face of the seat and lodge it against the leg. Hold the extension up a little, swing the support back out of the way and against the side rails, and allow the extension to assume a position vertical to the top. •——*by C. L. Widdicombe*

Brick Barbecue

This attractive model has no chimney, yet is an excellent outdoor fireplace

NINETY-NINE out of a hundred outdoor fireplaces and barbecues have chimneys in spite of the fact that most of them don't need a chimney. All a chimney does is carry smoke high enough so that it blows over your head instead of into your eyes, and it creates a draft which makes a fire burn brighter, and sometimes hotter.

If, however, your fuel is charcoal, a chimney may be more of a hindrance than a help. It may create too much draft, and draw a good deal of cooking heat up the flue, instead of leaving it under the steak where it belongs.

Charcoal makes hardly enough smoke to bother an outdoor chef of strong spirit. It is a fuel which will sustain combustion without artificial aid as long as it has air. This fact is borne out by the number of manufactured grills which are nothing more than a steel pan on legs with a steak holder over the top.

Simple Model

Unless you are sold on the tradition and the looks of a barbecue with chimney, you may like this simple model. To make it, build up with bricks to form a firebed; then a few inches beyond that to form a support for a grill of one sort or another at a convenient cooking height. Such a unit in somewhat elaborate form is shown in the photo here. It has the refinements of a storage place underneath for charcoal, plus a quarter-rounded woodbox at the side for kindling (a feature which would be equally or more useful as a spot to plant a low-growing, attention demanding shrub).

The drawings illustrate a more basic, though entirely adequate flueless barbecue of a type which was introduced several years ago. It's principal features are simplicity of construction, excellent perform-

BARBECUE IS MADE of bricks which match texture

ance and great capacity. And it looks good.

In substance, it is nothing more than a trough with partially open ends in which a long, stretched out fire of charcoal can be built, or in which a small fire can be concentrated in the middle.

The material which seems most appropriate for this barbecue is bricks, probably because that is the way it first appeared. However, there is no reason why it could not be duplicated in adaptation from these drawings for construction of 4x8x16 light-aggregate concrete blocks.

Regardless of the masonry material, you

and mood of basketweave floor. Table is round piece of exterior plywood on nail keg filled with sand.

should first buy the grates or grills so that construction can be made to fit them exactly. They are normally available in a 16-inch or 24-inch dimension in one direction, providing a cooking area of 16 or 24 inches from front to back. The length of the barbecue can be varied, falling within the dimensions which a combination of grates require.

Best Grates

Building, masonry and fireplace supply houses carry these grates. Those made of cast iron are best, both for durability and reduced tendency to soften and sag when heated.

Since it is not feasible to provide adjustable grate or firebed with this barbecue as a means of bringing the cooking closer to or farther from the fire, the best method is to establish eight inches between the actual firebed bottom and the grates. This means four courses of bricks, including the one which supports the grills. Refinements in height can be accomplished by the degree to which ashes are allowed to accumulate on the firebed. Such an accumulation not only raises the fire, but has

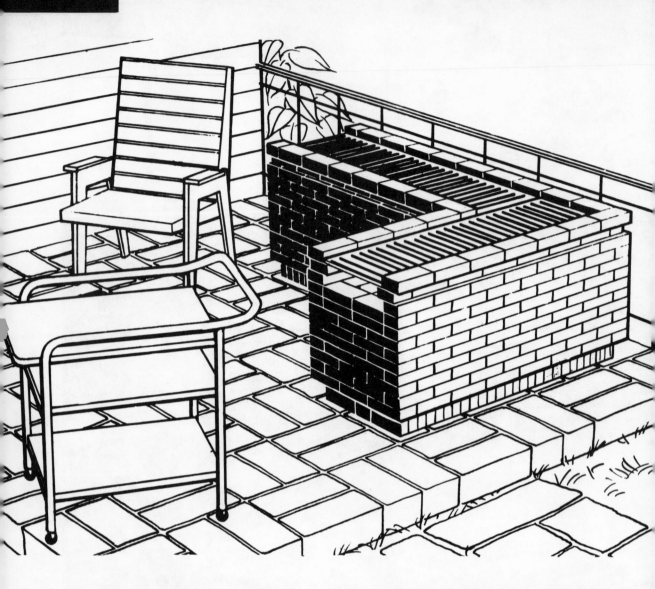

RIGHT-ANGLED MODEL of flueless barbecue shows how it could be used at corner of terrace. It is no more difficult to build than is straight version. In both cases purchase grills first to establish size of unit.

the additional value of insulating the masonry against too much heat. And the fire burns better for it.

The masonry techniques involved in this barbecue are rudimentary, departing in only two ways from the simple process of piling bricks atop one another with mortar.

First Course on Edge

To begin with, the first course of bricks is laid on edge. Don't be alarmed at the way this method of laying them seems to eat up bricks; no more are required than you need for the same height of bricks laid normally. This course hangs in two inches front, back, and ends, providing toe space which allows you to stand close to the

barbecue. Toe space is important to the cook.

The second course is laid "header"— which means flat but all with the ends exposed. The reason for this is that header bricks which overhang the toe space by two inches still have six inches of their length anchored on the previous course, and therefore have no natural desire to fall off. It is recommended, however, that you call a halt to brick laying when the header course is finished all the way around, and fill the space with concrete, as shown. This will anchor the headers against tipping when the remaining bricks are laid, and it will anchor the entire job to its footing or floating slab.

When you resume laying bricks, you'll

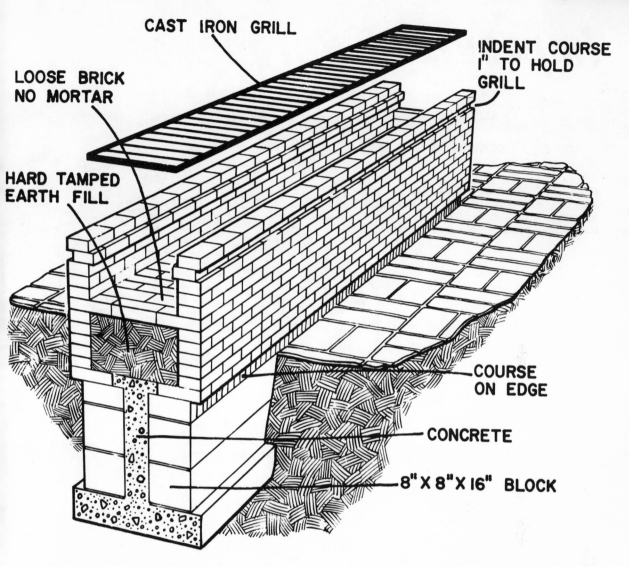

CAST IRON GRILL

INDENT COURSE
I" TO HOLD
GRILL

LOOSE BRICK
NO MORTAR

HARD TAMPED
EARTH FILL

COURSE
ON EDGE

CONCRETE

8" X 8" X 16" BLOCK

CROSS SECTION of flueless barbecue is shown here. Footing provides maximum foundation with concrete block interfilled with concrete. Add one more course of block for very cold areas, or to maintain precise level.

run them up in a normal manner until you reach the course just below the level of the firebed. Again call a halt. Fill the construction with earth, tamping it firmly.

You now lay another course of headers, letting them extend out over the earth fill, supported by it.

Above these headers go three more normal courses.

The fourth course hangs in one inch, providing a ledge on which the cast iron grates or grills will rest.

Above that, another course lines up with the man wall of the barbecue. And that's all. No lintel, no damper, no worries about whether it will "draw."

The firebed is finished with bricks laid on the earth fill without mortar. This al-lows them to expand and contract with changing temperatures without subjecting the entire job to stresses and strains.

The cross-section drawing shows this barbecue built with a footing of concrete blocks. This is necessary in very cold climates, or where it is important to hold the barbecue at a precise permanent level, as when it must always be stationary in relation to a terrace. If you are building on an unpaved area or other location where precise level is not critical, you can use a floating slab of reinforced concrete the size of the barbecue, six inches thick.

Study the drawings shown on these pages before undertaking job. Drawings and photos may give you ideas of your own. •

Improvised Barbecues

Wheelbarrows, oil drums and kettles are easily converted into grills for outdoor cooking

JUST ABOUT the best grill you can get is the grid from an old-fashioned "pipeless furnace." It's big, sagproof and usually fits perfectly on a simple base you make of concrete block or of brick.

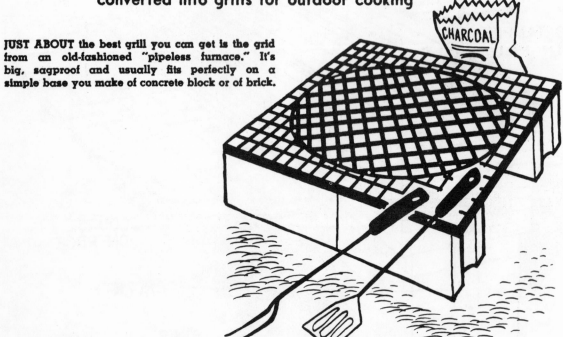

AN OUTDOOR cooking center does not need to be an elaborate piece of construction in order to produce an elaborately flavored charcoal broiled steak. Ever since the idea of eating and cooking out of doors began, ingenious and simple facilities for confining and controlling a fire have been devised.

Several years ago somebody hit upon filling a wheelbarrow nearly full of sand and using it as a barbecue. The idea was such a striking departure from outdoor fireplaces of romanesque or gothic grandeur that just about every how-to magazine published the idea. Thousands of wheelbarrows had their bottoms burned out. Thousands more will because it's still a good idea for a quick, workable, portable outdoor grill. Just be sure there is enough sand to insulate the wheelbarrow's bin from too much heat. Don't leave the sand in it and let it stand around all summer. The bottom will rust.

From the wheelbarrow, many ideas have emerged as workable and more novel.

One of them is the use of a 55-gallon oil drum as a barbecue. These drums can be bought for prices ranging from "glad-to-get-rid-of-it" to about $12, depending on what came in the barrel, and whether the man who bought its contents wants to bother to return it for the deposit. People use oil barrels to cook on in several ways. One way is to cut out the head, stand the drum on end, and fill it to about 8 inches from the top with dirt to provide a fire bed. If you punch a dozen holes in the barrel just above this 8-inch level for draft, it will burn wood or charcoal, it will support a grill, it will cook well and last many years without any bother or attention.

Split Drums

Another way steel drums are used for outdoor grills is split in half, lengthwise. Find a friend who goes along with the idea, and you get two for the price of one. This is fairly heavy steel, and you'll get it cut in two most quickly by using a cutting torch. Then, bend the edges over in a hem to keep them from being dangerously sharp. Mount the half-barrel on some sort

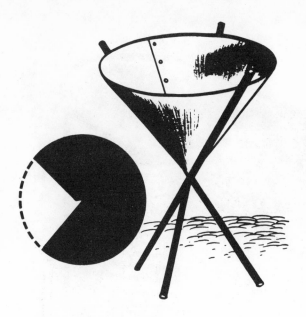

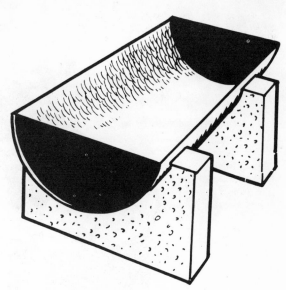

SMART, SIMPLE, functional, this home-made portable grill is merely a piece of sheet metal and three lengths of half-inch steel pipe. Cut "piece of pie" out of circle, rivet joint, weld or rivet to legs.

A BIG OIL DRUM, split lengthwise and mounted on concrete piers makes a good grill with large cooking area. Fill bottom of cavity with sand to raise fire and to prevent bottom from burning out.

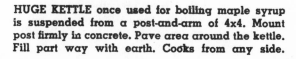

HUGE KETTLE once used for boiling maple syrup is suspended from a post-and-arm of 4x4. Mount post firmly in concrete. Pave area around the kettle. Fill part way with earth. Cooks from any side.

A LARGE-SIZE BELL TILE is a ready-made outdoor grill. Mount it in a circular slab of concrete so it won't tip. Fill it with sand or earth so fire will be about 8 inches down. Use charcoal.

of supports. Cast concrete piers are a good method, cradling the half-barrel solidly and attractively. Of course the barrel is partly filled with sand. Owing to the larger area, there is usually no need for punching draft holes in it, especially if charcoal is the fuel. However, if you will puncture it on the bottom, preferably at the points where it bulges in two rings, there will be a place for rain water to drain out.

This split-barrel idea will work with any drum-like object, one being an old hot water heating tank. Such tanks of heavy steel are often four feet high and more than a foot in diameter. They have a lot of cooking area.

A visit to the junk yard will often pay dividends to the person looking for something from which to improvise a barbecue grill. A wheel from a wrecked automobile or its gas tank split open can be the start. I once saw a beautiful grill made from a huge old gear of some dismantled machine, the spokes cut out and a steel bottom welded in place. Large, wide

wheels once used as flat belt pulleys would work the same way.

If you're lucky enough to run across one of those great kettles used to boil maple sap into syrup, you have the makings of the most distinctive grill in the neighborhood.

Just set a rugged post in the ground with a cross-arm from which a chain is suspended in an eye-bolt. Hook the bail of the kettle on the chain. This can be done with half an oil barrel, too.

Most lumberyards sell big bell tile, the kind with one end flared so that the smaller end of another tile can slip into it. Ready made for a grill, set on end.

Secondhand shops sometimes have old copper boilers of the kind we used for doing the family wash. Makes a perfect grill with two handles already in place, so that you can take it into the yard, store it in the garage between times.

Sheet metal, a material much easier for many people to work with than masonry, can be fabricated into various, good-looking, good-cooking grills, too. •